Contents

The Gulf Region

A New Hub of Global Financial Power

Edited by
John Nugée and Paola Subacchi

CHATHAM HOUSE

Helmut Reisen, Chapter 14, '*How to Spend It: Distinguishing the Origins of Sovereign Wealth Funds*', is based on '*How to Spend It: Sovereign Wealth Funds and the Wealth of Nations*', Development Centre Policy Insight No. 59, OECD, February 2008, and reproduced with permission.

First published in Great Britain in 2008 by
Royal Institute of International Affairs, 10 St James's Square,
London SW1Y 4LE
www.chathamhouse.org
(Charity Registration No. 208 223)

Distributed worldwide by
The Brookings Institution, 1775 Massachusetts Avenue NW,
Washington DC 20036-2188, USA

British Library Cataloguing in Publication Data
A CIP catalogue record for this book is available from the British Library.

ISBN 978 1 86203 194 4

Typeset in Berling Nova by Koinonia
Printed and bound in Great Britain by Latimer Trend and Co. Ltd

Cover design by SoapBox, www.sopaboxcommunications.co.uk
Cover photo: Karim Sahib/AFP, Getty Images

Part 3: Building an international financial centre

List of tables and figures

Tables

Figures

Preface and acknowledgments

The seeds of this book were sown at a Chatham House workshop of the same name, 'The Gulf Region: A New Hub of Global Financial Power', held in Doha in June 2007 and supported by the Qatar Financial Centre Authority and State Street Global Advisors. The quality of speakers and discussants was so impressive that it was decided to compile their contributions into a coherent edited volume. The majority of the authors were participants at the workshop, but the editors commissioned several additional chapters. We also took the decision, as sovereign wealth funds have increasingly come to prominence in policy circles and the media in the year since our workshop, to expand the book into this field. We believe that the various topics addressed here represent an important study of a major new force in world economics and finance that has the potential to shape much of the world's financial activities for the rest of this century.

We are indebted to the various authors for their wisdom and insights and for the time they have given to this book. We also thank the reviewers for the many useful corrections, comments and suggestions they made during its preparation. We are particularly grateful to Ruth Davis, whose support was crucial in bringing the book to completion, to the copy-editor, Kim Mitchell, and to Margaret May for her editorial guidance. We would also like to thank Rod Ringrow and Steve Martin for their enthusiastic support for this project. Any remaining errors are of course our sole responsibility.

September 2008

J.N
P.S

About the authors

Ahmet Akarli is an Executive Director in the Goldman Sachs European Economics team, covering Turkey, Middle East and North Africa. Prior to joining Goldman Sachs in 2005, he worked for FinansInvest Securities and for HSBC as Chief Economist. He has also taught in a number of universities in Turkey and the UK, including the London School of Economics, University of Southampton, Istanbul Technical University and Bosphorus University. He holds a B.Sc. in Economics (Middle East Technical University – Turkey) and M.Sc. and Ph.D. degrees in Economics and Economic History (London School of Economics).

Alexander Böhmer currently oversees the MENA-OECD Investment Programme, an initiative involving 18 countries from the MENA region which is hosted by the OECD in Paris, where he has worked for the last six years. Prior to this, he worked on international trade and investment policies with the Federation of German Industry (BDI) where he was responsible for the working group of the German industry on export/investment guarantees and project finance. Previous professional experience includes the German Ministry of Economy and the European Commission. He holds a Ph.D. in Law and a Master's degree from the London School of Economics.

Ruth Davis is a researcher in the International Economics Programme at Chatham House. She has recently been working on a project on the Gulf as a global financial centre, another on key financial hubs in Asia and a report on the competitiveness of the City of London's financial services. She has also been involved in a number of other research projects coordinating high-profile workshops at Chatham House and in the Gulf, Tokyo and Brussels. Before joining Chatham House she worked in a supporting capacity at the Cabinet Office and Department for International Development and as a reporter for World of Information, a business and economics publication. She read English at the University of Cambridge and Economics at Birkbeck College, University of London.

Florence Eid is Managing Director, Middle East & North Africa at Passport Capital, LLC. Previously she was Vice President and Senior Economist for MENA at JPMorgan, and Professor of Finance and Economics at the American University of Beirut. She holds a Ph.D. in Organization Economics from the Massachusetts Institute of Technology (2000), and has been Visiting Professor at INSEAD and HEC – Paris. She has worked for the World Bank, the Ford Foundation and Save the Children. She has been a contributing author to the World Economic Forum's *Arab World Competitiveness Reports* (2003, 2005). She is a member of the Young Arab Leaders, the YPO and LIBAN.

Tarek Fadlallah is Executive Director at Nomura Investment Banking (Middle East). He has over twenty years of experience in the international capital markets, including more than ten years focusing on the Middle East. He has authored several strategy notes on the GCC equity markets including 'The Great Arabian Bubble' in 2005. He has been a speaker at numerous events and conferences, including CFA Arabia, CFA Bahrain, the Saudi Economic Forum and Hedge Fund World. He is a graduate of the London School of Economics (B.Sc. Economics), a Certified Financial Analyst (2002), a founder member of CFA Bahrain and a Member of Hawkamah Institute for Corporate Governance.

Ghaleb O. Faidi heads a Dubai-based strategy and management consultancy, ILMAM LIMITED. Until the spring of 2007, he served as Chief Strategy Officer at the Dubai International Financial Centre (DIFC) Authority, where he was responsible for the overall strategy of the Centre. He had joined the DIFC in September 2003 when it was in its pre-launch phase. Prior to this, he was based in Washington, DC, where he assisted Fortune 500 and medium-sized US companies doing business in the Middle East and worked on a variety of projects relating to regional commerce and investment, including Islamic banking, trade agreements, high-level bilateral initiatives, and development projects. He holds an undergraduate degree with a dual major in International Business and MIS as well as an MBA.

Andrea Goldstein works at the OECD. He has been involved in various research projects on multinationals from emerging, transition and developing countries – a topic on which he recently published *Multinational Companies from Emerging Economies*. He has published 26 articles in refereed journals on topics as diverse as regulatory reform in network industries, the political economy of the global aerospace industry, and the impact of the emergence of China and India on other developing countries. During the past few years, he has also published op-eds in the *Financial Times*, *Helsingin Sanomat*, *Le Monde* and the *South China Morning Post*.

Daniel Hanna is currently on sabbatical at the London Business School. He is the former Treasurer and Head of Global Markets for Standard Chartered Bank in Qatar. Prior to this, he was a Visiting Fellow at Chatham House and a Senior Economist with Standard Chartered. In 2003, he established Standard Chartered's Middle East economic research team in Dubai. He has acted as a consultant for Gulf governments, institutions and companies and has been a regular commentator on regional issues on the BBC, CNN and CNBCArabia. He graduated from Exeter University in the UK and the Institut d'Etudes Politiques in Strasbourg, France.

Michael Hume is Executive Director and Chief European Economist for Lehman Brothers. He joined Lehman Brothers in 1997 and has held a variety of positions based in London and New York, including Emerging Markets Economist, Chief UK Economist, Senior Europe Economist and Senior International Economist. He is a member of the *Handelsblatt/Wall Street Journal* ECB Shadow Council;

a member of the Lisbon Council's Board of Economists; a member of the Royal Society's working group on Innovation in Services; and has written for numerous newspapers, including *The Financial Times*, *The Observer*, *Les Echos* and *Il Sole 24*. He read Philosophy, Politics and Economics at Oxford University and holds a Master's degree in Economics from the University of Warwick.

Stephen Jen is a Managing Director at Morgan Stanley and serves as the Global Head of Currency Research for the firm. He is based in London. Prior to joining the firm in October 1996, he spent four years as an economist with the International Monetary Fund in Washington, DC. In addition, he was actively involved in the design of the IMF's framework to provide debt relief to highly indebted countries. He has also worked for the Board of Governors of the Federal Reserve and the World Bank, and has been a lecturer at the Massachusetts Institute of Technology (MIT) and Georgetown University School of Business. He holds a Ph.D. in Economics from MIT, with concentrations in International Economics and Monetary Economics. He also earned a B.Sc. in Electrical Engineering (*summa cum laude*) from the University of California at Irvine.

John Nugée is a Managing Director of SSgA, and head of SSgA's Official Institutions Group. He is responsible for relationships with SSgA's central bank and official sector clients. He joined SSgA in November 2000 after a career in central bank reserves management, including spells as the Executive Director in charge of reserves management at the Hong Kong Monetary Authority, and as the Chief Manager of reserves management at the Bank of England. He was also a director of the European Investment Bank and European Investment Fund, and a lecturer and technical adviser at the Bank of England's Centre for Central Banking Studies. He has a Mathematics degree from Cambridge University and a diploma in Business Studies from the London School of Economics.

Andrew Rozanov is Managing Director and Head of Sovereign Advisory at State Street Global Markets, the investment research and trading arm of State Street Corporation. For the last four years, he has been advising and servicing central banks and sovereign wealth funds on various aspects of reserve management. In the past, he worked in State Street's Japan office as a fund manager and product engineer, focusing on global fixed income, currency and asset allocation. He also worked as a Director in the Equity Capital Markets Group at UBS Investment Bank in Tokyo, originating and executing equity block trades and convertible bond transactions for Japanese corporate clients. He has a Master's degree in Asian Studies (with concentration in Japan) from Moscow University. He has lived, studied and worked in Japan for a total of 20 years, and is fluent in English, Russian and Japanese. He is a CFA Charterholder, and also holds designations of Financial Risk Manager (FRM) from the Global Association of Risk Professionals and Chartered Alternative Investment Analyst (CAIA) from the CAIA Association. In 2005 he introduced the term 'sovereign wealth funds' in one of his articles. His work has been published in *The Wall Street Journal*, *Central Banking Journal*, *The World Today*, *Professional Investor*, and *Vedomosti* financial daily. His research has been quoted or referenced in *The Economist, Euromoney, Finance Asia, Les Echos, Smart Money* and *RGE Monitor.*

Helmut Reisen is head of research of the OECD Development Centre and will coordinate the first OECD Global Development Outlook, to be published in 2010. He has written extensively in scholarly journals and the financial press, including two prize-winning essays in the Amex Bank Review competition. He writes a regular economics column in *Internationale Politik* and is a member of the editorial boards of *International Finance, Deutsche Bank Research Notes* and *Internationale Politik.* He holds a Ph.D. from Cologne University and is a Professor of International Economics at the University of Basel. Prior to joining the OECD, he worked at Commerzbank AG, the Kiel Institute for the World Economy, the Federation of German Industries and the German Ministry of Economics.

Vanessa Rossi is a Senior Research Fellow at Chatham House, specializing in international economics, finance and emerging markets. She is a frequent speaker at conferences in London and around the world. In addition, she has been Director of International Economics for Oxford Economics since 1994, helping develop econometric models and detailed analysis of the international economy including emerging markets and capital flows. She has previously worked as a Research Director for Swiss Bank Corporation (now UBS) and with the European Commission. She is co-author of a book on financial market analysis and has contributed to numerous other publications covering the BRIC economies, global energy policy and the development of the oil economies. She is co-author of a Chatham House report, *The Gulf as a Global Financial Centre: Growing Opportunities and Influence* (June 2008). She gained her first degree, with distinction, in Mathematics, Economics and Statistics from Birmingham University, and a Master's degree from Warwick University, where she specialized in mathematical economics. She was subsequently a graduate student and researcher at Princeton University, funded by Fulbright and Princeton University scholarships.

Fabio Scacciavillani is the Director of Macroeconomics and Statistics at the Dubai International Financial Center. Previously he was Head of Economic Research at the Gulf Organization for Industrial Consulting, Executive Director at Goldman Sachs International, Senior Economist and Adviser in the Research Directorate of the European Central Bank, and worked several years at the International Monetary Fund. He has published many scholarly articles, economic reports, market analyses and op-eds. He has been a consultant for corporations, hedge funds and the European Commission. His views are frequently cited on international media and news agencies. He holds a Ph.D. in Economics from the University of Chicago.

Paola Subacchi is Director of International Economic Research at Chatham House (the Royal Institute of International Affairs). Her research covers a wide range of international economic issues, focusing, in particular on the international monetary system, international capital flows and global imbalances. Her current work explores the emergence of new economic powers and the challenge that this poses to global economic governance. She is a contributor to leading journals, and has presented many papers and keynote addresses. She is a regular media commentator, working with print and broadcast media at home and overseas. She has been interviewed widely. Recent coverage includes the BBC, CNN, CNBC, Bloomberg, the *Financial Times*, *Wall Street Journal* and *Herald Tribune*. She studied at Bocconi University and at the University of Oxford.

Mina Toksoz has been working as Head of Country Risk at Standard Bank Plc since September 2001. She has been in investment banking for the past ten years, initially with Caspian Securities and then as the Equity Strategist for EMEA at ABN Amro, London. Prior to this she worked for the Economist Group's Economist Intelligence Unit as Middle East editor, director of EIU's Country Risk Service, and Regional Director for Europe. She has a D.Phil. in Economics from Sussex University, a B.A. in Economics from Bosphorus University, and more recently completed the Executive Programme on Infrastructure in a Market Economy at Harvard University.

Introduction

John Nugée and Paola Subacchi

Changing global financial dynamics

Man has always been fascinated by money. From the dawn of civilization, people have desired money, and the pursuit of money – and the power it represents – dominates much of social and economic history. But there is a special place in history and in human interest for fabulous wealth, for those who have money beyond measure and sometimes even beyond comprehension. The wealth of Croesus, a king of Lydia in the sixth century BC, was legendary even in his own time and gave rise to the expression, still in use, 'as rich as Croesus'. Crassus, the first-century BC Roman politician, general and triumvir, amassed a fortune that even today ranks him among the richest men of all time.[1] The wealth of John D. Rockefeller – whose worth at the start of the twentieth century has been estimated at $320 billion in today's money,[2] making him the richest individual in history – earned him a status and level of attention that today's celebrities would envy.

Against this background, it is not surprising that the stunning accumulation of wealth in the Gulf region in recent years has attracted huge comment and analysis. Both the scale of the wealth in the various Gulf Cooperation Council states[3] – the Abu Dhabi Investment Authority alone manages funds worth about three times Rockefeller's total assets[4] – and the speed of its accumulation in recent years place the Gulf states in a league of their own. Seldom in history has so much wealth been amassed so quickly. Seldom in history have states, and their rulers, found that the only limit to what they can achieve is their own imagination. And seldom in history

1 The list of the world's wealthiest historical figures is based on calculations by Forbes, updated annually and published on Forbes.com.
2 Forbes.com.
3 The GCC consists of Bahrain, Kuwait, Oman, Qatar, Saudi Arabia and the United Arab Emirates.
4 Various estimates from Morgan Stanley, Standard Chartered and others. The Abu Dhabi Investment Authority has not published a figure for the assets under its control but it has not actively denied or disputed the market's estimates.

have the eyes of the world been so keenly trained on such comparatively small countries to see what they will do with their wealth.

Since oil prices began to increase rapidly in 2004, the countries of the Gulf region have become a major force in world economics and finance. This fast rise, together with the huge infrastructure projects under way across the region, is posing many questions and challenges both to developed and emerging-market countries and to the world financial order.

The purpose of this book is to examine these developments and add to the understanding of the challenges facing the GCC states, the choices available to them and the direction in which they are taking their people and region. This volume is a collection of essays written by keen observers of the Gulf – some live in the region; all visit it regularly – and thus the contents are quite diverse. Their contributions cover various issues, from the challenge of diversifying economies that are still highly dependent on oil to that of integrating them into the international financial system. What emerges is a picture of governments determined to do the best for their people and their countries: the lessons of the 1970s and 1980s have been learned well and there is a clear collective will not to allow the second great oil bonanza to go the same way as much of the first round of oil wealth. The oil riches from the first great rise in the price of oil 35 years ago perhaps flowed too much into consumption, with not enough thought for the needs of wider society or preparation for leaner times.

Even allowing for its diversity and richness, the book has a marked financial flavour. This is no accident, nor is it just because the starting point for any analysis of the Gulf states today is their wealth. The GCC governments have collectively decided that the financial services sector is an attractive one for their economies to specialize in: it offers an enticing range of high-income, high-valued-added activities with much growth potential that complements well the resource extraction industries. The evidence from other financial centres around the globe is that creating a successful financial sector is one of the best ways for a country to provide fulfilling jobs for its people, to advance its economy and to increase its national wealth.

Part 1 provides an overview of the changing global financial dynamics of which the GCC is a part and the context of rising oil revenues and diversification that drives the supply of savings and their use in the Gulf and related Arab countries. Here Vanessa Rossi and Michael Hume, in their respective chapters, set the scene and explore this dynamic in detail. Discussing how high GDP growth rates in emerging markets have fuelled rises in asset prices, stock market capitalizations and bank deposits, Rossi highlights the need for a 'more balanced' development of the financial market. Hume explores the competing explanations for the rapid increase in asset prices and the resulting long boom – until recently – in financial markets. On the one hand, this may be due to excess liquidity resulting from unusually low interest rates; on the other hand, it may be that the forces of globalization, including low inflation and increased capital flows, have radically transformed the fundamentals of asset prices. Both authors emphasize the 'perverse transfer' of savings from poorer to richer regions of the world because of the underdevelopment of financial markets in emerging economies.

Their chapters place the financial services industry in perspective and explain the GCC states' decision to transform themselves from users of financial services into providers. They both point to the significant consequences – not just for the global economy, asset management and the ownership of capital but also for governance of the global financial system – of the growing capacity of emerging economies to supply their own financial assets. They consider how realistic the GCC states' intentions are and assess perhaps the most interesting question that the various governments and their ambitious plans face: is there room for more than one international financial centre in the Gulf?

The challenge of diversification and integration in the world economy

Unlike in the 1970s oil boom, this time the themes of every government in the Gulf are development, diversification and sustainability. Every government now accepts that oil is a finite resource, and with varying degrees of urgency they are all striving to create a non-oil economy. In part this is a simple matter of providing employment for their young people: the oil industry is capital-intensive and does not itself create many jobs. In part it is a matter of diversification, as no government wants to be wholly at the mercy of the oil market, which recent history has shown to be quite volatile. The memories of the economic challenges of the mid-1990s, when the price of oil sank to about $10 a barrel, are still vivid in the minds of today's decision-makers. And in part there is the desire to show the world what can be achieved when Arab culture, Arab creativity and Arab money are combined and to showcase the region as one of the dynamic centres of the world economy in the twenty-first century.

At the heart of any discussion of oil-based economies is the intrinsic instability of oil revenues. Uncertainty about the long-term trend of oil prices affects decisions on the use of surplus oil revenues and plans for diversification of the GCC economies. This uncertainty also heavily influences fiscal and monetary policies, and through those channels it affects the development of the region's financial centres.

Depletion is another major concern in the financial planning of the authorities in all oil economies. At the moment, the Gulf's financial sectors are thriving because in the region there is both an explosion of savings and an expansion of investment opportunities outside the oil sector. But what would be the outlook for these sectors if one or both of those conditions fell away? In the next decades, the most plausible scenario is one in which surplus oil revenues will decrease and eventually dry up.[5] Unless the GCC countries have by then established alternative sources of revenue for their economies, and especially unless their financial centres have established a role serving the wider international financial community, they will fall upon lean times. The window of opportunity that the present economic conditions provide for the development of international financial centres in the Gulf will not last for ever, and thus there is a vigorous and concerted effort to diversify the economy, to build and expand the financial services sector and to develop competences and international status beyond the region before the window closes.

Part 2 of the book addresses the question of diversification and integration in the world's economy. Ahmet Akarli's chapter looks at whether the 'massive oil and natural gas revenue windfall' that has allowed the GCC economies to grow so strongly in recent years is likely to be sustained. There will be strong energy demand from the BRICs and N-11 countries and it will keep oil prices high, especially for the next 10–15 years.[6] The GCC is set to capture an 'ever larger share' of global energy production, although this will require pumping in significant extra capital expenditure in order to increase production capacity at a fast enough rate. If this is done, the resulting windfall will enable the GCC countries to keep investment levels very high and to generate strong, welfare-enhancing economic growth.

The chapter by Florence Eid takes this discussion further and brings in one of the most far-reaching developments in modern global finance, the rise of capital flows between developing countries that bypass the developed economies and the leading financial centres of London and New York,

5 One cannot imagine the theoretical result of the oil price increasing in real terms for ever or of the volume of oil production increasing for ever. On this see John V. Mitchell and Paul Stevens, *Ending Dependence: Hard Choices for Oil-exporting States*, Chatham House Report (London: Royal Institute of International Affairs, July 2008).

6 In 2001 Goldman Sachs coined the term 'BRICs' to refer to Brazil, Russia, India and China, countries with large populations that may dominate the world economy by 2050. In 2005, Goldman Sachs introduced the Next Eleven (N-11) concept; these countries – Bangladesh, Egypt, Indonesia, Iran, Mexico, Nigeria, Pakistan, the Philippines, South Korea, Turkey and Vietnam – could potentially have a BRICs-like impact in rivalling the G-7.

Singapore and Hong Kong. Eid notes how, in contrast to the 1970s, the public and private sectors of the GCC states have 'taken a decidedly more regional approach to petrodollar recycling'. The current oil windfall is fuelling unprecedented domestic investments aimed at economic diversification and there is as well a 'record level' of intraregional FDI flowing into North Africa and the Levant. This demonstrates the GCC states' ambition to provide finance not only to the West but also to the emerging economies of the world, and they have the confidence to do so directly themselves.

Mina Toksoz analyses how robust this approach is likely to be and whether the risks to the Gulf states have been mitigated or increased by the redirection of financial commitments. Sustainability, she believes, will depend on the ability to generate more private sector jobs, progress towards liberalization of markets, the break-up of monopolies, reform of the labour market and new educational and skills programmes. 'Traditional rentier-state structures' will need to show greater adaptability to the existence of a stronger private sector and a more complex, globally integrated economy. With a small domestic market unable to cushion a decline in external demand, 'these regimes could be exposed to acute future instability unless they allow for real change and develop institutions with flexibility that can generate appropriate policies in response to changing conditions and external shocks'.

All contributors to Part 2 emphasize that the GCC countries are changing decidedly. But the scope and extent of the changes, and the political dynamics behind them, are difficult to predict. Unlike, for instance, China's rulers, who seem clear about what they want to change and what they want to conserve, there is less consensus in the Gulf states on how to approach and manage this change. It is difficult to gauge in many countries the correct balance between reform and the maintenance of traditional cultures and systems of government. There is no right 'answer' here, and the various GCC member states are pursuing a range of different strategies. What is clear, however, as Ahmet Akarli argues in Chapter 3, is that GCC leaders need to place more emphasis on improving the investment climate and facilitating strong growth of productivity. This would help them to avoid past failings and inefficiencies and to emerge as 'one of the most prosperous regions in the world in the next decades'. Failing this, the development of a 'dual' economic structure is likely, 'characterized, on the one hand, by ultra-modern Dubai-like "growth poles" and, on the other hand, by continuing inefficiency and waste in general resource utilization'.

International financial centres in the making?

Part 3 provides an in-depth analysis of how exactly a financial centre is created, focusing on the advantages and difficulties inherent in such an undertaking. It highlights what would be needed to make the Gulf, or one city in it, a global or international financial centre. It also sets out most of the difficulties that beset development of the financial sector: no regulatory track record; competition between centres; difficulties of GCC currency and economic integration; population issues; and the problem of overcoming them by attracting migrant professionals and getting them to stay.

After John Nugée's chapter, setting out the role and functions of an international financial centre, Chapters 7–10 consider different aspects of this theme. Daniel Hanna explores the Gulf's changing internal financial landscape, assesses the strengths and weaknesses of the various states in the region as financial centres and concludes that 'consensus and further reform in the region is needed in order to fully cement its emergence as another major financial hub.' The Gulf 'can no longer be characterized as a passive, one-way investor', since 'a burgeoning financial sector is emerging'. He does note, however, that the region's 'aspirations outstrip its current capabilities' and that competition between the centres 'has hampered effective government coordination'. Regulatory differences have widened rather than narrowed, and a single regional capital market is still far off.

Ghaleb Faidi places the Gulf financial centres in a world perspective and considers how they fit in among the globally recognized financial hubs, drawing on the City of London Corporation survey. Using a detailed definition of financial centres, he looks at four imperatives that must be fulfilled for the GCC states to secure a sustainable position in the rankings of IFCs. He also proposes that the different centres should develop specialities based on identified comparative advantages in order to gain 'well-defined' positions. This is not, he believes, a zero-sum game.

Good supervisory and regulatory structures are of critical importance to all the Gulf's IFC projects, as the risks of a regulatory failure somewhere in the region would taint them. Alexander Böhmer emphasizes this and discusses why the governance of financial markets is now 'back on the international agenda' – partly prompted by the financial crisis in the United States, which raised issues of transparency, market integrity, regulation and institutional supervision. The proliferation of alternative and less regulated products has underscored the necessity of adequate regulatory and supervisory models for all and has raised doubts over notions of best practice and superior models based on long legal traditions. Böhmer explores evolving practice in OECD countries, which has informed practice in the Gulf region, and takes a detailed look at the current structures in the GCC states.

Rules and supervision are essential to the creation of a financial centre, but what about the *je ne sais quoi* that attracts the best talent and ensures that there is a steady stream of available and well-qualified financial sector workers in cosmopolitan cities such as New York, London and Hong Kong? In their contribution Tarek Fadlallah and Ruth Davis consider the softer side of establishing an international financial centre. They look at the rapid transformation of the Gulf states as increasingly desirable locations for the 'creative class'[7] of very skilled international executives. Factors such as the establishment of a high-luxury, low-tax lifestyle are discussed, along with other 'bread and butter' issues such as education, healthcare and housing. But while these are moving towards international standards, economic dynamism and demographic expansion are creating social problems such as congestion, pollution, growing inequality and friction among the local population that in the long run could tarnish the glamorous image of the Gulf countries.

SWFs: where politics meets economics

The chapters in Part 4 bring the arguments together and consider the wider issues arising from the size and activities of sovereign wealth funds (SWFs). They are a critical link in the construction of international financial centres in the Gulf. Rulers or state agencies provide most of the funding for diversification projects through SWFs, so their participation in them or at least their explicit consent is necessary if not sufficient.

Two contributions – by Paola Subacchi and Helmut Reisen – set out the major funding sources of SWFs, the economic motives for them and the differences between them. Reisen looks at the decision-making behind the management of public sector commodity booms, principally such as the oil boom in the Gulf. He looks at SWFs against the wider backdrop of the political dimension of decisions over the use of state resources. His contribution complements to an extent that by Andrea Goldstein and Fabio Scacciavillani. They consider the thorny subject of national interest, economic state activism and the Western response. Both contributions warn about restricting the operations of SWFs, a temptation for industrialized countries, but they also encourage SWFs to embrace funda-

7 See Richard Florida, *The Rise of the Creative Class: And How It's Transforming Work, Leisure, Community and Everyday Life* (New York: Basic Books, 2002).

mental principles such as transparency, disclosure and reciprocity apropos of different countries' level of openness to foreign investment.

The issues of transparency and governance are discussed by Andrew Rozanov, who, by bringing in the financial market practitioner's perspective, considers what information is required, by whom and at what level of detail. He distinguishes between supervision and regulation and between information gathering and disclosure, and this goes to the heart of the matter of SWF transparency. Indeed, transparency and disclosure may 'carry a very real economic cost'. These issues are much in the media and the public eye. Rozanov recommends that GCC countries take the lead in organizing a dedicated policy forum for SWF states, and so foster a more sophisticated debate.

The market's point of view also emerges in Stephen Jen's chapter. This addresses the challenges that the Gulf states face from the perspective of portfolio management and asset allocation. Jen argues that in order to maximize their investment returns, the members of the GCC should 'aggressively accumulate financial wealth through their SWFs', converting wealth underground (oil) into wealth above ground (financial or physical assets). SWFs' investment of this capital will have 'powerful implications' for the financial markets because the rise of the SWFs will favour equities over bonds and also emerging-market states at the expense of dollar and euro assets.

A common theme runs throughout the book. The opportunities that oil wealth is creating in the Gulf are enormous, and the changes in the world's financial system will be both significant and long-lasting. The GCC states stand poised on the threshold of an exciting period of development and diversification. Many will be watching to see what they, and their peoples, can achieve in the coming decades.

Part 1

Setting the scene

1 Global financial markets: how emerging-market economies are enlarging the playing field

Vanessa Rossi

Introduction

Rapid growth across emerging markets[1] in 2003–07 not only made a significant impact on economic conditions within these countries but also delivered about half the $20 trillion increase in global GDP, which reached almost $55 trillion in 2007 (at current prices). Thanks to this unexpectedly strong performance, the world economy was able to sustain real growth of close to 4% per annum even in the face of a sharp slowdown in the United States from 2006. The evidence from 2006 to mid-2008 confirmed the potential for decoupling[2] based on the scale and dynamics of the emerging markets, thereby reducing traditional reliance on US consumers. World trade expanded even faster than global GDP, with exporters successfully diversifying away from the United States in favour of both intraregional trade and growth markets, such as the Middle East and Russia.

Notably, wealth and capital flows have grown faster than global GDP. Asset prices, stock market capitalizations and bank deposits have risen throughout the emerging markets. More surprisingly, external wealth has increased sharply too, especially in terms of highly visible foreign exchange (FX) reserves and sovereign wealth funds (SWFs). This growth is creating an ever greater demand for financial services around the world and the need for more balanced financial market development. Asia, especially China,

1 It is assumed that 'emerging markets' and 'developing world' include the Gulf states (despite their economies recording per capita GDP well above developing-country levels). This is in line with classifications such as that used by the International Monetary Fund. The terms 'Gulf' and 'GCC' will be considered as interchangeable, and refer to the six states of the Gulf Cooperation Council.

2 'Decoupling' can be defined as growth in one region of the world economy becoming less dependent on growth in another. More specifically, it refers to the possibility that in contrast with a marked weakening in US demand growth, other regions (especially China and other emerging markets) may continue to enjoy high growth rates. This outcome contradicts the traditional 'coupling' (or synchronization) of global growth cycles with the business cycle in the US, previously the dominant driver. A popular way of explaining the recent phenomenon of divergence in growth rates is 'diversification'. The Asian economies in particular appear to have successfully diversified trade away from the US centre of gravity.

Figure 1.1: Per capita GDP of leading and 'mega-emerging' economies, 2007

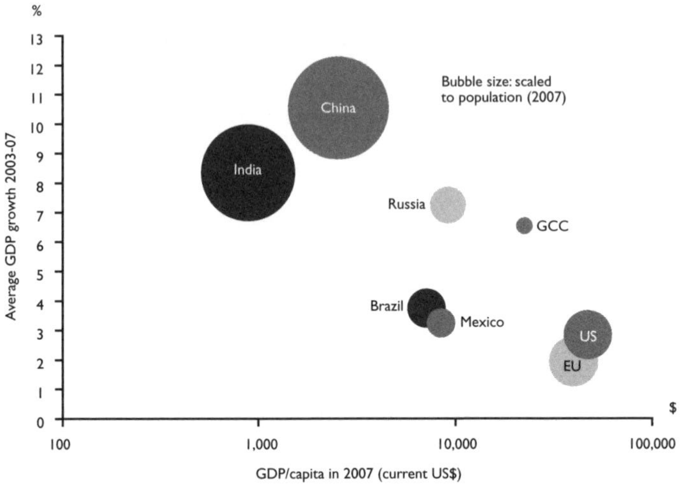

Source: World Bank.

and the GCC countries are at the heart of this new boom owing to their pole positions in world trade, investment and wealth-generation and to their status as key drivers of financial services.

Because of high global commodity prices and potential difficulties in increasing resource supplies, many analysts believe that the world economy will continue to be threatened by a generalized slowdown, possibly a recession, even if the rate of growth remains high in 2008. However, provided commodity bottlenecks can be resolved, any downturn would most probably be followed by a powerful recovery. The rapid development of the 'mega-emergers', chiefly the BRICs (Brazil, Russia, India and China), as well as Mexico and the Gulf, looks set to continue to 2020–30,[3] before convergence with OECD levels of per capita GDP dampens their growth potential. As Figure 1.1 shows, China's per capita GDP is still low even compared to that of Brazil or Russia, while India's is well below that of China. There remains ample scope for catch-up with the leading OECD economies, and that will eventually push the total GDP of the populous 'mega-emergers' well above the US and EU levels (as illustrated by relative bubble size).

3 This proposition is based on own estimates, on stated targets (e.g. those of China) and on estimates provided by other reviews, for example Gordon Cookson and John Hawksworth, 'The World in 2050: Beyond the BRICs: a Broader Look at Emerging Market Growth Prospects', PricewaterhouseCoopers LLP, London, March 2008; and Goldman Sachs Global Economics Group, *BRICs and Beyond* (London: Goldman Sachs, November 2007) and subsequent BRICs reports. (The term BRICs, it is understood, was first coined by Goldman Sachs in a report of 30 November 2001 entitled 'Building Better Global Economic BRICs'. The phenomenon has subsequently been a continuous subject of emerging-market research.)

Rapid development will need servicing in terms of the real resource stream (energy, food and other raw materials) and financial services. This has crucial implications for the future role of the commodity economies and for interregional growth in trade and finance. Strong trade and investment linkages across the Middle East and Asia, together with the two regions' substantial financial resources, will strengthen their financial ties. This could be the seedbed for major changes in global financial markets over the next decade.

The global economy: a surprising transformation

The landscape of the global economy, and global finance, has been radically reshaped over the last decade owing to the sustained surge in GDP growth (see Figure 1.2) and wealth creation throughout the emerging-market world. This is frequently referred to as a 'tectonic shift' in economic and financial power. It is all the more amazing because just a decade ago, in 1997–98, Asia was in the midst of a severe crisis, and many saw it as inevitable that China's growth would deteriorate.[4] Speculators bet on a collapse of the currency peg and devaluation in both China and Hong Kong. How very wrong this proved – and how times change. As a further illustration of the sea change in perspectives, in 1997–98 few energy analysts expected to see oil prices reach $30 per barrel, let alone $100 per barrel. Indeed, many thought that prices might even remain below $20 per barrel. These 'surprises' are interlinked, and they are important in understanding the outcomes seen today.

Crises in Russia in 1998 (linked to the collapse of oil prices) and then in Latin America followed on from Asia. After these episodes came the global recession of 2001. Nevertheless, China kept on growing strongly throughout all this turbulence[5] and the rest of Asia recovered rapidly from the 1997–98 crisis and then the setback linked to the recession of 2001 (which hit its IT sector hard). Recoveries in the energy and commodity economies, largely fed by Asian demand, also started to boost global growth from 2003–04.

4 Although some experts questioned the statistics; see, for example, Thomas G. Rawski, 'What's Happening to China's GDP statistics?', *China Economic Review*, vol. 12, issue 4, 2001, pp. 347–51, and other articles by the same author as well as forecasts from institutions such as the IMF.

5 Its growth was assisted by the momentum built up ahead of and during accession to the World Trade Organization in December 2001, although most assessments at the time greatly underestimated the benefits versus costs of entry and failed to predict the subsequent strong performance of exports, investment and GDP growth. A catalogue of these assessments is provided in Charles A.. Pigott et al., *China in the World Economy: The Domestic Policy Challenges* (Paris: OECD, 2002), Annex II, 'Summary of Studies of the Impact of WTO on China', pp. 759–84.

Figure 1.2: GDP growth at market exchange rates (MER)

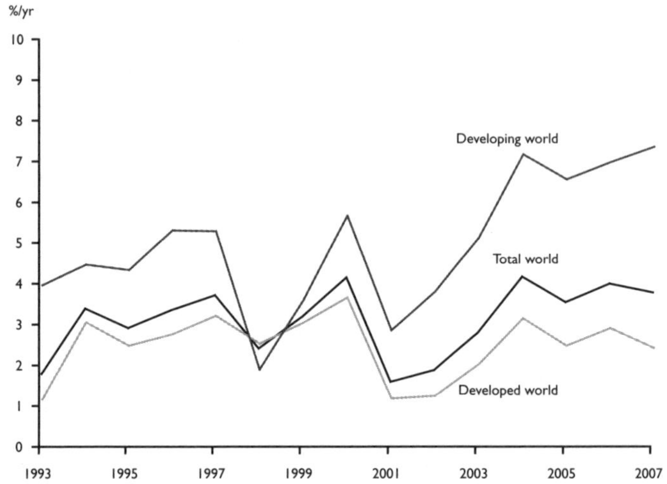

Source: Oxford Economics.

Figure 1.3: Emerging markets: GDP growth

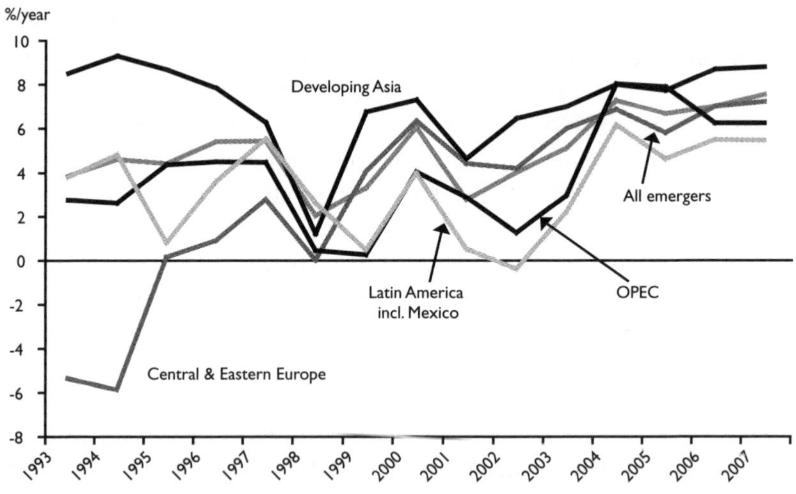

Source: Oxford Economics.

These trends culminated in a remarkable run of persistently high growth rates for the world economy starting in 2003. All the emerging markets did well, while developing Asia, led by China and India, performed spectacularly well, as shown by Figure 1.3.

Boost to commodities markets and emerging economies

Unexpectedly high growth has had consequences that were also unforeseen, such as raising commodity prices as well as increasing emerging-market wealth and capital outflows (which will be discussed later in this chapter).

The long-lived boom in China has delivered a strong boost to energy and raw material consumption because growth was largely driven by an extraordinarily rapid development of infrastructure (dependent on energy-intensive steel and cement) as well as by rising manufacturing capabilities. In 2007, China's shares of both global investment and world manufacturing were about double its 6–7% share of global GDP (recent estimates for 2008 put these shares even higher), which greatly increases its impact on those parts of the world economy and on demand for resources such as energy and metals. Thus it is not surprising that China alone has been responsible for as much as 70–80% of the growth in global demand for some raw materials, such as coal and metals. China now accounts for approximately 40% of global coal and iron ore consumption and 25–35% of aluminium and copper consumption – much higher than its share of oil consumption, which is just under 10%, held back in part by the late development of its car market.

Similar rapid development in other emerging-market economies has pushed global commodity demand up even more. The emerging markets have been the prime drivers of the surge in oil demand, accounting for about 7 million barrels/day (almost 90%) of the total increase of 8 million b/d in 2002–07. By 2012, they will probably consume about half of total world output. They already take 50% of global electricity output,[6] for which their demand is rising at annual rates of 7–8%. This puts pressure on coal supplies, especially in countries such as China and India that depend heavily on coal for electricity generation.

As commodity prices spiked up from 2004 to mid-2008, producers' revenues and profits soared, inducing a spurt of high growth in the commodity economies themselves – and also a sharp rise in wealth formation, as only part of the windfall profits have been spent. Although a few obvious problem spots have not been eradicated, even Africa has seen a welcome pickup in GDP growth, to annual rates of 5–6%. However, the greatest gains from the boom in commodity prices have accrued to the major oil and gas producers, chiefly Russia and the Gulf states, where annual GDP growth has averaged some 7% over the past five years. At peak, as

6 IEA database and *World Energy Outlook*, 2007.

new gas projects came on stream, Qatar saw its growth soar to high double digits, even greater than China's growth rate, and its per capita GDP is now one of the highest in the world, probably exceeding $100,000 in 2008 (at current prices).

The effective rerating of energy and commodity prices is now seen as a permanent phenomenon linked to the impact of sustained development throughout the emerging markets.[7] This growth is squeezing global raw materials capacity to the limit but it benefits producers in the process. Analysts continue to predict a prolonged period of global economic growth associated with the rise of China, India and other developing countries, a rise now seen as more certain than it appeared to be 10 or 20 years ago thanks largely to the very visible, sustained success of the Chinese economy since the 1990s. The contributions to world GDP growth of the emerging markets, especially China, have already reached a level that puts these countries in the driving seat of the global economy.

Emerging markets: from back seat to driving seat

The developing world has quadrupled its GDP in 20 years, from just $4.5 trillion in 1987 to $8 trillion in 1997 and as much as $18 trillion by 2007 (as shown in Figure 1.4). It accounted for about $10 trillion (40%) of the $25 trillion rise in global GDP over the past decade, with $9 trillion of this coming in the past five years alone (the previous five years having been affected by the Asian, Russian and Latin American crises).

Collectively, the developing world now represents about one third of global GDP (at market exchange rates, the MER measure), up from just over 26% in 1987–97. About half this increase is due to China, where GDP growth, supported by rapid investment and productivity gains, has averaged almost 10% per annum in the past decade and over 11% in 2006–07. From 2003, India has seen growth shoot up from its typical 4–6% range to a more China-like pace of 8–10% while the energy economies (including Russia and the Gulf) have also enjoyed higher average growth rates (above 6%), contrasting sharply with previous years of low growth (often below 3%) and even recessionary conditions.

Further fast growth in the emerging markets means that their share of global GDP (at MER) will probably reach 50% by about 2020 and continue to rise. In fact, their share of world electricity, oil and metals consumption

7 For example, oil price futures and consensus forecasts have been steadily upgraded for several years; and by mid-2008, they pointed to oil prices remaining above $100, although these dropped back from peak in late 2008

Figure 1.4: The developing world's share of global GDP, 1987–2017 (GDP at current MER)

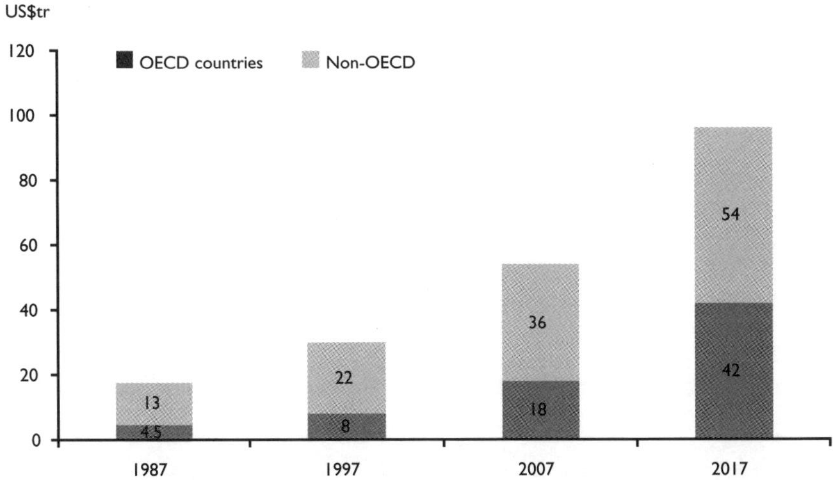

Sources: World Bank and own estimates.

is already close to 50%, similar to their share of global GDP at PPP[8] (these shares better represent the significance of developing countries in the context of global resources). In PPP terms, it is estimated that the developing world has recently accounted for as much as 60–70% of global GDP growth (although the exact scale of this depends on assumptions adopted concerning appropriate PPP weightings).

In terms of global impact, size clearly matters. When the first Asian tigers burst on the scene with a similar pattern of rapid industrial development and productivity growth, they were too small (in terms of population and thus total GDP) to make a noticeable impact on global trends except in specialized niches of industry and trade. Now the big developing economies are booming and are amply demonstrating not only their current strength but also their future potential. China is currently just behind Japan as the world's fourth-largest economy (counting the European Union as one

8 Purchasing power parity (PPP) measures of GDP are based on adjustments that aim to reflect estimated discrepancies between actual living standards in a country and its GDP measured at market prices and exchange rates (MER), which tends to underestimate the living standard of people in poorer countries. As a comparable measurement of economic performance across countries, many see the PPP-adjusted GDP figure as more appropriate. This adjusted measurement affects the ranking of GDP for China in relation to the US, with China appearing much closer in size to the US using PPP. With high-growth China having a larger GDP in PPP terms, the PPP measurement of global GDP growth is also higher than the MER measurement. For example, for 2007 these measurements of global growth were estimated at about 3.7% and 4.8% respectively. PPP-based data are supplied by the World Bank (its figures were revised heavily in late 2007, indicating uncertainty about PPP assessments).

block) (see Table 1.1). Indeed, as the US economy slowed in mid-2007, news headlines reported that China had overtaken the United States as the main contributor to growth in world GDP. Even so, China's per capita GDP is still well behind that of the United States. As productivity catches up, its GDP will eventually rise to four or five times that of the US, although this will not occur for many years.

Table 1.1: World GDP rankings: the top 10, 2007

Rank	*Region*	*GDP estimates ($trn), 2007*
1	European Union	17
2	United States	14
3	Japan	4.4
4	China	3.3
5–7	Canada, Brazil, Russia	1.3–1.4
8–9	India, South Korea	1.0
= 10	GCC, Mexico, Australia	0.8–0.9

Sources: World Bank and National Accounts data.

World trade, commodities and financial markets all experienced significant gains from steady high GDP growth in 1997–2007. Compared with a rise of just over 75% in global GDP over the past decade, world trade soared by 150% (more than $10 trillion) to about $17 trillion (measured as total exports of goods and services). Global wealth approximately doubled and the total for gross financial wealth is now close to $200 trillion (own estimate based on financial market data and IMF historical estimates), almost four times annual GDP.

Emerging markets have accounted for a large proportion of the rise in world trade, with the $1 trillion increase in China's exports from 1997 representing 10% of this growth (more than the United States' contribution of about $700 billion). The energy economies, in aggregate, have more than matched China's gains. In the past five years alone, the Gulf's exports of goods and services have approximately tripled, from just under $200 billion to almost $600 billion in 2007. The scale of Russia's contribution has been similar. The other emerging Asian markets have also added some $1 trillion to global exports since 1997. China is now the world's third-largest exporter (after the EU and the US); the GCC is in fifth place, just behind Japan.

The growing influence of the emerging markets on the developed economies and on each other is also illustrated by their contributions to import growth (see Figure 1.5). China has overtaken the United States as

Figure 1.5: Leading emerging markets' contribution to the growth of imports, 2001–11

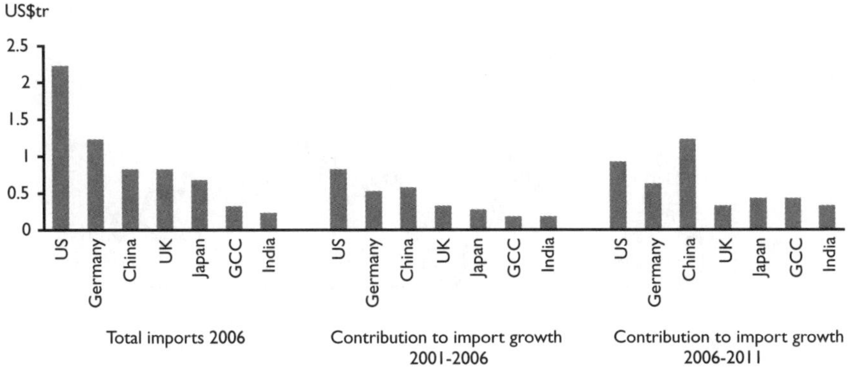

Sources: WTO, National Accounts data and own estimates.

Figure 1.6: US imports and real GDP in emerging Asia

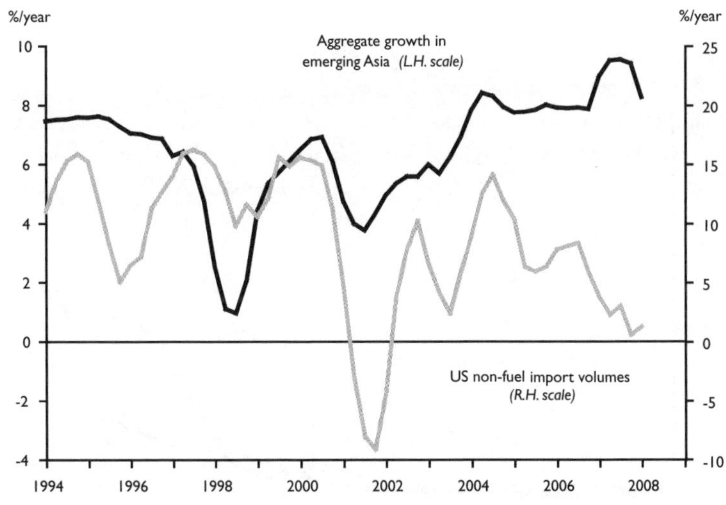

Source: Oxford Economics.

the key driver of world demand while the GCC and India are nudging up alongside Japan. Over the coming decade, this influence will grow. Even if a large part of this expansion of trade has been driven by the funnel effect of China sucking in raw materials and semi-finished goods and spewing out manufactures, more of the finished goods are now being sold back to Asia, the Gulf, Russia and other emerging markets, not just to the US and the EU.

Figure 1.7: China: destination of exports

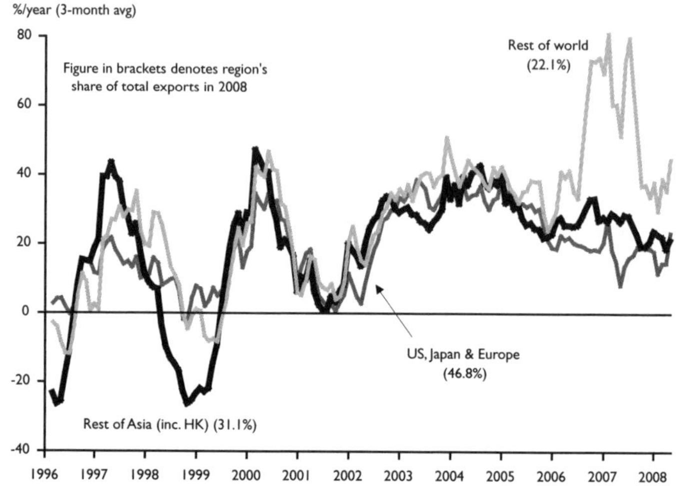

Source: Oxford Economics.

Figure 1.8: Exports to UAE from leading trade partners

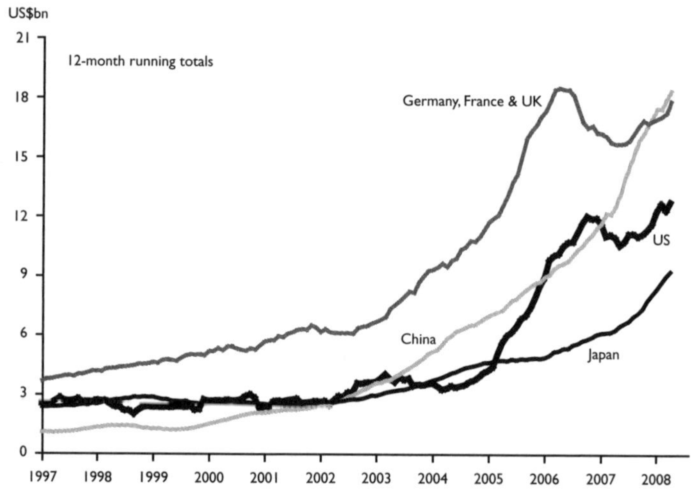

Source: Oxford Economics.

This new pattern of trade is helping to sustain world (including US) export growth even as US import growth has ground to a halt (see Figures 1.6 to 1.9). It is also forging new partnerships in business, investment and finance.

Figure 1.9: Korea: destination of exports

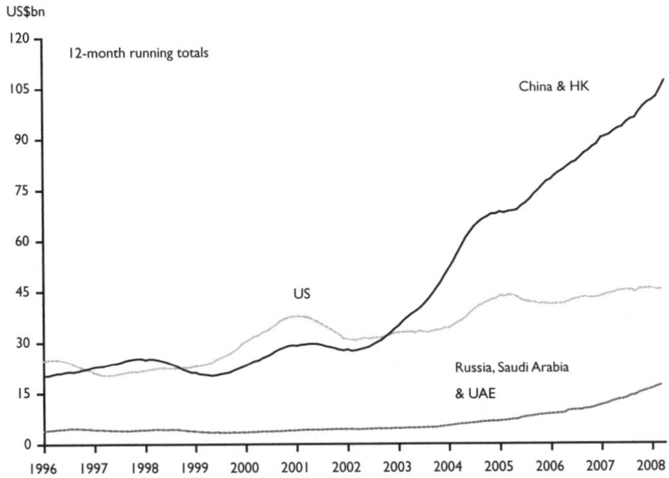

Source: Oxford Economics.

Emerging markets sustain lower risk premium

The coming together of a number of benign influences presented a golden opportunity for improvements in finance, external balances and debt structures across most of the developing world, especially during 2002–07. Emerging-market risk premiums tumbled and – a significant milestone – Brazil was rerated to investment grade in early 2008.[9]

The sharp decline in the emerging markets' risk spread (see Figure 1.10) reflected a perceived improvement in policies, performance and prospects, especially emphasizing the shift towards firmer exchange rates and lower inflation. In the historical perspective, the emergence from late 2007 of a 'hump' in inflation represents only a modest setback caused by soaring oil and food prices. A few developing countries are at risk of spiralling wage–price inflation, among them Vietnam, Egypt, Ukraine and some other east European states, but so far this threat has been contained in most of the key economies. Core annual inflation (excluding food and fuel) is still in the 2–3% range in the United States and Europe, close to central bank targets; and on average, annual inflation in the developing world also remains low, [10]in the 7–8% range (see Figure 1.11) or below 5% excluding food and fuel.

During the banking crisis in 2007–08, the shock waves have been concentrated in the United States and Europe. Although there have been some

9 Standard and Poor's, ratings review of 30 April 2008, as reported in the press.
10 Inflation started to drop sharply in China in mid-2008, for example.

Figure 1.10: Global bond markets: risk spreads

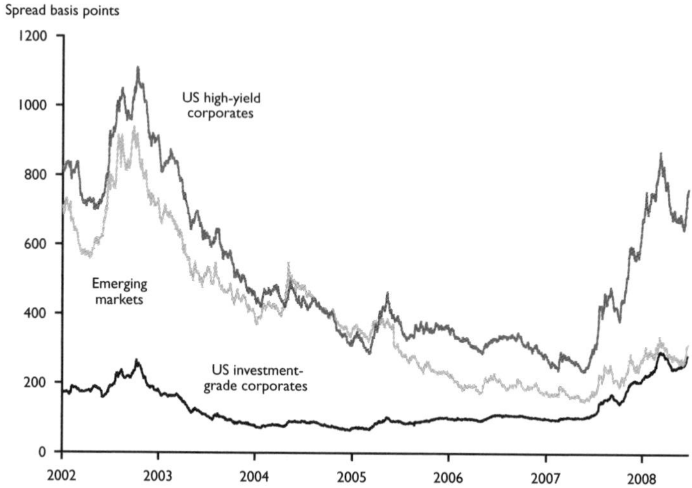

Source: Oxford Economics.

Figure 1.11: Emerging markets: GDP growth and inflation

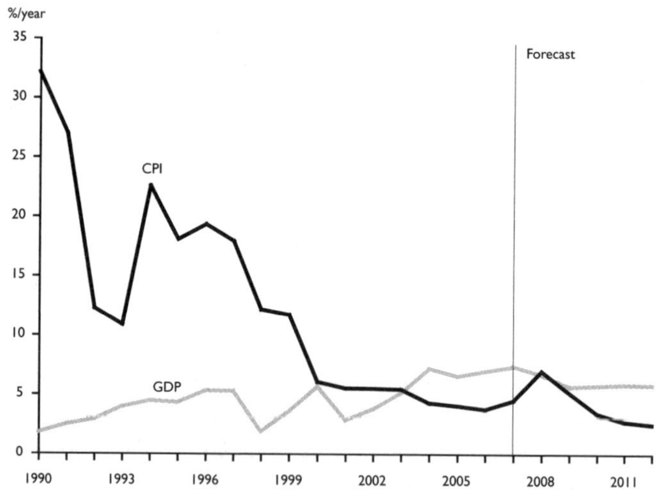

Source: Oxford Economics.

ripple effects on property and mortgage markets elsewhere, the banking sector in most emerging markets has seen little impact, partly because of its focus on domestic development, raising local savings and loans rather than expanding in international finance. Countries that have benefited from easier access to credit and property investment from abroad (e.g. those in eastern Europe, funded largely by EU banks) will see this growth curtailed owing to the credit crunch and to greater risk aversion. But in general, there is little direct exposure across emerging markets to the complex securitization and interbank dealing that exacerbated the debt crisis in the United States and its spread to European banking.

It is possible that the banking crisis also had indirect impacts on countries with substantial surplus savings, such as China, Japan and the energy economies. For example, the lack of confidence in international markets, particularly in US assets, created a dilemma for the investment of surplus funds, probably leading to a temporary bottling up of excess liquidity at home. However, after serious setbacks for the dollar and the equity markets in early 2008, capital flows into US securities resumed, helping the dollar to recover and release surplus funds.

Despite greater risk aversion, the rise in inflation and the possibility of a cyclical slowdown in global growth, emerging markets have been able to sustain underlying investor confidence, as illustrated by their relatively steady risk ratings as opposed to volatile equity markets. There may be more turbulence ahead, but if so, markets have not anticipated it.

Overall, the 2007–08 banking crisis has left the better-funded emerging markets and their banking sectors in relatively good shape compared with their weakened US and EU counterparts. This offers current and future advantages, for example in terms of liquidity, the cost of funds and potential acquisitions. This is especially true for cash-rich countries such as China and the Gulf states, probably accelerating their emergence as important forces in global finance.

Wealth build-up a surprise – impacts contentious

Despite the 2007–08 financial crisis, the US, the EU and Japan together still account for about 70% of the world's recorded gross financial market wealth, currently estimated at about $200 trillion. They also possess most of the world's stock of financial assets, boosted by their large bond markets. This needs to be kept in perspective when assessing the impact of rising emerging market wealth and the need for more balanced financial market development.

However, China and the GCC have built up financial market wealth of some $10–12 trillion and $4–5 trillion respectively, each with external wealth of approximately $2–3 trillion according to recent estimates (excluding any assessment of private external wealth, which may be worth several trillion dollars).[11] In total, financial wealth in the developing world (chiefly held in bank accounts and local equities) can be estimated at approximately double its annual GDP, $40–50 trillion, largely accumulated over the past five to ten years.

Gains in wealth (at home and abroad) represent both the accumulation of annual savings and the revaluation of existing asset holdings. Since 1997, the fast-rising emerging markets have become wealthier as the developed world's wealth has expanded. Asset prices have gained on a global basis, in part driven by fundamental reratings (alongside the rerating of commodities and long-run growth prospects) and by the impact of surging liquidity. Rising wealth has generated a correspondingly substantial expansion in demand for banking and other financial services. The emerging-market financial sector has been a beneficiary of global growth. In particular, fast growth in trade directly stimulates demand for global financial services (FX, trade finance, insurance, etc). International expansion and experience tend to encourage private capital flow activity as well.

Of course, burgeoning trade has a more direct impact on wealth formation. Large current account surpluses have appeared in the emerging economies, resulting from excess domestic savings that directly feed into the build-up of external wealth (see Figures 1.12 and 1.13).

From the point of view of the developed world, it is the management of this external wealth (and related capital flows) that has created most of the interest, and concern. In particular, central bank foreign exchange reserves have approximately quadrupled over the past five years to about $5.5 trillion in early 2008, fed chiefly by the stream of current account surpluses in Asia and the energy economies that reflects excess national savings. SWFs have also grown rapidly, especially in the energy economies.

For prudential reasons, central bank FX holdings are mostly in government securities such as US and EU government bonds. This fast-growing segment of global capital flows is seen as a contributing factor to the persistence of unusually low levels of bond yields and market rates in the United States in 2003–07. Indeed, foreign investors now hold roughly half the stock of US government bonds (compared to an average share in US financial assets of about 20%).[12] This increasing demand for US treasury securities could not be met by expanding supply (avoiding a fall in yields); thus the creation of 'cheap money' was largely plugged into consumer credit and

11 These are estimates for 2007, and they are based on FX reserves, SWFs, local equity market valuations and savings deposits. Government debt and bond markets are only a very small part of financial markets in these countries, e.g. China's government debt is less than $500 billion, most of which is held in the domestic banking sector. Estimates for SWFs are in line with figures quoted by International Financial Services London.

12 Measured in mid-2008 before the US Treasury bail-outs of the US mortgage and insurance system.

Figure 1.12: Emerging Asia: foreign exchange reserves

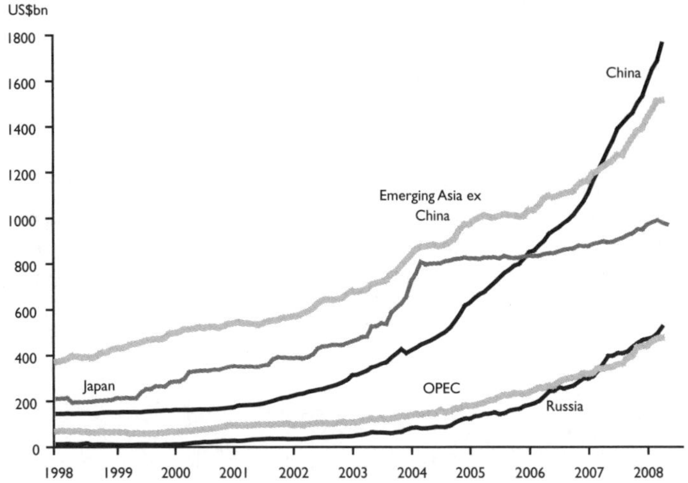

Source: Oxford Economics.

Figure 1.13: Current account imbalances of leading world economies, 1990–2012

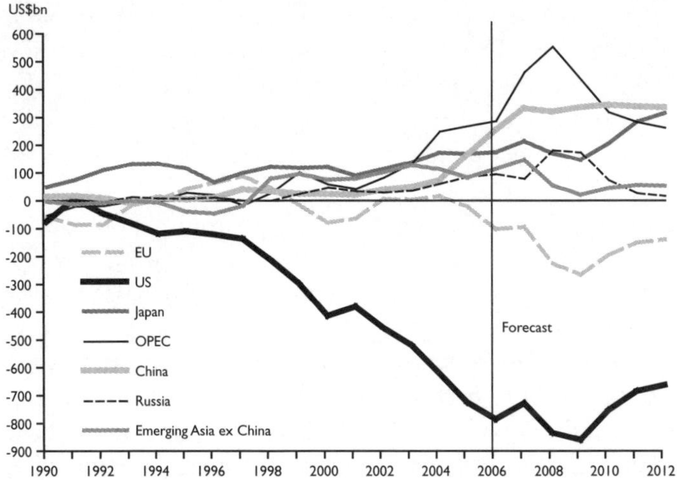

Source: Oxford Economics.

mortgage market expansion, part of the background to the recent property bubble.

Low interest rates also provided support to equity markets and leveraged finance around the world. In consequence, this flood of cheap money has been blamed for exacerbating risks from asset price bubbles to the expansion in subprime debt. The resulting excesses are still unwinding, particularly in the US and UK banking sectors but also in Eurozone banking.

The ramifications of asset imbalances

The problem highlighted above is that a rise in global FX reserves generates a disproportionately high demand for government bonds in the major, liquid markets, primarily the US and to a lesser extent the EU. However, this FX effect serves only to highlight the asset allocation–supply imbalance caused by the dominance of the US and the EU in global bond issuance. Increasing investment in bonds will tend to damp down yields in these key markets. In addition, swings in asset allocation across the two main markets will generate volatility in the exchange rate.

As long as the United States was the prime destination for surging FX reserves, this flow helped to support the dollar, despite the large US current account deficit. But as central banks started to diversify their asset positions, primarily into the euro and SWFs, this reduced the level of support. On its own, this change may have been quite small, but in the midst of events that probably shifted private investor preferences, even a small reallocation of FX holdings may have exacerbated the move away from US assets and thus the downward trend in the value of the dollar. Divergent central bank policies have also encouraged the currency cycle, with European monetary policy remaining relatively tight versus steep rate cuts in the United States.

After hovering at about $1.25 in 2004–06 (up from an average of $0.90 in 2001), the value of the euro shot up in 2007–08, reaching $1.60 by the second quarter of 2008 as investors sought a secure alternative to US securities and the dollar. However, as confidence in the Eurozone started to evaporate by August, the euro's value began to fall back sharply. The amplitude of the dollar–euro cycle is very high – most other currencies have seen far less turbulence – and the cross-rate is clearly driven by swings in asset allocation and capital flows, largely linked to bond and currency investments. As there are few options for large-scale investments outside the liquid US and EU bond markets, shifts in asset allocation will imply that this volatility in the dollar–euro rate will continue, broadly in line with the economic cycle.

This is hard on Eurozone businesses, which find the timing, as well as the scale, of such currency cycles difficult to absorb. Yet in the midst of the March 2008 debacle over the collapse of Bear Stearns and fears for other major banks, even the United States became concerned to avoid a further dollar rout.

If there were another option for bond investors, it would help to relieve the tensions created by the bipolar bond market world. In principle, Japan could help to provide that option. But in practice, foreign holdings in Japanese bonds are very low, and this market remains dominated by domestic savers. Another way of relieving the pressure needs to be created.

Although shifting funds from FX reserves into SWFs may reduce the global asset imbalance by spreading asset holdings more widely outside US and EU bonds, it would ease the pressure only slightly. The world could address the problem more effectively by creating a better balance in the global structure of assets. Essentially, this means creating larger and more liquid debt markets in other parts of the world (and another global currency, whether actual or synthetic) so as to offer serious alternatives to the bond markets (and currencies) of the US and the EU.

Asset market imbalances should be understood as an important facet of the more general global imbalances threat. Indeed, these asset imbalances may even hinder the exchange rate corrections many see as appropriate for reducing trade imbalances. The rise in financial markets and centres across the newly wealthy emerging-market economies should become part of the solution instead of posing an investment dilemma.

Exchange rate regimes questioned as FX reserves rise

Exchange rate regimes in the emerging markets have also come under increasing scrutiny. This is largely in response to the appearance of substantial balance of payments surpluses across most of the emerging market world, especially in Asia and the energy economies. These surpluses are the counterparts of the US trade deficit and the source of EU concern over competition in some industries.

This is especially true for China, where a bulging balance of payments surplus has led to the build-up of massive FX reserves from less than $150 billion in 1997 to over $1.5 trillion by the end of 2007. These reserves are now far beyond normal prudential requirements (typically not more than six months of imports cover) – indeed key countries, including not just China and Hong Kong but also Brazil, Russia, India, Taiwan and Japan, have reserves equivalent to more than one year's cover. However, it was China that attracted most attention as its exports and FX reserves soared following WTO entry yet its currency remained pegged to the dollar. International pressure to revalue the renminbi has been intense. The question of currency manipulation has even been raised in conjunction with the threat of trade sanctions against Chinese goods. In July 2005, the Chinese authorities did announce a move to a more flexible basket float but, in practice, this has turned out to be a managed crawling peg, with the renminbi only gradually revaluing against the dollar. So there continues to be pressure for more substantial change, including a move to a free float.

China is not the only country under scrutiny, as most Asian central banks (including the Bank of Japan) have accumulated substantial FX reserves. By contrast, the energy economies have tended to channel their surplus savings into SWFs, and their FX reserves have risen less rapidly despite large trade surpluses. With global FX reserves at $5.5 trillion in early 2008 and sovereign wealth funds accounting for an additional $3–4 trillion, the build-up of government-managed external wealth has been impressive. Most of these currencies are in some way managed in relation to or directly pegged to the dollar. Although there is less concern in the US and the EU over the implications for competitiveness *vis-à-vis* the energy economies, those countries too have been encouraged to consider floating their currencies.

Despite pressure for change, the surplus countries look set to continue in

Figure 1.14 Estimated value of SWFs, 2007–12

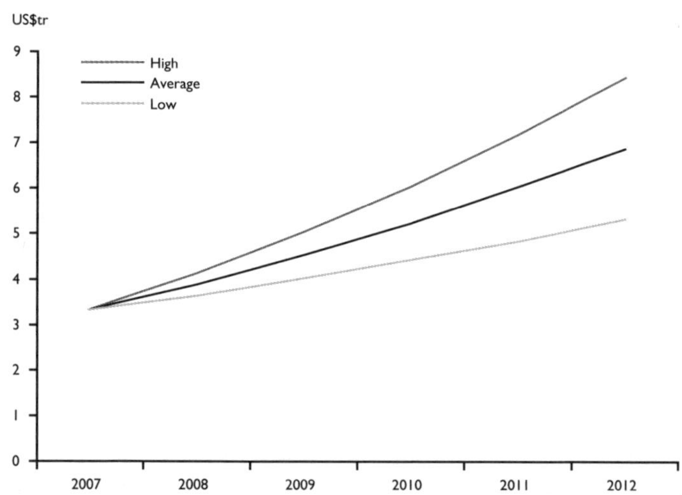

Note: It is assumed that existing FX reserves are kept separate from SWFs. High estimates for SWFs are based on cash inflows of $500 billion per annum and investment returns of 10% per annum (by 2015, this methodology produces a forecast of about $12.5 trillion for SWF holdings, just a little above the estimate made by Stephen Jen in 'How Big Could SWFs Be by 2015?', Morgan Stanley Research, London, 2007). Low estimates are based on no further cash inflows and 10% investment returns only.

Source: Historical data from IFSL and estimates provided in Royal Institute of International Affairs, *The Gulf as a Global Financial Centre: Growing Opportunties and International Influence*, London, June 2008.

surplus, partly because of policy preferences to maintain a positive balance of payments (for economic and financial security) but also because adjustments in net trade are typically too slow to create a rapid, marked change. Slow adjustments reflect the underlying inability of the surplus economies to spend as fast as they earn. Although domestic demand has started to pick up relative to exports, especially in China where the savings rate is now estimated to be falling, the process of unwinding excess savings takes time. For example, even if export growth were to come to a dramatic halt by the end of 2008, the level of annual imports into China would have to increase by a further 20% in order to eliminate the trade surplus; for the GCC, its level of imports would have to almost double. In consequence, FX reserves and SWFs look certain to grow, and these substantial external funds will need to be managed for the foreseeable future.

In principle, SWFs could be drawn down if governments wanted to use fiscal policy actively in order to support growth in a downturn. However, there seems little likelihood of this happening in the near future, especially as budgets remain in surplus, allowing ample leeway for more expansionary policy. At present, the savings surplus is still high and is adding to the

Figure 1.15 Estimated value of combined SWFs and FX reserves, 2007–12

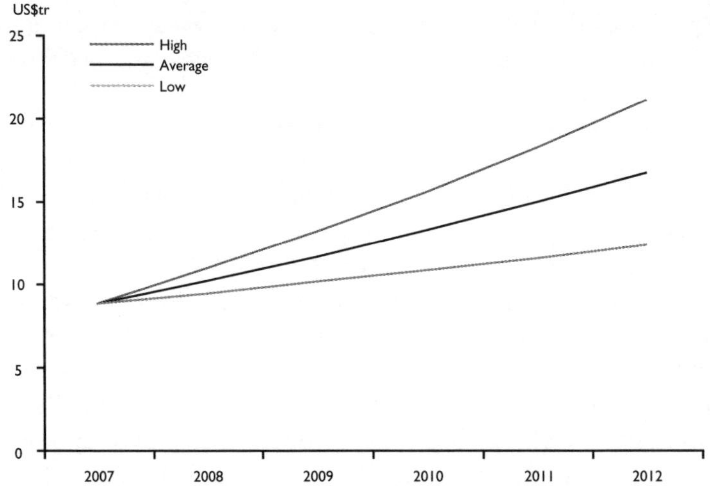

Note: The high estimates utilize the high estimates for SWFs alone plus high estimates for FX reserves based on cash inflows of $1 trillion per annum and investment returns of 5% per annum. The low estimates use the low SWF values plus FX estimates based on no further cash inflows (5% investment returns only).
Source: Estimates provided in Chatham House, *The Gulf as a Global Financial Centre: Growing Opportunities and International Influence*, London, June 2008.

build-up of wealth – it probably accounted for about half the estimated rise of nearly 20% in the global value of SWFs in 2007 – and this contribution is likely to increase in 2008.

Estimates based on plausible assumptions for savings flows and investment returns suggest that SWFs and FX reserves combined could more than double to over $20 trillion by 2012, as shown by Figures 1.14 and 1.15. In five years' time, these funds will be approximately equal in value to the combined size of the US and Eurozone government bond markets (up from about 50% of its value today). Even if SWFs adopt less conservative investment strategies, central banks' FX investment policies will tend to remain cautious, implying that significant proportions of these funds will have to be placed in the major bond markets. Therefore, the share of foreign investors in the US government bond market may rise from its present level of 50% even in the case of further diversification of FX reserves (across other currencies) and transfers to SWFs.

Impacts on capital flows and markets

As highlighted above, global wealth has changed even more surprisingly and radically than world trade and GDP, and it has affected capital flows. Not only has wealth increased but also more of this wealth is being moved around the world as investors adopt a more global view and as FX reserves and SWFs have grown.

The global capital account used to be composed of modest FDI flows, IMF packages and aid – all at relatively low levels compared with the scale of trade flows, which dominated both the balance of payments and exchange rate analysis even into the 1990s. In 1980, capital flows were still small, only about 5% of world goods trade worth $2 trillion, while services trade was worth about 20% of goods trade (see Figure 1.16). By 1990, capital flows were close to 15% of goods trade and almost on a par with services trade. But over the past 20 years, global financial flows have risen sharply and are now roughly equivalent to one-third of goods trade, which totalled about $15 trillion in 2007. Although services trade has also picked up rapidly in the past few years, it is only around half the size of global capital inflows. This change has transformed balance of payments analysis and the forces shaping exchange rates and investment trends.

Capital inflows now make up roughly one-third of FDI (typically including substantial M&A (mergers and acquisitions) activity) and one-third of portfolio flows; the rest are banking and official capital flows. The marked shift towards larger two-way global capital flows across the major

Figure 1.16: Evolution of global GDP, trade and capital flows

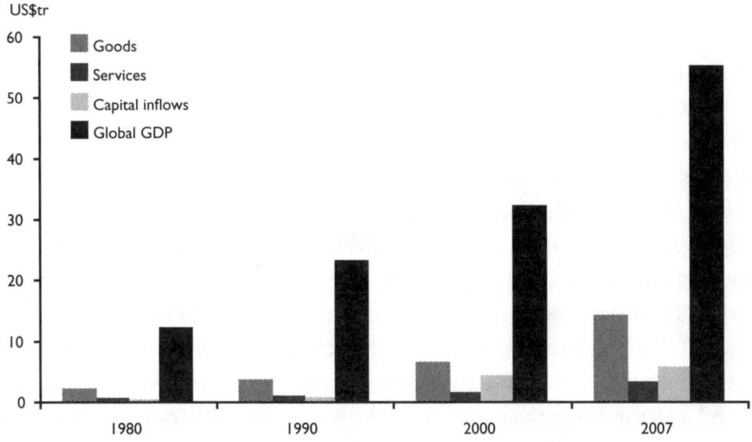

Sources: IMF, WTO and National Accounts data.

developed economies reflects global business patterns, M&A activity and global wealth-management. Now emerging markets have also started to play a much more active (and dual) role. In 2007, estimates indicate that capital inflows to the developing world alone rose sharply to nearly $800 billion[13] and capital outflows were probably very similar – even larger if SWFs and FX reserves are included.

The rise of the emerging-market countries has opened up the potential for greater capital flows to developing countries from the developed world and, more unexpectedly, it has also led to a surge in capital outflows from the emerging markets themselves. Development economics has had to re-examine its traditional model for global capital as a flow from rich to poor countries. Although a very poor economy's take-off into growth may still need a helping hand to enable essential investment and development to take place, not all emerging-market economies need to rely on capital inflows.

China has clearly not needed foreign capital from a purely financial point of view – it has ample and excess savings of its own – but it has nevertheless been open to substantial FDI inflows (recently some $40–80 billion per annum), as they have enabled it to rapidly connect with the global economy and trade. FDI has formed the backbone of the export sector's capital base: estimates point to cumulative FDI (foreign ownership) making up about 50% of this capital. And export performance has been very strongly correlated with the build-up of this base. But it was expertise

13 Institute of International Finance, 'Capital Flows to Emerging Market Economies', 6 March 2008.

and trade linkages, not strictly finance, that have played the critical role, opening up the previously closed Chinese economy and enabling a massive and rapid change in its position in world trade and the global economic order. Excess local savings have thus been accumulated into a build-up of wealth at home and abroad.

China's example of a debt-free, and very successful, development strategy has not been lost on other aspiring emerging-market economies. Although general economic conditions have favoured the improvements seen in developing countries' policies and financial positions, such as reduced reliance on external debt, the build-up of reserves, stronger currencies and lower inflation rates, these changes are to an extent also due to the adoption of a more 'Chinese style' approach to growth and development. This concept of financially prudent development was undoubtedly reinforced by the experience of the Asian crisis and its aftermath. It is remarkable that the IMF no longer has 'invalids' in its care and that so few countries are threatened by debt and balance of payments crises even in the midst of a US slowdown and a widespread banking crisis.

Increasing participation in the financial sector

The increasing importance of the emerging economies means that the previously rarefied pursuit of development economists has become the daily business of business – everyone now knows about BRICs, 'S curves', catch-up and the likely transformation of the world's economic order by 2050. Rapid gains in GDP and living standards have increased the number of consumers in all sectors of the world economy, from users of mobile phones and the Internet to purchasers of electrical appliances and processed foods. Alongside these consumer trends, participation in banking, insurance and financial markets has also boomed.

Although the major markets of the US and the EU plunged into a banking crisis in 2007, the developing world emerged largely unscathed. Developing countries have started to expand their presence in banking, M&A activity, private wealth management, insurance and all forms of financial services. China has begun to set up SWFs in order to cope better with managing its large FX reserves; Indian companies such as Mittal have engaged in large M&A deals in the major markets; and new financial centres have sprung up in the Gulf. The speed of the change has taken everyone by surprise. And even though the new players are still a long way behind the global leaders, their potential is substantial and their challenge will grow. This raises issues of wealth management, regulation and governance that were not even on the agenda until several years ago. Nor was the thought of emerging-market SWFs bailing out leading Western banks.

The developing world's swelling pools of liquidity, along with its aspirations for a greater role in global financial markets, will have further widespread impacts on the global economy, asset management and the ownership of capital. The rules for governance of the global financial system may well be challenged. The current high-profile debate over these issues illustrates the great importance attached to potential threats and to the possible implications for the world's leading economies, companies and financial markets.

Data and forecasting sources

Institute of International Finance (IIF)
International Energy Agency (IEA)
International Financial Services London (IFSL)
International Monetary Fund (IMF)
Organisation for Economic Co-operation and Development (OECD)
Oxford Economics (for the supply of charts)
World Bank

2 Global financial markets: liquidity vs globalization

Michael Hume

Introduction

The rapid increase in asset prices and the boom in global financial markets over the past decade has been unprecedented and has contributed to the word 'bubble' being applied to a very wide range of asset markets and financial innovations: stock markets, bond markets, housing markets, leveraged buyouts, collateralized debt obligations, subprime mortgages and more. 'Bubble' evokes the notion of something that cannot be sustained; and in the recent period, it has often been associated with the idea that the increase in asset prices has been fuelled by 'excess liquidity', administered by central banks that have maintained interest rates too low for too long. This chapter examines the theoretical case for linking liquidity and fundamentals to asset price increases over the past 10 years and relates it to changes in the level of real interest rates and to global imbalances.

The clearest indication of excess liquidity is that the historically stable relationship between the global broad money supply and the global nominal GDP has been definitively broken. At around the turn of the millennium, the rate of increase in broad money began to exceed that of nominal GDP by a wide margin. This has been sustained. With the rise in money supply having been matched by rises in asset values of a similar magnitude, some economists have concluded that it was excess liquidity that drove asset prices higher.

But it is reasonable to ask whether the link between liquidity and asset prices has been running in a different direction. Is 'excess liquidity' really behind the rapid growth in asset prices or is it that the fundamentals which determine asset prices have improved substantially and that there has been a rise in the demand for money as a consequence? The forces of globalization, insofar as they have radically transformed the fundamentals of asset prices, are certainly a rival explanation for the long boom in the financial markets. It may have been that, owing to the downward pressure on inflation from globalization, the pursuit of these inflation targets permitted a policy of low official interest rates that generated strong growth in both liquidity and asset prices.

The drivers of globalization have been well documented by many researchers. The reduced costs of transport and communication, rapid advancements in information technology and also political stability, among many other factors, have contributed to the growth of the emerging economies to such an extent that the balance of economic and financial power is shifting. As part of this process, capital flows across the economies of the world have risen sharply, with significant influences on asset prices. At the macroeconomic level, these forces appear to have been powerful enough to lead to changes in interest rates and in a whole range of asset prices.

One issue that has perhaps received less attention than it should do in this debate is the role played by the development of financial markets in the emerging economies. Although these economies have grown at rapid rates for several years, in many cases their financial markets remain underdeveloped: the share of emerging economies in global GDP has now increased to about 30% but their share in global capital markets amounts to only 15%. It is the discrepancy between the capacity of their economies to generate savings and the capacity of their financial systems to absorb them that, arguably, explains the perverse transfer of savings from poorer regions to richer regions of the world. However, there are already many signs that the development of the emerging countries' financial markets is beginning to catch up with economic fundamentals. Many chapters of this volume deal with this issue in connection with the Gulf Cooperation Council countries.

Monetarist roots

Like so many relationships in economics, money and asset prices should be seen as being determined simultaneously. The modern-day representation of the monetarist model draws a link between money and inflation over the longer term. But this representation is too simple and does not do justice to monetarism. Somewhere along the way, the richness of the monetarist model was put to one side and replaced with something far too basic to be of help in interpreting the behaviour of modern economies. Now is perhaps the time to retrieve some of that early richness.

In their Raffaele Mattioli lecture of August 1988, Karl Brunner and Alan Meltzer set out a more sophisticated macroeconomic model in which money, credit, asset prices and the broader economy are jointly determined (Brunner and Meltzer 1993). The key insight of this model is that asset prices affect the demand for money and that the supply of money affects the level of asset prices. From this emerges the conventional monetarist viewpoint: a loose central bank policy, by creating excess credit and money, will result in asset prices being chased up. Other things being equal, this will continue until asset prices have increased by an amount that is sufficient to bring the demand for money back into line with the new level of supply.

However, in this model an alternative sequence can occur. In the modern world in which central banks target the level of the interest rate, an increase in demand for money will always be met by an automatic increase in its supply. Consequently, an increase in asset prices precipitated by a change in fundamentals will also lead to a rise in the demand for *and* supply of money. This means that the rise in money and credit could be the consequence of higher asset prices, not just their cause.

Distinguishing which sequence has been operating in recent years therefore requires an assessment of the extent to which changes in the fundamentals can account for the increase in asset prices. To the extent that they can, the growth in liquidity should be viewed as a symptom of changing fundamentals rather than as the cause of an asset price boom.

Understanding asset prices

What are the fundamentals in this model that could account for a change in the level of asset prices? The simplest asset pricing model, the Gordon model, is a good place to start:

$$P = D / (R + r - g)$$

P is the asset price, D is the asset's cash-flow yield, R is the risk-free real long-term interest rate, r is the required return to compensate for the risk of the asset and g is the expected growth rate of real dividends. Within the framework of this simple model, there are four factors that could account for the asset price boom: an increase in D, a fall in R, a fall in r and an increase in g. It is possible that all these changes have taken place over the past decade.

Perhaps the most important factor has been a decline in the risk-free real long-term interest rate (R) as it affects all assets. Consequently, identifying the causes of the decline in real interest rates is essential. But there are likely to have been effects from the other factors too. At the global level, GDP growth has been sustained at its highest rate for over 30 years, with, until very recently, few signs of inflation. This has probably raised expectations about the growth rate of dividends (g). The profit share of GDP has also been rising, and this may have helped to boost the level of corporate profits and cash-flow yields (D). (It may additionally have raised expectations about the future growth of dividends.) Finally, the Great Moderation, i.e. the damping of the business cycle, may have reduced the volatility of cash-flow yields, and thus it would justify a reduction in the required return of assets to compensate for risk (r).

Globalization has probably played at least some role, if not a dominant one, in all these fundamentals-based explanations for higher asset prices. This much is reflected in the wide range of debate that has taken place since the late 1990s, from the interest rate conundrum and the sources of stronger world growth to the rise in the profit share of GDP and the origins of the Great Moderation.

Low interest rates: fact or fiction?

It is generally accepted that over the past 10 years, interest rates have been unusually low and that this has been a significant factor behind the increase in asset prices. However, Robert Shiller of Yale University has challenged this view. In a recent paper (Shiller 2007), he sets out the case for thinking that the strong rise in asset prices stems not from low interest rates but from agents becoming confused about the distinction between nominal and real interest rates as nominal interest rates have come down. As part of his case, he also casts doubt on the idea that real interest rates are low, suggesting that although the nominal long-term interest rate has fallen very sharply, the level of real long-term interest rates is not low in a long historical context. He then presents behavioural evidence to suggest that the rise in asset prices reflects something akin to 'money illusion' as agents incorrectly equated the decline in nominal interest rates with a fall in the real interest rate.

Whether long-term real interest rates are unusually low is an empirical question. If they are not, then that would be a fatal blow to the case for a fundamentals-based explanation based on the forces of globalization. Shiller (2007) presents data showing that the average long-term nominal US interest rate between 1871 and 2007 was 4.72%, which is about the same as the rate that has prevailed over the past decade. More importantly, the same is true for real long-term interest rates. The ex-post long-term real US interest rate between 1871 and 1997 was 2.40%.[1] This is lower than it

1 This average includes a period of sustained negative real interest rates in the 1970s. Excluding that period would result in a slightly higher average real interest rate.

was in 1997; and taking the current inflation rate as a forecast for inflation over the next decade, it is not obviously low compared to the level that has prevailed over the past one. Thus, according to Shiller (2007), 'The best we can say for the popular low long-term interest rate view is that today interest rates remain relatively low when compared with twenty or thirty years ago' .

However, although it is interesting that the *level* of real long-term interest rates may not be low compared to the long-run historical average, it nonetheless remains the case that real long-term interest rates have declined substantially from about 4% in the early 1990s to some 2% since 2000. And it is the change in real interest rates that matters most when understanding the change in asset prices. Thus, on balance, it still seems reasonable to think that the real interest rate has been a significant factor behind the rise in asset prices.

Even so, given that the level of the real interest rate appears to be historically normal, it is also necessary to ask whether the decline deserves a special explanation – of which globalization is potentially the most important – or whether the decline can be seen as a mere normalization. On balance, it seems likely that a special explanation is necessary. Even if the level of real long-term interest rates is not historically abnormal, this needs to be seen in the context of much higher potential growth at the global level, which would tend to put upward pressure on real long-term interest rates. It does, then, seem reasonable to think that a special explanation for the 'low' level of real long-term interest rates is warranted.

Explaining the interest rate conundrum

The idea of the interest rate conundrum first came to prominence when Alan Greenspan, the then chairman of the US Federal Reserve, expressed puzzlement at the lack of response by the long end of the yield curve to monetary tightening in 2003 and 2004. One recent study has argued that this can be accounted for, from the perspective of finance, by a decline in the term premium (Backus and Wright 2007). It highlights lower macroeconomic and financial volatility, more predictable monetary policy and the state of the business cycle as possible causes.

However, there are other, more powerful explanations for the origin of the decline in the term premium. It is the current chairman of the US Federal Reserve, Ben Bernanke, who is most closely associated with the idea of the low level of real long-term interest rates being a consequence of a global savings glut (Bernanke 2005). The argument here is that at the global level, there has been an increase in planned savings relative to planned investment. As a result, there has been persistent downward pressure on real interest rates, and this low level of real interest rates has helped to fuel the asset price boom.

In his book *The Age of Turbulence*, Alan Greenspan (2007) has emphasized not only the significance of the global savings glut but also the disinflationary effect of the integration into the world economy of the major emerging markets and their previously untapped labour forces. This, he argues, has contributed to an increase in global aggregate supply that has had a downward effect on inflation across the world. And this, in turn, has permitted central banks in the advanced economies to run much looser monetary policies, with fewer consequences for their own domestic inflation rates, than would otherwise have been the case. Coupled with the downward effect on real long-term interest rates from the global savings glut, this provides a powerful explanation, one that is intimately tied to the process of globalization, for the rise in asset prices.

Some economists, notably those from the Keynesian tradition such as Brad de Long from the University of California at Berkeley, have argued that these explanations need to be fused (de Long 2005). On its own, the savings glut hypothesis is inconsistent with world growth having been so strong. Typically, an increase in planned savings relative to planned investment would drive down not only the level of real interest rates but also the level of real activity. But, de Long argues, this misses how monetary policy has responded. Owing to the disinflationary forces of globalization, central banks have been in a position to offset the negative effect on activity from the rise in planned savings relative to planned investment with loose monetary policy. It is only the combination of the savings glut, the disinflationary shock from globalization and loose monetary policies pursued by central banks that can account for all the key phenomena: a low level of real interest rates, a high level of asset prices, robust world growth and low inflation. To the extent that this is the correct explanation, it suggests that a combination of globalization (the savings glut) and excess liquidity (an accommodating central bank policy) underlies the low level of real interest rates and rising asset prices.

Does this, in itself, exonerate monetary policy from all responsibility for the asset price boom? Judged by the central banks' own mandates, in most cases price stability, they have been successful over the past decade. But because of the downward pressures on inflation from globalization, the pursuit of a constant inflation target has nonetheless had the effect of permitting strong growth in both liquidity and asset prices. This may be a weakness of the inflation-targeting framework. Michael Woodford of Columbia University has argued that for inflation-targeting to be an optimal (or desirable) monetary policy, central banks may have to pay more attention to the details of how it is implemented, including the possibility that longer forecast horizons may be warranted (Woodford 2007). In other words, it is possible that central banks ought to have operated a more restrictive monetary policy, even if it required accepting below-target inflation in the short term.

The role of global imbalances

One problem with the explanations of the interest rate conundrum given above is that they take place within a closed-economy framework. For example, the savings glut hypothesis need not be inconsistent with robust global growth in the way that Brad de Long suggests if the rise in savings has come about because of strong growth in the emerging economies, where saving rates are structurally high. Another problem is that it fails to shed any light on persistent global imbalances and the rise in the share of US assets in global portfolios. For example, why, given their strong growth potential, have the savings generated in emerging markets not been matched by a corresponding rise in their investment?

An attempt at answering this problem has been made by Ricardo Caballero of the Massachusetts Institute of Technology (Caballero et al. 2006). It is, he and his colleagues have argued, the inability of the emerging economies to supply financial assets that has both generated the savings glut and required it to be intermediated internationally. Here a distinction should be made between the Asian economies and the oil exporters, including those of the GCC. For the former, the 1997 exchange rate crisis is seen as having undermined the ability of domestic Asian financial markets to supply financial assets to invest in. For the oil exporters, their economies may not, at least until now, have had the domestic growth possibilities upon which financial markets could be based.

As a consequence, the increase in savings of the emerging market countries and the oil exporters has ended up being channelled into the financial market that has the greatest capacity to supply financial assets, the United States. In most cases, this has taken the form of very large official flows because many of the large emerging economies have capital account restrictions and pegged exchange rate regimes. But whatever form they take, these inflows to developed markets have had the effect of driving down real interest rates, and the low level of real interest rates has encouraged the supply of financial assets. Thus, in addition to global imbalances, there has been rapid growth in asset markets and financial products in the developed markets.

This supply-driven story depends crucially on there being a distinction between the United States and Europe as desired places to invest in for those who demand financial assets. Were this not the case, it would be hard to account for the very large US current account deficit coexisting with Europe's current account being broadly in balance. After all, Europe's financial markets are similarly mature to those of the United States. The reason Ricardo Caballero gives for this is the relatively low growth potential in Europe, which has undermined its attractiveness as a place to invest in.

This explanation seems to be confirmed by regional patterns across Europe and the rest of the world. For example, the United Kingdom and Australia, with their relatively high potential growth rates, have followed a similar path to the United States in running a large current account deficit. And within the euro area, strong-growth performers, such as Spain and Ireland, have also experienced large current account deficits. For Europe as a whole, however, this has been more than offset by Germany, which has grown more slowly and has correspondingly run a large current account surplus. Quite possibly, then, it is the need to intermediate the savings glut towards economies with high potential growth that is behind both the low level of real interest rates and persistent external imbalances in some countries.

Other explanations for higher asset prices

The main 'other' explanations worthy of consideration, as identified using the Gordon model, are the role of the rise in the profit share of GDP and declining macroeconomic volatility. The former has been a far from uniform feature of the advanced economies, but the United States, Japan and Germany have all seen rising profit shares over the past few decades. Although economists' understanding of the forces behind this tendency is as yet embryonic, a recent study by an IMF staff economist suggests that the rise in the global profit share of GDP can be attributed to both capital-augmenting technological progress and factors related to globalization (Guscina 2006). A more recent study by economists at the Bank for International Settlements suggests that the role of technological progress is the main explanation and that other possible causes, such as globalization, play a much smaller or even non-existent role (Ellis and Smith 2007).

As for the role played by declining macroeconomic volatility, Kenneth Rogoff of Harvard University has endorsed the ideas of Martin Lettau,

Sydney Ludvigson and Jessica Wachter in speculating that 'lower macroeconomic volatility has rationalized sharply higher prices for risky assets' (Rogoff 2006). To the extent that the damping of the business cycle is a consequence of better macroeconomic policy, this factor may have little to do with globalization. But to the extent that Alan Greenspan is correct that lower global inflation pressures have made central bankers' jobs that much easier, globalization may still be a factor: in a world of low inflation and higher potential growth, it is easier to adjust policy pre-emptively in order to head off economic slowdowns and cyclical growth surges.

Conclusion

The debate about whether the rise in asset prices over the past 10 years has resulted from excess liquidity or from globalization should be based upon an analysis of the extent to which higher asset prices can be justified by a change in fundamentals. The forces of globalization unleashed on the world economy during this time have been so evident in so many spheres that it does seem plausible that it is these forces that have driven asset prices higher rather than excess liquidity *per se*. However, this is not to suggest that the processes of change will be sustained indefinitely and that the higher level of asset prices will be maintained. At some point as emerging economies grow richer, their structurally high saving rates will decline. The downward pressure on global inflation from the increased integration of workers in emerging markets is likely to fade. And the capacity of the emerging markets to supply their own financial assets – a subject that is intimately connected with the contents of the rest of this volume – is likely to increase over time.

Recent developments in financial markets also suggest another possibility: the capacity of the advanced economies to supply financial assets may diminish. It is possible that the debt levels of households and firms, having been driven so high, are now generating higher default rates and risk premiums that will be elevated for some time. That would tend to short-circuit the transfer of capital from the emerging economies to the advanced economies and undermine asset prices in the process. In the absence of an offsetting increase in the capacity of emerging economies to supply financial assets it would also raise the possibility of the global savings glut leading to a period of very weak global growth or even recession.

This would suggest that an additional fundamental element in asset price determination is the functioning of the financial system. For much of the past decade a healthy financial system was taken for granted and this expectation was embodied in asset prices. Recent developments indicate that that should no longer be the case and that a period of deleveraging in both the broader financial and economic system is now likely to lead to sustained falls in asset price.s

Such an outcome would probably be associated with weak money supply growth and be seized upon as evidence of an independent influence from liquidity on asset prices. But, as with the boom itself, it would more accurately be described as a reflection of a change in the fundamental determinants of asset prices, with the health of the financial system playing a particularly important role.

References

Backus, D. and J. Wright (2007), 'Cracking the Conundrum', NBER Working Paper 13419, Cambridge, MA, September.

Bernanke, B. (2005), 'The Global Saving Glut and the US Current Account Deficit', remarks at the Sandridge Lecture, Virginia Association of Economics, 14 April.

Brunner, K. and A. Meltzer (1993), 'The Monetary Mechanism: Markets for Assets', in *Money and the Economy: Issues in Monetary Analysis*, Raffaele Mattioli Lectures, Cambridge University Press.

Caballero, R., E. Farhi and P. Gourinchas (2006), 'An Equilibrium Model of "Global Imbalances and Low Interest Rates"', BIS Working Paper No. 222, Basel, December.

De Long, B. (2005), 'Global Excess Liquidity?', 17 August, available at www.j-bradford-delong.net.

Ellis, L. and K. Smith (2007), 'The Global Upward Trend in the Profit Share', BIS Working Paper No. 231, Basel, July.

Greenspan, A. (2007), *The Age of Turbulence: Adventures in a New World* (London: Allen Lane).

Guscina, A. (2006), 'Effects of Globalization on Labor's Share in National Income', IMF Working Paper 06/294, Washington, December.

Rogoff, K. (2006), 'Impact of Globalization on Monetary Policy', Federal Reserve Bank of Kansas City symposium on 'The New Economic Geography: Effects and Policy Implications', Jackson Hole, Wyoming, 24–26 August.

Shiller, R. (2007), 'Low Interest Rates and High Asset Prices: An Interpretation in Terms of Changing Popular Economics Models', NBER Working Paper 13558, Cambridge, MA, October.

Woodford, M. (2007), 'Forecast Targeting as a Monetary Policy Strategy: Policy Rules in Practice', NBER Working Paper 13716, Cambridge, MA, December.

Part 2

The GCC's integration in the world economy

3 The GCC: economic powerhouse between the BRICs and the developed world

Ahmet Akarli*

Introduction: the hydrocarbon revenue windfall

The Gulf Cooperation Council countries have benefited from the surge in global energy prices in recent years. The resulting massive oil and natural gas revenue windfall has allowed the GCC economies to improve their net foreign assets and their fiscal position over the past four years and to realize strong, investment-driven economic growth. The GCC region's current account and budget surpluses soared to 35% of regional GDP in 2006 and economic growth rebounded strongly to an estimated 7% in 2007, double the 3.5% average for 1990–2002. This robust economic performance is likely to continue uninterrupted in the next few years as the region continues to benefit from high energy prices, which will be reinforced by a combination of strong demand growth and supply-side constraints.[1]

Not surprisingly, the GCC region's growing importance in energy markets and as a supplier of capital to the world is commonly acknowledged and widely discussed. Less clearly appreciated but of particular interest is its ongoing economic transformation and long-term economic potential. It is becoming an economic power to be reckoned with. The GCC countries currently boast a combined GDP of about $800 billion, comparable to that of sizeable economies such as Mexico ($810 billion), Australia ($745 billion) and the Netherlands ($665 billion) (see Figure 3.1). Their average per capita income is also fairly high at $20,500. The GCC ranks 27th globally, just after Cyprus ($21,000) and above Israel ($20,000), Portugal and South Korea (both $18,000) (see Figure 3.2).

The GCC region has much more to offer as it continues to benefit from the strong growth of global energy demand in the coming decades. The

 Special thanks to Jim O'Neill, Willem Buiter, Rory Macfarquhar and Dominic Wilson for their useful comments and contributions to this chapter.

1 For a more detailed discussion of the medium-term outlook for the GCC region, see 'Gulf Cooperation Council: How to Handle the Oil Price Windfall', *New European Markets Analyst*, Goldman Sachs Economic Research No. 06/10, 11 May 2006.

Figure 3.1: Major economic powers by GDP (2006 prices)

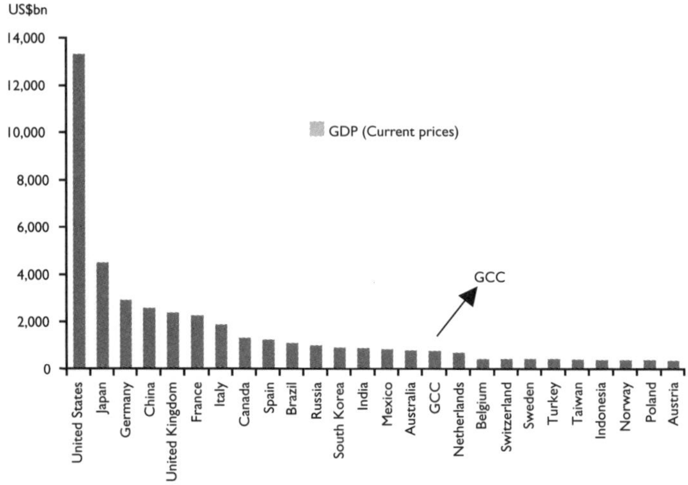

Source: GS.

Figure 3.2: The most prosperous countries by per capita GDP (2006 prices)

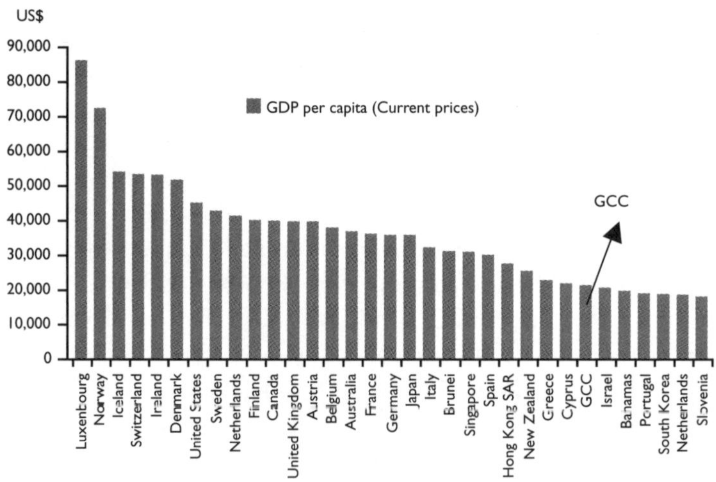

Source: GS.

rapid economic development of the BRICs and the N-11 countries[2] will exert considerable upward pricing pressure on global energy markets, especially over the next 10–15 years. This strong demand-side stimulus will,

2 The 'N-11' (next 11) countries, a category conceived by Goldman Sachs, are those with large populations and growing economies. They are Bangladesh, Iran, Turkey, the Philippines, Nigeria, Vietnam, Pakistan, South Korea, Indonesia, Egypt and Mexico. They are seen as next in line to the BRICs for rapid economic growth.

Figure 3.3: Global demand for energy: percentage year-on-year growth to 2050

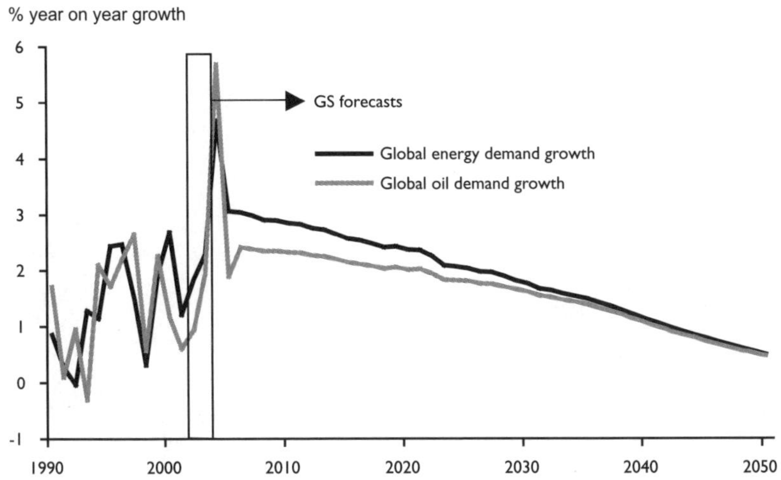

Sources: Peterson Institute for International Economics (IIE) and GS projections.

in turn, bring in a substantial oil and natural gas windfall for the GCC, enabling the region's economies to sustain very high investment levels and to generate strong, welfare-enhancing economic growth.

The region's economic growth towards the living standards of the developed countries is unlikely to be as explosive as that of the BRICs or some of the leading N-11 economies. Certain economic rigidities, political constraints, such as strong rent-seeking motives, and general regional instability will probably continue to prevent the GCC countries from realizing their full economic potential. But with a little extra effort – if they place more emphasis on improving the investment climate and facilitating strong total factor productivity (TFP) growth – they can emerge as one of the most prosperous regions in the world in the next decades.

Global energy demand and the revenue windfall

Over the next 15 years, there will be strong global demand for energy. Earlier work by Goldman Sachs (GS) suggests that this demand could grow at an average per annum rate of 2.9% to 2020, well above the previous 15 years' 1.85% per annum average.[3] The growth of energy demand is expected to retreat gradually to an average 2.1% per annum through the 2030s and to stabilize at about 1% per annum thereafter, as depicted in Figure 3.3.

3 See 'The BRICs and Global Markets: Crude, Cars and Capital', Global Economics Paper No. 118, Goldman Sachs Economic Research, 12 October 2004.

Figure 3.4: GCC countries' share of the world's proven oil and natural gas reserves

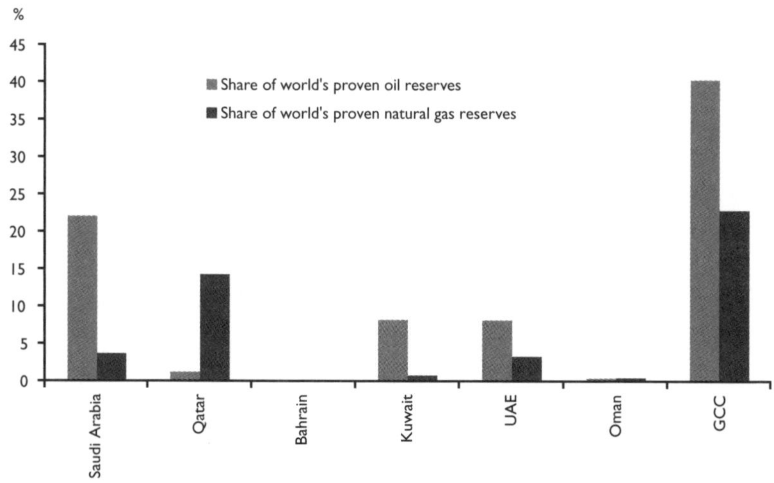

Source: BP.

The bulk of demand growth is projected to come from the fast-developing BRIC economies. GS projections put the growth of the BRICs' energy demand at an average of 5.3% per annum over the next 15 years. This growth is projected to fall gradually to 2% per annum in the 2020s and to stabilize at about 1.3% per annum in the following decades. This will come about as the BRICs complete the very energy-intensive early stages of their economic development (characterized by rapid industrialization, urbanization and infrastructure development) and as more subtle demographic factors kick in to bring down economic growth rates gradually.

The above projections do not, of course, constitute exact forecasts. They are intended mainly to illustrate the potential impact of growing BRIC demand on global energy markets. In reality, supply-side constraints and ensuing price pressures may not allow for such rapid demand growth, and eventually they may lead to calls for greater energy efficiency and diversification into alternative energy sources.[4] This could, in turn, push demand growth somewhat lower. Even so, energy (and specifically hydrocarbon) demand is likely to remain strong, supporting relatively high prices in the next decades – much to the benefit of global energy producers. The GCC, as a major energy supplier, would clearly benefit from emerging strong demand-side pressures and higher energy prices.

4 See Box 3.1 for a more detailed discussion of the environmental implications of increased growth in energy demand. See also 'Why the BRICs Dream Won't be Green', *BRICs Monthly*, No. 06/06, Goldman Sachs Economic Research, 18 October 2006.

Figure 3.5: GCC countries' share of global crude oil and natural gas production

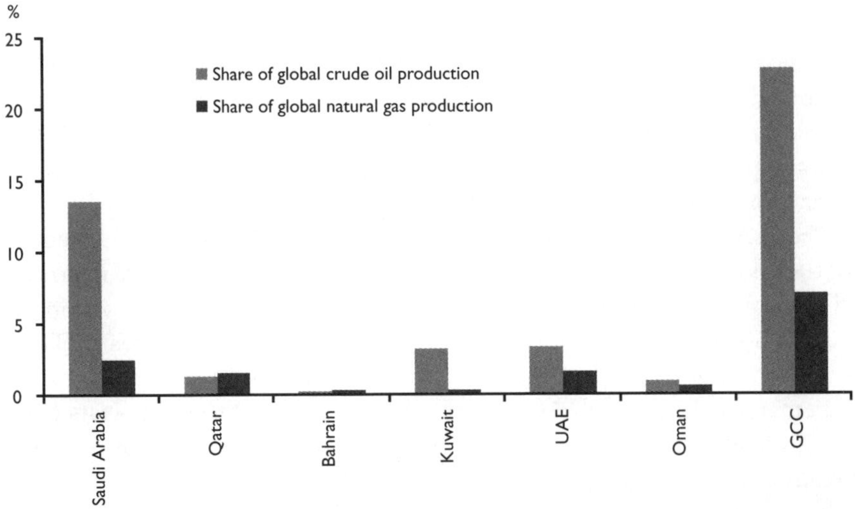

Source: BP.

The GCC countries, exceptionally well endowed with crude oil and natural gas reserves, will continue to play a crucial role in global energy production in the decades to come. Currently, their proven oil reserves stand at 484.3 billion barrels and their natural gas reserves stand at 41.4 trillion cubic metres – 40.3% of the world's proven oil reserves and 23% of its natural gas reserves respectively (see Figure 3.4). They produce roughly 6.7 billion barrels of crude oil and 195.9 billion cubic metres of natural gas every year. Even if production levels were to rise substantially over time, the vast natural resource base of the GCC region would still be sufficient to increase oil and natural gas production steadily for a long time, particularly in the next 15 years, provided that the necessary capital expenditure to uphold increasing levels of production comes through (see below).

More importantly perhaps, the GCC is set to capture an ever-larger share of the global energy production pie in the next decades. Its share of global oil production (22.8%) and natural gas production (7.1%) is currently below its share of proven reserves (see Figure 3.5), which suggests that its members will contribute increasingly to the global oil and natural gas supply. The International Energy Agency (IEA) estimates that in 2005–2030, roughly 38% of the projected increase in the global oil supply will come from the GCC region, whose production will grow by 72%. Its natural gas production is also projected to grow rapidly, by more than 200%, in the same period, thereby accounting for roughly 46% of the total projected increase in the global supply of natural gas.

Nonetheless, it will be quite a challenge to increase the region's production capacity at a pace that will match the world's growing demand for energy, and much capital expenditure will be required in order to bring new capacity on stream. Its crude oil reserves are abundant, but some of its giant oilfields are ageing, with natural 'decline rates' approaching 12% per annum in places. Similarly, the region (especially Qatar) boasts some of the largest natural gas reserves in the world, but much investment is needed in order to bring existing reserves into production.[5]

The IEA conservatively estimates the total capital expenditure needed for the GCC countries to sustain a steady 2.2% per annum increase in crude oil production and a 5.6% per annum increase in natural gas production at roughly $650 billion (measured in 2006 prices) over the next 25 years.[6] This is a substantial figure, but the GCC governments see further opportunities emerging in the global economy. They understand the importance of providing affordable energy for the health of the world economy and are already committing large resources to expanding capacity.

Financing an expansion of capacity is not as pressing a problem for the GCC region as it is for the less developed African, Middle Eastern and Central Asian energy producers. The latter are subject to more serious sovereign risks and do not enjoy the financial means available to the more prosperous GCC economies. They also face much higher extraction costs upstream. The likelihood of serious 'investment failure' remains relatively limited in the GCC region. It is thus quite likely to consolidate its lead as the world's prime energy exporter. But this implies a sustained, and increasing, flow of oil and natural gas revenue into the region, probably well beyond the level of previous decades.

The potential 25-year revenue windfall: two scenarios

The GCC's net cumulative energy windfall could reach $5 trillion in the next 25 years. To put this potential into quantitative perspective, GS has projected GCC oil and natural gas revenues up to 2030. Two scenarios have been developed: the base and the historical trend.

The base scenario more or less captures the picture depicted above: sustained strong global demand for carbon-based fuels coupled with

5 For a more detailed (albeit somewhat speculative) discussion of some of the supply-side constraints in global energy markets, see K.S. Deffeyes, *Hubbert's Peak: The Impending World Oil Shortage* (Princeton, NJ: Princeton University Press, 2001); J. Leggett, *Half Gone: Oil, Gas, Hot Air and the Global Energy Crisis* (London: Portobello Books, 2005); and J.H. Kunstler, *The Long Emergency: Surviving the Converging Catastrophes of the Twenty-First Century* (London: Atlantic Books, 2005).

6 IEA, *World Energy Outlook: Middle East and North Africa Insights* (Paris: OECD/IEA, 2005).

robust growth of capital expenditure and a steady expansion of production capacity. All parameters were set in line with GS global energy demand forecasts. More specifically, it was assumed that:

- Oil exports and natural gas exports from the region will grow on average by 2.5% and 5.5% respectively per annum in 2005–2030, consistent with GS global energy demand growth projections.
- The average oil price will be $48 per barrel, above the $35/bbl postwar average (both measured in 2006 prices). Basically, it was assumed that prices would be 'sticky' in the next 15 years, mainly owing to strong demand growth and supply-side constraints; and that beyond 2020 the pressure would ease as new production capacity comes on stream and as demand pressures moderate somewhat, allowing the oil price to retreat gradually towards $40/bbl. Also, a flat $6.5/Mbtu (million British thermal units) was assumed for the average natural gas price (measured in 2006 prices).
- A capital expenditure of $1.2 trillion (measured in 2006 prices) was assumed for the forecast period, well above the $650 billion projected by the IEA. In doing so, GS accounted for potential supply-side challenges involved in raising production levels to match growing demand.

The historical trend scenario is intended mainly to relativize the baseline scenario – by setting prices and the net export growth rate at their respective 35-year average. This time frame encompasses two major oil shocks (1974 and 1979), one major investment cycle (1972–82) and three regional wars (the Iran–Iraq war and the two Gulf wars), which all led to major price increases.

- A 1.8% net crude oil export growth and a 3% net natural gas export growth were assumed for the 2005–30 period, well below the assumptions of the base scenario.
- The average crude oil price was set at the historical $35/bbl average and natural gas was set at a flat $4.7/Mbtu (both measured in 2006 prices).
- Capital expenditure was set at $600 billion, in view of the very low extraction costs that have prevailed in the region for the past 40 years.

Needless to say, the projections are highly stylized and do not constitute exact revenue forecasts. We provide a more detailed sensitivity analysis in Box 3.1, discussing in particular the potential impact of environmentally friendly economic policies on the outlook for the region's oil and natural gas revenue. The exercise does give a good sense of the windfall that is likely to accrue in the coming decades. Our main findings are as follows:

Box 3.1: A green policy scenario: slower growth of hydrocarbon demand?

The growing energy needs of the global economy will exert much pressure on the world's natural resources and the environment. The IEA's projections suggest that global CO_2 emissions are set to increase by 50% by 2030 in view of current energy consumption patterns and efficiency levels. GS energy demand projections are more aggressive than the IEA's projections, and assume an average consumption growth rate of 2.5% per annum over the next 30 years. Other things being constant, this implies an explosive growth in CO_2 emissions. At some point, consumers might have to switch to more environmentally friendly policies that would help to check CO_2 emissions – emphasizing in particular increased energy efficiency and the use of alternative (non-carbon-based) energy sources. This could lead to slower demand growth and perhaps to lower prices for carbon-based resources.

However, the transition to a greener world will take time. More importantly, the world economy will continue to depend on carbon-based fuels as its primary energy sources, as Figure 3B1 depicts, for two reasons:

- Carbon-based fuels constitute the most robust energy source available to humankind and will continue to play a key role in meeting the world's growing energy needs. A major technological breakthrough on alternative energy sources could change this picture fundamentally. However, it would probably take a great deal of time, investment and (ironically) carbon-driven energy input to develop, introduce and diffuse the new technology and then to adopt it for mass consumption. In any case, such a breakthrough is currently not on the cards.

- There is much path dependency in our energy consumption patterns, and kicking the world's growing carbon-based energy addiction would require strong political commitment and cooperation among consumer countries. Environmental concerns are becoming more widely expressed by key decision-makers globally, and there are some encouraging signs that policy-makers and politicians are taking environmental constraints more seriously. However, much still needs to be done in the United States and even in Europe. But more significantly, it will not be easy for rapidly developing emerging-market economies (especially the BRICs) to secure a more energy-efficient path to economic development.

Widespread implementation of environmentally friendly economic policies could reduce the oil and natural gas revenue windfall substantially. But the GS view is that this is unlikely to end the windfall entirely. The technological path dependency mentioned above and strong demand from the BRICs and the N-11 are likely to ensure steady growth in net oil and natural gas exports from the GCC region and to keep energy prices fairly high through the next decade. After this point, however, demand growth might slow down and prices might decline, which could push oil and natural gas revenues somewhat lower, relative to the baseline forecasts discussed above. To measure the likely impact of green economic policies on the GCC energy windfall, we assumed:

- An annual export growth rate of 1.8% for crude oil and 5.2% for natural gas. In this way, net export volumes for 2050 were cut by 17.6% for oil and 5.8% for natural gas compared with the base scenario.
- A gradual retreat of oil prices from $55/bbl in the 2010s to $35/bbl by 2030. It was also assumed that the natural gas price would be $6/Mbtu.
- $1 trillion of capital expenditure. This arbitrary assumption reflects the substantial costs associated with increasing production while simultaneously replacing the natural decline in upstream capacity.

These assumptions brought the projected oil and natural gas revenue of the GCC countries to $4.4 trillion (measured in 2006 prices, expressed in NPV terms), significantly below the base scenario figure of $5.1 trillion but still substantially above the $3.6 trillion implied by the historical trend scenario. In per capita terms, the projected windfall was $103,000, below the $115,500 implied by the base scenario and above the $84,250 suggested by the historical trend scenario.

Fig 3B1: Carbon-based fuels will remain the primary source of energy in coming decades

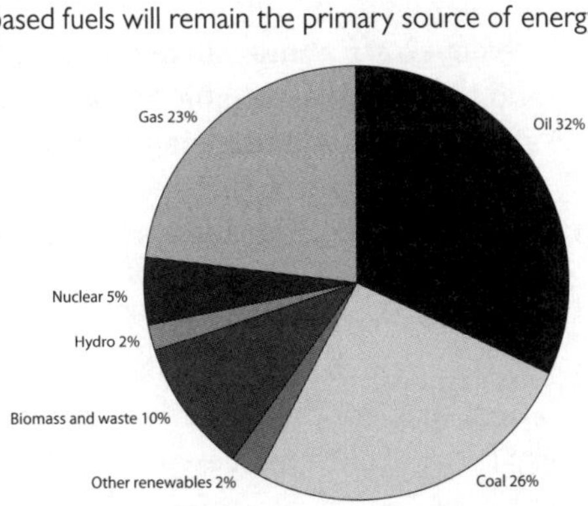

Source: GS.

- **There will be a huge windfall.** The oil and natural gas revenues projected under the base scenario will remain well above what is suggested by the historical trend scenario, implying an extra-normal revenue flow. Specifically, measured in net present value (NPV) terms (using a discount rate of 6.5%), projected cumulative oil and natural gas revenue for the 2005–30 period will amount to $5.1 trillion in the base scenario, significantly higher than the $3.6 trillion implied by the historical trend scenario (see Table 3.1).
- **There will be massive wealth creation.** Population growth is expected to remain fairly robust throughout the region during the forecast period (see below), so there will be more GCC citizens to share the windfall. But reducing forecasts to per capita terms does not change the picture fundamentally. GS projections put the cumulative per capita oil and natural gas export revenue (again measured in NPV terms) at $115,500 in the base scenario, well above the relatively modest $84,250 implied by the historical trend scenario. Regional (nominal) per capita income currently stands at about $20,500, which implies serious wealth creation in the region under the base scenario in the forecast period.
- **Hydrocarbon revenue will peak in the next 15 years.** GS projections suggest that the bulk of the windfall is likely to accrue in the next decade or so, when the BRICs' demand is expected to peak, and that alternative energy use and energy efficiency gains will remain limited. In the base scenario, roughly 65–70% of the total projected revenue accrues within the next 15 years. Beyond 2020, the pace of revenue accrual normalizes somewhat.

Old challenges and new opportunities

The 'natural resource curse' and regional instability will continue to haunt the GCC countries. The sizeable windfall implied by GS projections suggests that they will remain a structural current account surplus region in the global economy and that they will be able to sustain high investment levels and to generate strong, welfare-enhancing economic growth in the coming decades.

The key question is whether or not this potential will be realized. Important challenges will have to be overcome, and there are macroeconomic and institutional weaknesses that could undermine the region's long-term growth potential, which will be discussed in detail below. However, with some effort and good economic management, the GCC countries can make a leap forward and emerge as one of the most prosperous regions of the world.

GS sees two main, overarching impediments/rigidities: one related to

Table 3.1: Projected oil and natural gas revenues (total and per capita)

		Base scenario	*Green policy*	*Historical trend*
Nominal oil and natural gas exports ($bn)		13,493	10,935	8,234
Nominal Capex ($bn)		1,969	1,395	450
Net nominal oil and natural gas exports ($bn)		11,524	9,541	7,784
NPV net nominal oil and natural gas exports (2006 dollars, bn)		5,070	4,449	3,618
NPV net nominal oil and natural gas exports per capita (2005 dollars, bn)		115,687	103,174	84,235
Crude oil prices (2006 prices)	2005	50.6	50.6	50.6
	2010	55.0	55.0	35.0
	2020	50.0	40.0	35.0
	2030	40.0	35.0	35.0
Average annual net export growth	Crude oil	2.5%	1.8%	1.7%
	Natural gas	5.5%	5.2%	3.0%

Source: GS.

the broader Middle East risk and the other linked to the 'natural resource curse'.[7]

- **The Middle East risk:** The GCC is in one of the most unstable regions of the world. Many complex examples from the past and today are well known, including the Arab–Israeli conflict, Iraq's ongoing instability, Iran's external relations and growing Sunni–Shia friction. These all still stand as key risk factors that could destabilize the Middle East (and the rest of the world) in a major way. The GCC countries, controlling a good chunk of the world's hydrocarbon reserves, may have to commit significant resources to enhancing their defence capabilities, diverting them from possibly more efficient uses. The need constantly to secure domestic political stability in countries surrounding the GCC could dent its members' political and economic reforms, making it more difficult to address deep-rooted incumbency problems.[8]

7 For a thorough discussion of the 'natural resource curse' and its implications for long-term economic growth, see Jeffrey D. Sachs and Andrew M. Warner, 'Natural Resource Abundance and Economic Growth', in G. M. Meier and J. E. Rauch (eds), *Leading Issues in Economic Development* (New York: Oxford University Press, 1995) and Xavier Sala-i-Martin and Arvind Subramanian, 'Addressing the Natural Resource Curse: An Illustration from Nigeria', IMF Working Paper, WP/03/139, 2003.

8 For a comprehensive discussion of regional challenges to the GCC's economic and political stability, see *The Gulf: Challenges of the Future* (Abu Dhabi: The Emirates Center for Strategic Studies and Research, 2005).

Figure 3.6: Significant improvement in GCC growth environment, 1996–2006

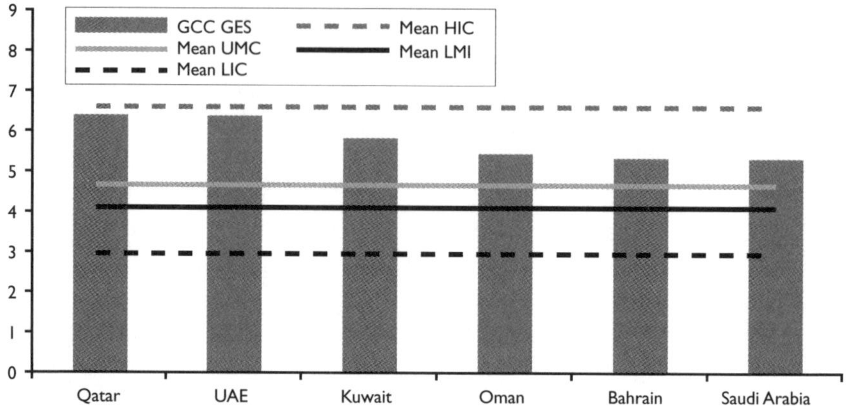

Source: GS estimates.

Note: HIC: High-income country; UMC: Upper-middle-income country; LMI: Lower-middle-income country; LIC: Low-income country.

- **The 'natural resource curse' – rent-seeking and 'voracity'**: The GCC is an extreme resource-endowment case, characterized by strong rent-seeking motives and opportunities and by relatively weak institutional (market) structures. All too often in the past, networks of patronage and clientelism have led to inefficiency in the distribution and use of economic resources.[9] Windfalls have resulted in dramatic increases in government spending, leading to much economic waste.[10] It is possible that a future revenue windfall could repeat past tendencies and create significant inertia in the region's transition to a more market-based economy characterized by a more commonly accepted rule of law and strong market institutions.[11]

But over the past decade, the GCC's growth environment has improved significantly, as suggested by Figure 3.6, and the GCC economies are undergoing a major economic transformation. The GCC governments now place a great deal of emphasis on economic diversification, openness and market regulation, as well as on the development of infrastructure

9 A thorough examination of the historical connection between growth retardation and rent-seeking behaviour is D. North, J.J. Wallis and B. Weingast, 'A Conceptual Framework for Interpreting Recorded Human History', NBER Working Paper No. 12795, Cambridge, MA, 2006.

10 For a detailed discussion of the links between resource endowment, rent-seeking and 'voracity', see Aaron Tornell and Philip R. Lane, 'Voracity and Growth', NBER Working Paper No. 6498, 1998.

11 A more detailed discussion of rent-seeking motives in the Middle East is in Steffen Hertog, 'Segmented Clientelism: The Political Economy of Saudi Economic Reform Efforts', in P. Aarts and G. Nonneman (eds), *Saudi Arabia in the Balance: Political Economy, Society, Foreign Affairs* (London: Hurst & Co., 2005), pp. 111–43.

and human resources. These reform efforts, combined with the oil and natural gas revenue boon, are helping to improve the growth environment and are pulling the region's long-term growth potential above the rather disappointing 3.5% per annum average of the past few decades.[12]

GS's Growth Environment Score (GES) indices capture the fundamental improvement that has taken place across the region and its solid growth potential. The GES is an objective summary measure of 13 variables that drive productivity and help to achieve a country's growth potential. A set of key socio-economic and demographic parameters are looked at. Then the GES measures are used to compare growth conditions across a broad range of countries and to assess whether or not long-term GS projections about GDP and per capita income growth are likely to become a reality.[13]

The results of the recently updated GES indices show an encouraging picture for the GCC region. Without exception, the GCC economies now occupy top positions in the GS global ranking of 177 countries. Qatar and the UAE rank 24th and 25th respectively. Kuwait, Oman, Bahrain and Saudi Arabia occupy the 32nd, 39th, 42nd and 43rd places respectively in the GES rankings, above, for example, Greece (44th), Hungary (47th), Poland (54th), China (58th) and Mexico (68th).

Among developing economies, the region stands out: Qatar and the UAE rank 1st and 2nd, and Kuwait, Oman, Bahrain and Saudi Arabia follow in 4th, 8th, 9th and 10th place respectively – all well above the BRICs and the N-11 (except South Korea). Among developed high-income-group countries, Qatar and the UAE compare quite well with their peers. Kuwait, Oman, Bahrain and Saudi Arabia also do fairly well, but there is much room for improvement, especially in human resource development and technology use. In any case, the GES indices show that the region's growth potential remains as good as that of any developing economy.

The baseline: solid growth and rapid convergence

In order to put the GCC region's potential into quantitative perspective, the GS model for GDP projection was used. It is based on neoclassical growth theory and sets labour, capital and total factor productivity as key determinants of long-term economic growth (see Appendix 3.1 for details of this model).

12 For recent reform efforts in the GCC region, see M. Malik and T. Niblock, 'Saudi Arabia's Economy: The Challenge of Reform', in Aarts and Nonneman, *Saudi Arabia*, pp. 85–110.

13 For a more detailed discussion of the GES, please refer to 'You Reap What You Sow: Our 2006 Growth Environment Scores (GES)', Global Economics Paper No. 148, Goldman Sachs Economic Research, 8 November 2006.

In projecting GDP levels for the GCC to 2050 as a baseline, a conscious effort was made to keep assumptions as conservative as possible:

- **Investment levels at average for past 10 years:** The underlying gross investment rate was set at the average over the past 10 years for each GCC economy: 1.2% for Bahrain, 15.6% for Kuwait, 15.7% for Oman, 17.9% for

Figure 3.7: Projected narrowing of GCC/G-7 income gap, 2006–50

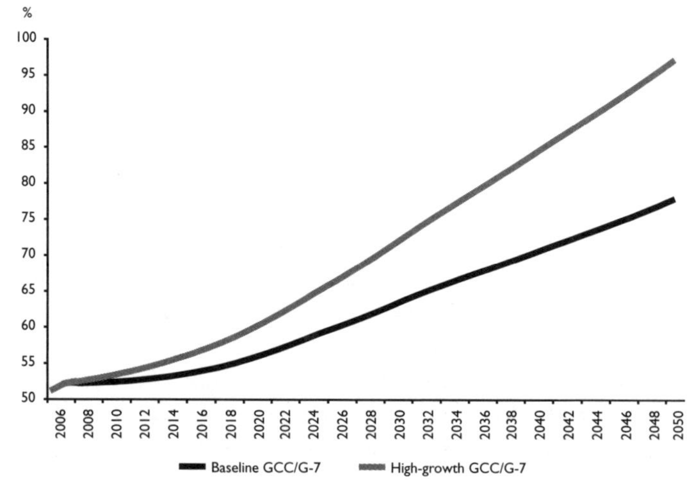

Sources: IEA and GS projections.

Figure 3.8: GDP of leading global economies, 2050

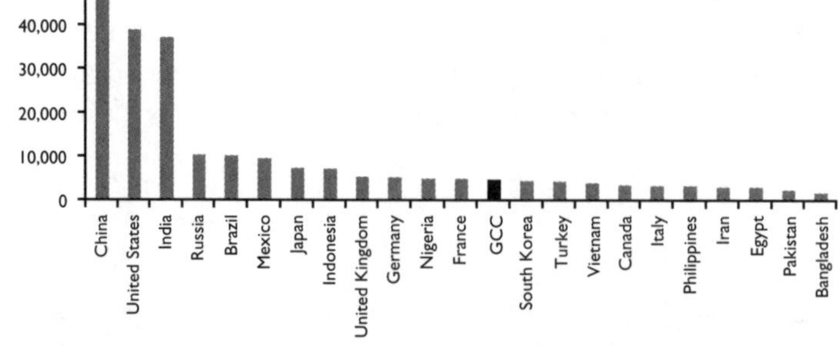

Source: GS.

Figure 3.9: Per capita income of leading global economies, 2050

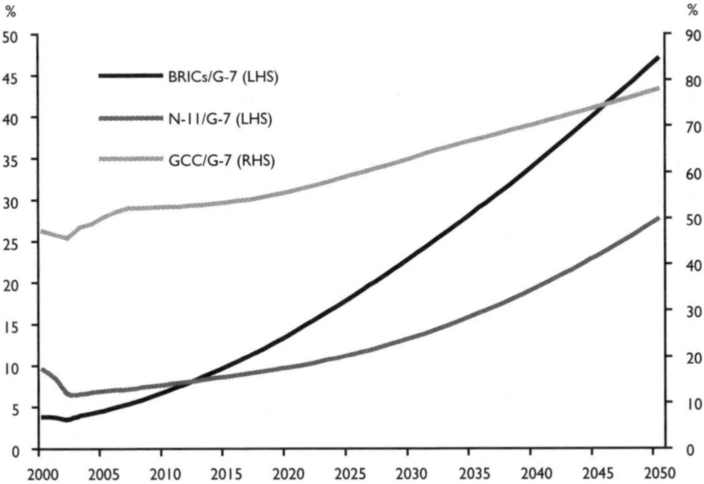

Source: GS.

Saudi Arabia, 24.7% for the UAE and 28.5% for Qatar. A major improvement in the investment climate was not included in constructing the baseline projections; and reasonably low investment levels were assumed, notwithstanding the extra-normal revenue inflow. In other words, it was assumed that the region would remain a capital exporter and would diversify more gradually as it developed.

Figure 3.10: Projected GCC, G-7, N-11 and BRICs per capita income levels

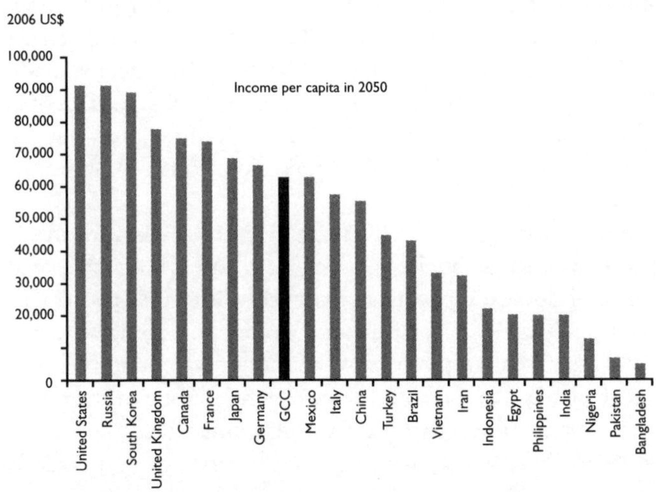

Source: GS.

Box 3.2: The case for greater exchange rate flexibility

If global energy demand grows strongly in the coming decades and if, as argued, it generates a steady inflow of extra-normal revenue to the region, then reconciling price stability and rapid economic development objectives will become increasingly difficult under the current fixed exchange rate regime.

There are four reasons for this. First, with local currencies fixed firmly to the dollar, the terms of trade shock (from high energy prices) will be passed on directly to domestic prices. This is because energy figures prominently both in the consumption bundle and as a productive input in the non-carbon sectors.

Second, the wealth effect of the oil and gas income windfall will raise domestic spending, which will fall in part on non-traded goods. Compared with a scenario without that windfall, this will result in an appreciation of the real exchange rate (an increase in the relative price of non-traded to traded goods). Resources will also be drawn into the production of non-traded goods and services, and out of the non-carbon tradable goods sectors. This 'Dutch disease' scenario need not signal a problem, as an increase in the demand for non-traded goods and services is a natural consequence of greater wealth. It is, however, essential that the (relative) reduction in the size of the non-carbon-tradable producing sectors does not 'overshoot' and result in excessive reliance on oil and gas exports. At a fixed nominal exchange rate *vis-à-vis* the dollar, the required real exchange rate appreciation can occur only through a rate of inflation of domestic costs and prices that is higher than that in the United States and the dollar-pegging countries. But this higher inflation should only be temporary in that the required adjustment involves an increase solely in the level of a key relative price. This wealth effect is in addition to the direct price level effect of an increase in the dollar price of energy. It would also occur, for instance, if the windfall resulted not from an increase in the dollar price of oil and gas but from a new discovery of carbon reserves.

Third, in addition to the 'Dutch disease' effect of a hydrocarbon windfall, there is the Balassa–Samuelson effect, associated with the successful convergence of domestic productivity levels with those in the advanced countries. If and when successful catch-up or convergence occurs in the non-oil and gas-producing sectors of the economy, productivity catch-up in the traded goods sectors tends to be more rapid than in the non-traded sectors. The implication is that if factors of production can flow relatively easily between these two sectors, the relative price of non-traded goods will rise. This supply-side-driven real exchange rate appreciation is quite distinct from the demand-driven 'Dutch disease' appreciation described in the previous paragraph, and it can also be expected to persist for as long as real catch-up or convergence takes place. For the GCC region, this could be several decades. With a fixed nominal dollar exchange rate, Balassa–Samuelson real exchange rate appreciation requires inflation in excess of that in the rest of the dollar-pegging world.

Lastly, although GS expects the GCC countries to be net exporters of capital for the foreseeable future, the desire of regional monetary authorities for large foreign exchange reserves and periodic large inflows of private capital could easily lead to the excessive creation of money and liquidity. This could, in turn, lead to excessive domestic credit expansion and speculative excess.

All these factors will make it increasingly difficult to maintain price stability with a fixed exchange rate peg to the dollar. Under a more flexible monetary policy regime, it would be easier to reconcile price stability and diversification/growth objectives: more effective liquidity management, on the one hand, and greater exchange rate flexibility, on the other hand, would help to absorb the ensuing pressure on domestic prices.

A more flexible exchange rate regime is not without risks, however. One risk is excessive exchange rate appreciation, which could lead to a crippling form of the 'Dutch disease' and undermine efforts at diversification. A more flexible regime would have to be supported by institutional and structural reforms that would enhance the ability of the monetary authorities to resist exchange rate 'overshooting', facilitate productivity growth and bolster the flexibility of the labour market. Also, fiscal policy would have to become increasingly counter-cyclical, rather than pro-cyclical, so as to smooth the cycles.

At any rate, a transition from existing pegs to a more flexible exchange rate regime would have to be gradual. The dollar pegs served well as solid nominal anchors in past decades, but the institutional structure needed to support more flexible exchange rate regimes is not in place. The first step would probably be towards greater exchange rate flexibility via the adoption of a composite currency basket peg, which would help to reduce the inflationary effects of sharp movements in major currency crises. The next step would be to prepare the institutional basis for the implementation of more flexible monetary policy regimes, placing much emphasis on developing local debt markets and also proper central bank independence. Lastly, size matters. The GCC countries would be well advised to maintain a fixed exchange rate among themselves while introducing greater flexibility for their common external exchange rate.

Figure 3.11: GCC region's human resource development, 2006

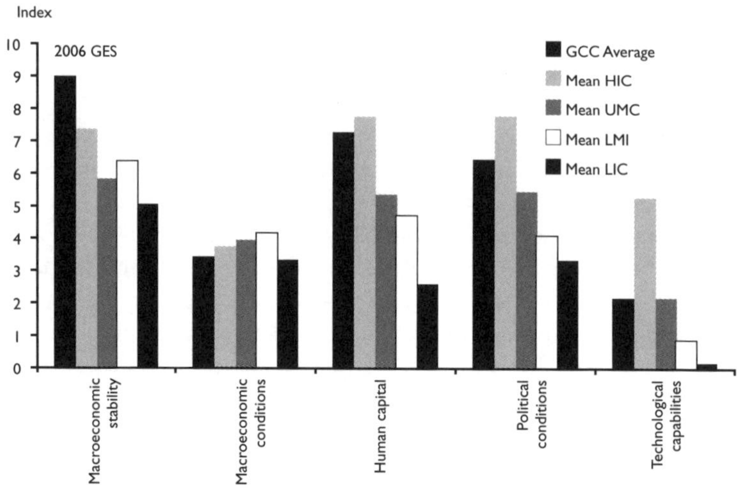

Source: GS projections.

- **Relatively subdued productivity growth**: Despite the high GES rankings of the GCC economies, the convergence ratio (the other key parameter in our projection models capturing TFP growth) was set at 0.8% for the entire 2006–50 period. This is below the 1.0–1.5% we use for our BRIC projection and most of our N-11 projections. A conservative assumption was made that there would be relatively subdued TFP growth for the region (comparable to the underlying assumption used for, say, Pakistan), reflecting the overall growth-retarding effects of the above-mentioned structural rigidities and geopolitical challenges.
- **Gradual demographic normalization**: Lastly, regional population growth rates were set at about 2.0–2.5% until 2015, 1.5% until 2040 and slightly above 1% until 2050.

Under these fairly conservative assumptions, the projections suggest reasonably rapid economic growth and convergence. By the middle of this century, the GCC could be comparable to major developed economies in terms of both size and per capita income. The region's total GDP in 2050 is projected at $4.5 trillion, just under the projected GDP levels of Germany ($4.9 trillion) and equal with France and Nigeria (see Figure 3.7). The region's 2050 per capita income is estimated at $63,250, which compares favourably with that of leading industrial economies such as Japan ($69,000), Germany ($67,000) and Italy ($58,000), as shown by Figure 3.8. Accordingly, the income gap with the G-7 is projected to narrow quite significantly, to roughly 77% of the projected G-7 average, up from the current 50% (see Figure 3.9).

An alternative, 'dream scenario'

The GCC region could have much more to offer than the conservative baseline projections suggest. The growth and convergence potential implied by the base scenario is impressive, but, as Figure 3.10 shows, it does not suggest as robust a convergence as that of the BRICs or some of the stronger N-11 economies. To realize its full potential, the region will have to put stronger emphasis on improving the investment climate and, more importantly, on developing technology and human resources.

The human resource base is not strong enough now. On human resource development, the GCC region is ranked just below the high-income-country average and slightly above the average for upper-middle-income countries (see Figure 3.11), but there is still much room for improvement. Specifically, it would benefit immensely from further improvement in education and health standards, which would help to bolster TFP growth and to further economic development over the longer term. Another major constraint is the low proportion of women in the workforce; this still hovers at a disappointing 25–30%. There are cultural obstacles here, but it would be quite advantageous for the GCC countries to incorporate women into the active labour force: it would strengthen their demographic dynamics even further.[14]

To demonstrate the hidden potential here, two key parameters of the GDP projection model were adjusted in order to capture the impact of a more robust investment climate and a stronger technology and human resource base.

- The **investment ratio** was set one standard deviation above the 10-year average for Saudi Arabia (19.7%), Kuwait (21.6%), Oman (18.9%) and Bahrain (19%). The investment ratios for the region's big spenders, the UAE and Qatar, were left unchanged at 24.7% and 28.5% respectively.
- The **convergence ratio** was set at 1% until 2035 and at 1.2% until 2050 – above the 0.8% assumed in the baseline and more consistent with the region's exceptionally high GES scores – with a view to incorporating the productivity gains to be reaped from technology transfer and diffusion and from human resource development.

Under these assumptions, the region will comfortably achieve promotion to the league of advanced economies. Its GDP will hit $5.5 trillion by 2050 (well above the $4.5 trillion projected in the baseline scenario), overtaking leading industrial economies such as the United Kingdom and

14 For women's participation in Gulf labour markets, see A. A. Fakhro, 'The Changing Role of Women in the Gulf Region', in *The Gulf: Challenges of the Future*, pp. 391–422.

Germany (both of whose GDP will be at about $5 trillion) and moving closer to the GDPs of Indonesia ($6.7 trillion) and Japan ($7 trillion). The GCC members' per capita GDP will reach $78,800 and the income gap between them and the G-7 will disappear almost completely, with their per capita GDP reaching 97% of the G-7 average (see Figure 3.9).

As discussed above, the odds against this 'dream' scenario are high, and there is a risk that deep-rooted structural weaknesses and regional instability might continue to hold back the GCC region from fully realizing its huge economic potential. It is more likely that the region will grow into a 'dual' economic structure characterized, on the one hand, by ultra-modern Dubai-like 'growth poles' and, on the other hand, by continuing inefficiency and 'waste' in general resource utilization.

However, the GCC region's long-term economic potential is immense. With a little bit of effort, it can capitalize on the new opportunities presented by the fast-globalizing world economy and emerge as a leading economic power in the coming decades.

This globally driven economic transformation and development process will also provide strong support for regional asset prices (particularly equity prices) and make the value of the regional currency substantially stronger in the next decades. In that sense, the GCC can be seen not only as a source of capital for the rest of the world but also as a long-term investment opportunity with a significant positive potential.

Appendix 3.1: Technical problems in projecting the GCC countries' GDP levels

Methodological problems and the terms of trade effect

GS long-term growth models project GDP levels in real dollar terms, based on the assumption that inflation differentials will be offset by purchasing power parity assumptions on the exchange rate side of the model. In other words, GS methodology does not control for the impact on GDP levels of the shifts taking place in the terms of trade (ToT). This simplifying assumption leads to methodological difficulties for the GCC economies. Basically, the consumer price index and GDP deflators tend to be substantially different for the GCC economies, where the hydrocarbon sector accounts for 20–50% of the economy and a sizeable amount of consumption goods are imported. A change in the ToT therefore leads to a corresponding shift in consumer price index and GDP differentials, which, in turn, leads to a substantially lower/higher GDP level, depending on the direction that the terms of trade move. For this reason, it is important to consider also the ToT effect in projecting GDP levels for the GCC economies.

The ToT effect: a model

Let P_C be the consumer price index, P_X the price of exports (oil), P_M the price of imports, P_T the traded goods price index and P_V the GDP deflator.

Let

$$P_C = P_T^{\alpha} P_N^{1-\alpha} \quad (1)$$

$$P_T = P_X^{\beta} P_M^{1-\beta} \quad (2)$$

$$P_V = P_X^{\gamma} P_N^{1-\gamma} \quad (3)$$

It follows that

$$P_V/P_C = (P_X/P_M)^{\gamma(1-\beta)} \quad (P_N/P_T)^{\alpha-\gamma} \quad (4)$$

where P_X/P_M is the terms of trade and P_N/P_T is the real exchange rate or relative price of non-traded to traded goods.

It is a reasonable approximation to assume that the share of non-traded goods in the consumption bundle is the same as the share of non-traded goods production in value-added, that is $\alpha=\gamma$. So the ratio of the value-added deflator to the consumer price index simplifies to

$$P_V/P_C = (P_X/P_M)^{\gamma(1-\beta)} \quad (4)$$

which is the terms of trade to a power (less than 1) equal to the product of the share of exports in value added times the share of imports in the consumption bundle of traded goods. If the share of exports (oil) in consumption is very small (that is, $ß \approx 0$) this further simplifies to

$$P_V/P_C = (P_X/P_M)^{\gamma} = (P_X/P_M)^{\alpha} \quad (4)$$

Implications for GS projections

A simple sensitivity analysis based on the terms of trade model suggests that every \$5/bbl fall in the average oil price would trim roughly \$210 billion off the GCC countries' 2050 GDP level and about \$2,950 off their estimated per capita income – assuming that the share of imports in the consumption bundle of traded goods is 60% for the region and that the ratio does not change in time (i.e. there is no diversification).[15] Thus if the oil price were to fall to \$40/bbl (from the current \$65/bbl) by 2050, this could imply a GDP level of \$3.3 trillion, significantly below our base scenario \$4.5 billion projection. Per capita income would also fall to \$47,300, from the baseline \$63,250.

If, however, the region can diversify and reduce its dependency on imports, it would be possible to compensate at least partly for the adverse ToT impact. It is calculated that every five percentage point fall in the import dependency ratio would add \$85 billion to the estimated 2050 GDP level and \$1,200 cumulative to the projected per capita income level. This suggests that extensive diversification will be required to minimize the region's sensitivity to potential ToT shocks.

As discussed extensively in the preceding analysis, our base scenario does not assume a major deterioration in the ToT in the next 20 years because fast-growing BRIC and N-11 energy/hydrocarbon demand will exert upward pricing pressure on global energy markets. Thus the next 20 years may be the GCC countries' prime opportunity to diversify and strengthen their economies. Those economies would also be best advised to diversify the region's vast savings base and to maximize long-term investment returns in order to minimize as much as possible the potential wealth losses that could emerge from adverse ToT shocks.

15 There are no official data on consumption in the GCC region, for which reason it is not possible to determine with accuracy the share of imports in the regional consumption bundle. The share of imports in its combined GDP stands at about 35–40%, and does not exceed 55%. The GS assumption of 60% looks sufficiently conservative here.

4 The new face of Arab investment

Florence Eid

Introduction

In contrast to the 1970s, the public and private sectors of the Gulf Cooperation Council (GCC) states have taken a decidedly more regional approach to petrodollar recycling. While the current oil windfall is fuelling unprecedented domestic investments aimed at economic diversification in the GCC, a record level of intraregional foreign direct investment (FDI) is flowing into the economies of North Africa and the Levant, generating significant positive externalities. This new picture contrasts markedly with the past three decades, during which intraregional FDI in the wider Middle East and North Africa (MENA) region[1] was at a negligible level (Eid and Paua 2003). Although a large proportion of capital outflows from the GCC is still invested in developed markets (and increasingly in emerging Asia), the pick-up in intraregional flows in absolute terms has considerable implications when contrasted to the relatively small initial absorptive capacity of MENA economies. This chapter will seek to map the implications of the new FDI picture in the MENA region, starting with the GCC, to understand its implications so far, to discuss its positive externalities through remittances, exports and tourism revenues and to point up the challenges in going forward.

Petrodollar recycling today: differences from the 1970s

The pattern in which the GCC countries are investing their petrodollars today is remarkably different from that of the first 'oil shock' in 1973, and it underlies the unprecedented focus on domestic and regional investment. In the 1970s, most of the recycling took place through the banks or securities markets of developed countries, which allowed the Bank for International

1 MENA comprises the Arabic-speaking countries of the Middle East, the Levant, the Gulf and North Africa.

Settlements (BIS) to track with precision the direction of financial flows (IMF 2006). Between 1974 and 1979, $108 billion, almost 47% of the $232 billion of total identified investments, were deposited in bank accounts in developed economies or used to purchase short-dated instruments in the American and British money markets (see Table 4.1). Bilateral and multilateral loan agreements over the period stood at $79 billion and accounted for more than one-third of the cumulative oil windfall. The main recipients were Latin American countries, where strong growth meant high loan demand, and a few industrialized European countries running current account deficits. The petrodollar recycling 'model' of the 1970s reflected in part the fact that the oil windfall occurred over a short time frame, causing the GCC states to save large portions of what was believed to be a temporary phenomenon. This is in sharp contrast to the present situation in which the perception is that of a more sustained rise in the equilibrium price of oil for reasons that are now well studied and around which there appears to be a broad international consensus.

Table 4.1: Fuel exporters' investment of current account surpluses, 1974–79

Type of financial investment	*Amount (US$bn)*
Bank deposits and money market instruments	108.0
Dollar deposits in the US	10.9
Sterling deposits in the UK	2.4
Deposits in foreign currency markets	88.8
Treasury bills in the US and the UK	5.9
Long-term investments	124.2
Bilateral agreements	69.7
Loans to international agencies	9.5
Sovereign securities in the US and the UK	9.2
Other (incl. equity and real estate investments in the US and the UK)	35.8
Total	232.2

Sources: BIS (2007) and IMF data.

Although anecdotal evidence demonstrates clearly that the recent rise in oil prices has allowed the GCC countries to focus on much broader domestic and international investment opportunities than in the past, an analysis as detailed as the one above unfortunately is complicated by shortcomings in data.[2] The Institute of International Finance (IIF)

2 Bahrain is the only GCC country to provide data on its international investment position. Capital account data for the GCC are fragmented and are generally recorded in net terms. In the mid-1990s, the BIS stopped producing data on cross-border banking claims on a basis comparable to earlier years.

(2007) has suggested that contrary to the 1970s, when a large proportion of petrodollars was accumulated in bank deposits, the proportion of bank deposits as a share of the total identified stock of external asset holdings had declined significantly, from 46.0% in 2001 to 27.9% at the end of 2006. Using various published counterparty data, the IIF has further estimated that $60 billion, 11% of the total build-up of GCC foreign assets implied by the cumulative current account surpluses in 2002–06, has been invested in the MENA region, excluding investments within the GCC (see Table 4.2). To put it in perspective, this figure represents 13% of the 2006 GDP of the MENA region, excluding the GCC, and it compares favourably to GCC capital outflows to the United States and Europe at 2% and 1% of 2006 GDP respectively. Furthermore, it is roughly equal to the *total* net FDI received by the MENA region, excluding the GCC, over the period 2002–06.

Table 4.2: Estimated geographical distribution of GCC states' capital outflows, 2002–06

Destination	*Amount (US$bn)*
United States	300
Europe	100
MENA	60
Asia	60
Other	22
Total	542

Source: Institute of International Finance (2007). The data combine FDI and portfolio flows, including asset classes such as bank deposits and real estate purchases.

Although lack of bilateral data on a balance of payments basis precludes an accurate estimation of intraregional FDI flows, data on intraregional investment is available from the Inter-Arab Investment Guarantee Corporation (IAIGC) on an 'approval basis'.[3] IAIGC figures point clearly to a growth in intraregional investment, with a particular surge in 2005 owing to large inflows ($28.8 billion) into investment projects in Saudi Arabia (see Figure 4.1). On the back of strong government and corporate balance sheets, the United Arab Emirates (UAE), Kuwait and Saudi Arabia

3 Inter-Arab investments refer to private and licensed investment flows conducted by Arab investors from one Arab country or more into another Arab country. This is different from the definition of FDI according to the United Nations Conference on Trade and Development (UNCTAD): an investment made to acquire lasting interest in and control of enterprises operating outside the economy of the investor; this investment will involve a long-term relationship and has three possible components (equity capital, reinvested earnings and intracompany loans).

Figure 4.1: Intraregional MENA investment transactions, 1995–2006

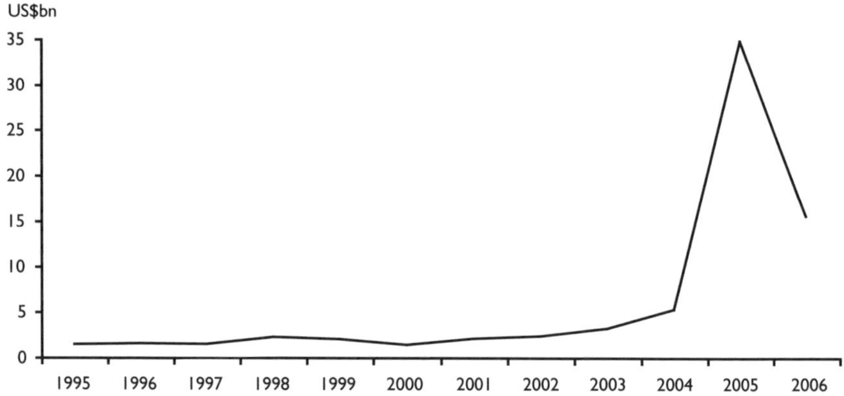

Source: Inter-Arab Investment Guarantee Corporation (2006).

Table 4.3: Average GCC intraregional investment transaction flows ($m), 2001–06

From / to	*Lebanon*	*Egypt*	*Tunisia*	*Syria*	*Morocco*	*Yemen*	*Rest of MENA (excl. GCC)*
Bahrain	20.0	43.0	10.8	0.1	3.3	0.0	12.5
Kuwait	383.0	72.8	28.4	75.1	52.6	0.3	134.8
Oman	0.0	1.9	0.0	0.0	0.0	0.6	0.0
Qatar	112.9	7.7	0.0	0.0	57.8	4.0	10.3
Saudi Arabia	273.3	143.5	9.5	197.4	99.2	209.0	227.2
UAE	308.3	589.8	469.1	207.4	259.7	7.8	150.5
GCC	1,097.5	858.7	517.9	480.0	472.7	221.6	535.3

Source: Inter-Arab Investment Guarantee Corporation (2006).

accounted for 69% of outward MENA intraregional investment in 2006, having averaged 88% in 2001–05. As Table 4.3 shows, the main recipients of GCC investments in 2001–06 were Lebanon, Egypt and Tunisia. A majority of investment went into the services (about 66%) and industrial sectors (about 32%).

One aspect of this picture has not changed very much. Higgins, Klitgaard and Lerman (2006) find that although the *primary* destination of GCC investments is difficult to determine, the bulk must *ultimately* end up in the US, either directly or indirectly through financial intermediation, given that the rise in the US current account deficit is the only counterpart to the rise in the current account surplus of oil exporters. Furthermore, a good portion of investment in North African and other Arab countries is debt-financed, according to the IMF's recent findings. As such, even though it does not constitute a *direct* recycling of oil revenues *per se*, the flow of finance appears, in our view, to be circular (given that a significant proportion of the debt offerings are being absorbed by GCC investors), and it is contributing to absorptive capacity through a deepening of the capital markets.

Investment absorptive capacity: improving with MENA reforms

Intraregional flows are supported by the reform stance adopted by many MENA countries, as regional oil-importing countries are pushing ahead at varying paces with economic liberalization and more investor-friendly policies. Notably among the pack, Egypt launched an ambitious reform package in July 2004 that has helped to offer investors a markedly more business-friendly environment. The government aims to reduce its budget deficit by 1% of GDP every year until 2010, and it has unified its exchange rate, reformed its trade regime and tax environments and set up a monetary policy committee that is looking at inflation targeting. It is also restructuring the financial sector through banking sector consolidation and credible privatization programmes.[4] As a result, net FDI in Egypt reached 11% of GDP in the past fiscal year,[5] compared to an average of 3% over the past three decades. On a more measured but nevertheless steady path, Tunisia is moving towards current and capital account liberalization and is focusing on privatizing state-owned banks and resolving non-performing loans. Along with carrying out a medium-term fiscal consolidation programme, Morocco is diversifying away from the volatile agricultural sector by focusing on tourism and enhancing its attractiveness as an outsourcing destination for European firms. Libya is broadening its privatization programme and has dismantled most import monopolies. It has significantly streamlined its tariff regime as a part of measures to reintegrate into the world economy after the end of decade-long UN and US sanctions. Again, it is too early to draw on data sets to establish this, but we see clear evidence that a wave of gradual reductions in domestic oil subsidies across oil-importing MENA countries will help to curb costs from

4 Egypt was the top reformer in the World Bank's Doing Business 2008 rankings.
5 The fiscal year runs from 1 July to 30 June.

high oil prices with respect to the benefits derived through GCC-country FDI and other portfolio flows.

The current reform drive is steadily increasing the investment-absorption capacity of the region. Local stock markets boomed, busted and have now recovered, and they are absorbing a good portion of the oil windfall while the regional real estate boom is attracting further GCC inflows. Privatization programmes pursued by oil importers, along with an improvement in the business climate, are providing new opportunities for GCC equity participation. As a result of stronger regional growth prospects, GCC corporates are strategically pursuing expansion into MENA markets where the combination of a large population and a low penetration of various goods and services offers many business opportunities. In particular, GCC telecoms firms have had a strong incentive to expand, in order to offset the near saturation of their domestic markets and the increased competition brought about by liberalization. Between March 2006 and March 2007 alone, GCC telecoms operators bought stakes or won licence auctions in North Africa and the Levant worth a combined $6.1 billion.[6] In North Africa, a large proportion of GCC inflows has gone towards developing infrastructure and tourism projects and has generally benefited from partnerships with national governments.

As an example of intraregional GCC investment, the UAE-based developer Sama Dubai announced plans to build over the next 15 years a $14 billion business and leisure park in Tunis, which, at 40% of its GDP, represents the largest FDI transaction ever committed to Tunisia. Another UAE real estate developer, Emaar Properties, is particularly active across North Africa as it seeks to replicate its Dubai luxury development model.[7] Morocco has received FDI commitments for the next 10 years, from the UAE alone, amounting to 33% of its GDP. In Jordan, the GCC states have invested heavily in real estate development projects, with the bulk of these projects going to the Aqaba Special Economic Zone.[8]

6 Intra-GCC investment in the telecoms sector is particularly buoyant too: in March 2007, the Qatar-based Q-Tel bought a 51% stake in Kuwaiti operator Wataniya for $3.8 billion and Kuwait's Zain won the auction for the third GSM licence in Saudi Arabia for $6.1 billion.

7 Emaar Properties is one of the largest investors in Algeria, Morocco and Egypt, with a portfolio of $20 billion, $6.8 billion and $5.5 billion respectively in tourism and residential development. It is currently negotiating a memorandum of understanding with the Libyan government over the development of a residential and industrial zone. Elsewhere in MENA, Emaar is active in the UAE, Saudi Arabia, Syria and Jordan.

8 One of the largest property developments in Jordan is the $995 million (6% of its GDP) joint project between Saudi Oger and Saraya Aqaba.

Figure 4.2: Quarterly remittances to Egypt by country of origin, 2001–07

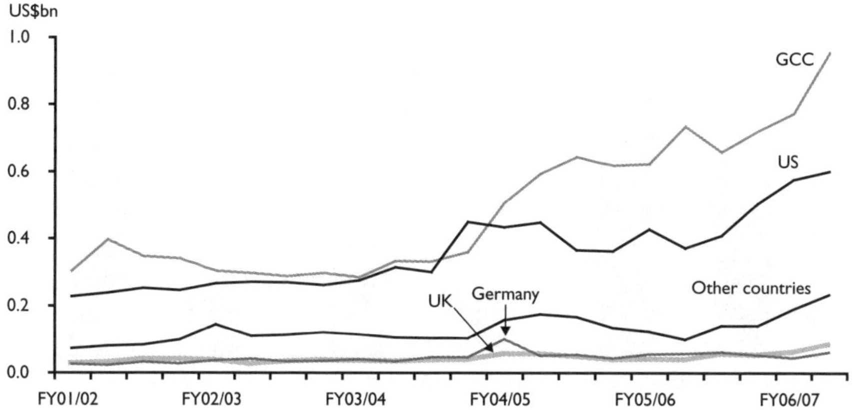

Sources: Central Bank of Egypt (2008) and Passport Capital (2008).

Figure 4.3: FDI inflows to Egypt by country of origin, 2000–07

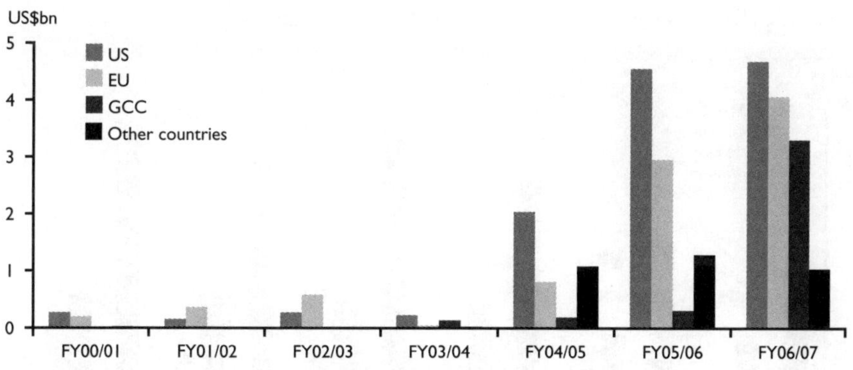

Sources: Central Bank of Egypt (2008) and Passport Capital (2008).

The GCC oil boom: further positive externalities

The GCC oil boom has also meant that the rest of MENA is benefiting, albeit to differing degrees, from positive externalities through increased remittances, exports and tourism revenues; and increased portfolio flows are contributing to already rising asset prices. This is perhaps nowhere more visible than in Egypt,[9] which among the MENA countries is the

9 The Egyptian equity market rose by 1,879% between 2003 and November 2007. Real estate prices in the main urban areas are estimated to have risen by close to 200% in 2005–07 owing to a combination of strong demand and supply shortage. Five of the 10 largest real estate projects in Egypt are being developed by UAE-based firms. See EFG-Hermes (2007).

Figure 4.4: Egyptian exports of iron and steel by main markets, 2004–07

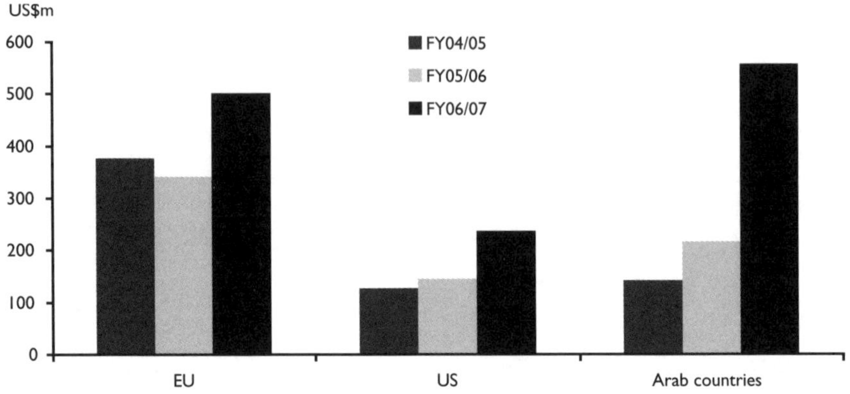

Sources: Central Bank of Egypt (2008) and Passport Capital (2008). The time series consolidates the export sales of cast iron, rolled iron, semi-finished iron products and finished iron and steel products.

Figure 4.5: Tourist arrivals in Egypt by region of origin, 2001–07

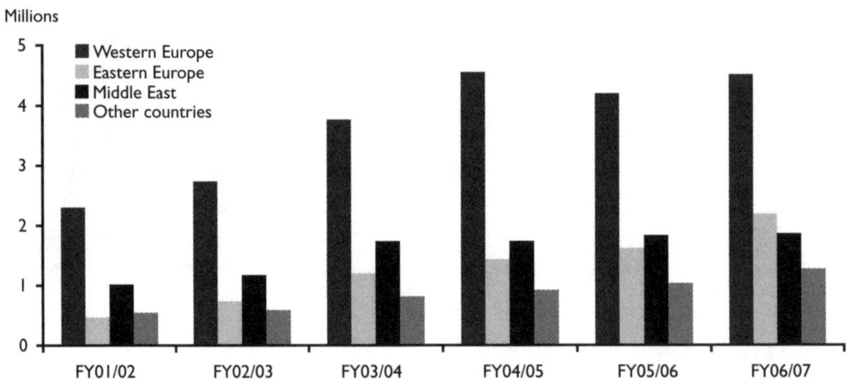

Sources: Central Bank of Egypt (2008) and Passport Capital (2008).

most integrated with the GCC investment programme. In the last quarter of fiscal year 2006/07, Egyptian workers in the GCC remitted close to $1 billion to their home country. This was more than 150% of Egyptian remittances from the United States, as shown in Figure 4.2. FDI inflows to Egypt from the GCC reached $3.3 billion in fiscal year 2006/07, up from just $0.3 billion in the previous fiscal year (see Figure 4.3). Egyptian exports of iron and steel, which represent some 30% of its non-hydrocarbon exports, soared significantly in the GCC markets in view of the ongoing construction boom,[10] reaching close to $550 million in fiscal year 2006/07 (see Figure 4.4). Although the increase in the number of tourist arrivals in Egypt from the Middle East is not as large as that from Europe (as shown in Figure 4.5), GCC citizens in particular tend to stay longer, and they spend more than all other tourists. Other positive externalities include strong and steady financial support to Lebanon, where the repercussions of the armed conflict in 2006 have necessitated further backing from the GCC, without which the economy would have suffered even more.[11]

Making a dent in unemployment?

The World Bank has aptly described the 1990s as MENA's 'lost decade', but the current 'virtuous' economic growth cycle could end up yielding a happier characterization of the 2000s, particularly apropos of its most formidable challenge, unemployment. Employment growth was strong during the 1970s oil booms, but demographic pressures and lower growth in the 1980s and 1990s meant that the rate of job creation fell below the growth rate of the labour force. With 35% of MENA's 300 million population under the age of 25, the World Bank estimated in 2004 that it needed to create 100 million jobs by 2020 in order to absorb new labour market entrants and to keep the average unemployment rate of 15% from rising further (see World Bank 2004). This level of job creation requires annual economic growth rates of between 6% and 8% to be achieved between 2000 and 2020, far higher than the 3.6% rate seen during the 1990s.

Although it is too early to assess its impact fully, clear signs are present that a structural transformation is being attempted in earnest in the MENA region, albeit with different levels of commitment and chances of success. As an early indicator of the changing economic fortunes of the region, MENA has already posted annual employment growth rates of over 4% between 2000 and 2005, the highest of any developing region and much higher than the 2.5% annual average recorded in the 1990s (Dyer and Yousef 2007). The regional unemployment rate still stood at a high 12.2% in 2006 (ILO 2007), down from 15.2% in 2000, but it is likely to have declined further since then, as growth and FDI have picked up. This has led the

10 The GCC has $1.5 trillion (200% of its members' estimated 2007 GDP) of infrastructure projects planned or under way, according to MEED (2007).

11 Saudi Arabia and Kuwait deposited $1.5 billion in the Banque du Liban in support of the dollar peg and pledged another $0.8 billion for humanitarian and reconstruction efforts at the onset of the war in July 2006 (a combined total of 9.7% of Lebanon's GDP). The GCC pledged $1.4 billion during the Paris III donor conference in January 2007 and $430 million at the Stockholm donor conference in August 2006.

World Bank to revise its estimates of job creation needs down to 68 million new jobs by 2020[12] – not a bad start by any measure.

However, despite the recent high economic growth rates across MENA, the increase in employment masks an uneven performance of the labour market. Most GCC countries have seen exceptional job creation, in excess of 9% annually, but expatriate workers have absorbed the majority of these new jobs, a particularly worrying conundrum for Saudi Arabia. Furthermore, Morocco and Tunisia have posted sluggish to stagnating yearly job-creation rates of 2–3%. And although the annual growth rate of employment reached 6.3% in Algeria between 2000 and 2005, nearly half of all additional jobs were due to growth in the 'work-at-home' sector, which includes military conscription and informal and unpaid activities (World Bank 2007). In Egypt, the unemployment rate declined to 8.9% in the first quarter of fiscal year 2007/08, down from 11.1% in the same quarter of the previous fiscal year (Egyptian Ministry of State for Economic Development 2008) but it is yet to be seen whether it will continue to decline and then be sustained at this lower level.

Female unemployment also presents a mixed picture, albeit with some positive developments. The MENA region now has a more active female labour force than ever before, but this has not been followed by an increase in levels of employment across the board. Female unemployment has in fact worsened relative to that of men in all MENA countries except Algeria and the United Arab Emirates. Unemployment among women has increased in Bahrain, Iran, Jordan and Tunisia while that among men has fallen. This is partly explained by the fact that women in the region are shifting from their inactive status to becoming openly unemployed, implying increasing unemployment rates. Although there has been an improvement in the situation of educated female workers in MENA's labour markets, there remain countries where both men and women with higher education face higher unemployment rates than those with lower levels of education. Examples are Algeria, Egypt, Iran, Jordan and Morocco, pointing to the structural problems impeding higher levels of employment. Gender differences are substantial at this level, as women with higher education have at least twice the unemployment rates of their male counterparts. As female participation in the labour market increases, female employment appears to be growing more rapidly than female unemployment, especially in the more dynamic labour markets such as Iran, the United Arab Emirates and Qatar, but also in Algeria and Egypt.

12 Still, the challenges remain daunting. Although the growth of MENA's labour force is slowly converging with that of other developing regions, it remains the highest in the world. See World Bank (2007).

Towards a new social contract?

Despite the growth of the past eight years, the MENA region still employs only a fraction of its potential workforce and has lower employment rates than, for example, Latin America and South-East Asia. The sustainability of higher job-creation rates depends largely on addressing long-term structural labour market rigidities. MENA has one of the highest percentages of public-sector employment in the world, and increased hydrocarbon revenues have allowed governments in oil-exporting countries to absorb some of the labour force entrants in targeted programmes.[13] Labour market regulations generally continue to be restrictive, and generous public-sector employment policies have contributed to crowding out private-sector employment. Although the *number* of jobs that need to be created is important, the *quality* of these jobs is a challenge that must be addressed given the educational attainments and wage expectations of young graduates.

Over the past decade, productivity in the MENA region rose by less than 9%, compared to a world average of nearly 26%. Low productivity levels help to explain why significant gains in human development since 2000 have not translated into the reduction of income poverty (Iqbal 2006). Even though some of the MENA countries are making significant progress in encouraging private-sector-led growth, long-term structural policies still need to be pursued further, particularly gender equality and better governance, and they would need to be assisted by more appropriate and responsible educational systems (Yousef 2005).

In the near term, positive growth prospects, the economic diversification under way in the GCC and the growing proportion of 'greenfield' intraregional FDI should help to sustain healthy levels of employment generation across most of the MENA region.[14] This is despite the fact that compared to the 1970s, some of the linkages between the GCC and the rest of MENA stand at comparatively weaker levels. To take one example, while Egypt's FDI, portfolio inflows and intraregional tourism have grown, worker remittances are lower as a percentage of GDP – 6% today compared with a peak of 14% in 1979.[15] Still, the quality of remittances, their use in Egypt and the investments they generate domestically are new key variables to watch for. This decade's liquidity boom certainly offers policy-makers a new set of tools for tackling an old set of problems.

13 Unemployment among nationals in the GCC states is in the low double digits, according to governments' figures.

14 'Greenfield' investments refer to the creation of a subsidiary from scratch by one or more non-resident investors, as opposed to cross-border mergers and acquisitions.

15 The decrease in labour remittances reflects mainly the GCC states' nationalization policies and the switch towards lower-cost South Asian labour. See World Bank (2006).

References

BIS (2007), official website www.bis.org and online database.

Central Bank of Egypt (2008), official website www.cbe.org.eg.

Dyer, P. and T. Yousef (2007), 'Will the Current Oil Boom Solve the Employment Crisis in the Middle East?', *The Arab World Competitiveness Report* (Geneva: World Economic Forum).

EFG-Hermes (2007), 'Sixth of October Development and Investment Co. Initiation of Coverage'.

Egyptian Ministry of State for Economic Development (2008), see www.mop.gov.eg and www.capmas.gov.eg.

Eid, F. and F. Paua (2003), 'Foreign Direct Investment in the Arab World: The Changing Investment Landscape', in *Arab World Competitiveness Report* 2002-2003, World Economic Forum (New York: Oxford University Press).

Higgins, M., T. Klitgaard and R. Lerman (2006), *Recycling Petrodollars*, Federal Reserve Bank of New York Research Paper Series – Current Issues in Economics and Finance (12) 9 (December): 2–8.

ILO (2007), *Global Employment Trends* (Geneva: International Labour Office).

IMF (2006), 'Oil Prices and Global Imbalances', *World Economic Outlook*, April.

Institute of International Finance (2007), 'Regional Briefing: Tracking GCC Petrodollars' (Washington, DC: IIF).

Inter-Arab Investment Guarantee Corporation (2006), *Investment Climate in Arab Countries* (Kuwait: IAIGC).

Iqbal, F. (2006), *Sustaining Gains in Poverty Reduction and Human Development in MENA* (Washington, DC: World Bank).

Middle East Economic Digest (MEED) (2007), online database.

Passport Capital (2008), unpublished MENA research.

UNCTAD (2006, 2007), *World Investment Report*.

World Bank (2004), Tarik Yousef, *Unlocking the Employment Potential in the Middle East and North Africa: Toward a New Social Contract* (Washington, DC: World Bank).

World Bank (2006), 'Economic Developments and Prospects: Financial Markets in a New Age of Oil', Middle East and North Africa Region Report.

World Bank (2007), 'Economic Developments and Prospects: Job Creation in an Era of High Growth', Middle East and North Africa Region Report.

World Bank (2008), 'Doing Business 2008', Washington, DC: World Bank Press.

Yousef, T. (2005), 'Structural Reforms, the Investment Climate and Private Sector Development in the Arab World', *The Arab World Competitiveness Report* (Geneva: World Economic Forum).

5 The GCC: prospects and risks in the new oil boom

Mina Toksoz

Introduction

This chapter argues that although the Gulf Cooperation Council region is economically and financially more robust than it was in the oil boom of the 1970s, significant vulnerabilities still exist. It is clear that the current boom has seen better management of oil windfall revenues than in the previous one. Most (but not all) governments in the Gulf have built up sufficient foreign exchange (FX) reserves to provide a temporary cushion against a drop in oil prices. The private sector is now strong enough to undertake many large-scale projects, implying a more efficient and commercial allocation of resources. Also, large oil revenues and the general conditions created by the emergence of Asia as a significant dynamic force in the world economy have given a new lease of life to diversification plans in the Gulf. Saudi Arabia is set to become a heavy industry base for the region and the lower Gulf region looks likely to regain its historical role as a trading/finance and logistics hub between Asia, Africa and Europe.

The boom this time has raised new challenges. There are worries about a property bubble in Dubai, the rapid rise in foreign borrowing by regional corporates and banks, and the sustainability of the dollar pegs in view of the falling value of the dollar and accelerating inflation in the region. But besides these short-term, cyclical challenges, there are medium-term issues that will determine whether the boom leads on to a more sustainable pattern of growth. The diversification project remains fragile owing to the cyclical character of oil revenues and the persistent heavy dependence of the region's exports on global demand. This is because of the small size of the national markets, the slow pace of integration of the internal market of the GCC, and political instability in the countries surrounding the GCC that would normally make up its natural economic hinterland. Sustainability will also depend on the ability of the lower Gulf economies to generate more private-sector jobs for the national workforce. This ability will be driven by progress in the liberalization of markets, the break-up of monopolies and reforms of the labour market, along with new educational and skills programmes. Finally, the traditional rentier-state structures will need to show greater adaptability to the existence of a stronger private sector and a more complex, globally integrated economy.

A repeat of the first oil boom and bust?

With the exception of a few (Lackner 1978), writing on the Gulf during the oil boom of the 1970s focused gushingly on the extraordinary pace and extent of infrastructural investment and development taking place in the region on the back of the double rise in oil prices. The vulnerability of these projects to a collapse in oil prices and the difficulties of transforming traditional social and economic structures were yet to be experienced. These quickly became apparent from the mid-1980s as oil prices began their almost two decades of decline. By the end of the 1990s, with per capita incomes and budget revenues falling sharply, several big projects were left half-complete; the diversification plans that had been embarked upon were achieved only in part. The GCC economies did not have the dynamism to generate sufficient jobs to employ a rapidly growing indigenous labour force. Given the inability of the mostly capital-intensive state enterprises to absorb new entrants to the labour market, the biggest source of employment remained the state bureaucracies. But even these were under pressure owing to the decline in oil revenues. Governments throughout the Gulf were forced to borrow domestically and abroad in order to cover their budget deficits. By the end of the 1990s, several years of running fiscal and current account deficits had brought the Saudi public debt to over 100% of GDP, and the Saudi Arabian Monetary Authority's net foreign assets were estimated to have dwindled to below $40 billion in 1999 (IMF 2001). Expectations about the survival of the traditional political elites in the region also turned pessimistic after the 1990–91 Iraqi invasion of Kuwait: many predicted either that there would be increased repression (Graz 1990) or, especially after 9/11, that traditional rule would be replaced by more democratic forms of governance.

The oil boom since 2002

But with the steady rise in oil prices since 2002, the situation has turned around again. Debts have been swiftly reduced and the traditional political structures mostly continue, with a few cosmetic democratic changes. The

Figure 5.1: GCC members' budget spending and revenues, 1990–2007

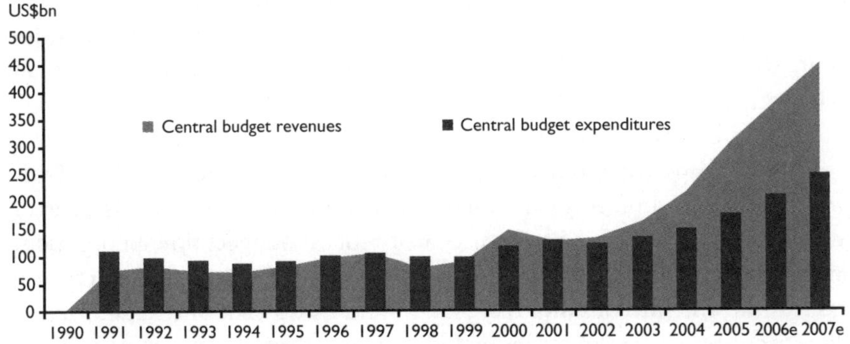

Source: IIF (2007a).

World Bank–IMF meetings in Dubai in 2003 and the holding of the Asian Games in Qatar in 2006 seemed to confirm that the GCC region is no longer a peripheral one that just exports oil; now it has a central position at the crossroads of the world. By 2007, Dubai had established itself as the third-biggest re-export centre, after Hong Kong and Singapore.

The combined GDP of the GCC countries has more than doubled since 2002, and was estimated to have reached $800 billion at the end of 2007. The combined external surplus of the members of the GCC stood at $200 billion in 2006, not far from the $250 billion current account surplus of China.[1] Their total foreign assets are estimated at $1.6 trillion (225% of combined GDP); this compares with China's foreign currency reserves of $1.1 trillion (42% of GDP). Projects valued at over $700 billion are planned for 2006–10. They include six new cities in Saudi Arabia, a $100 billion city in Kuwait and two new financial centres, one in Qatar and the other in Saudi Arabia (King Abdullah Financial District), in addition to the two existing ones in Dubai and Bahrain.

The Gulf regimes have shown a capacity for a rapid (and, so far, measured) response to this new round of accumulation of oil savings over the past four years. There has been a renewed expansion of public spending while conservative underlying oil price assumptions in budgets have been kept to (see Figure 5.1). With the exception of Dubai, where public debt has risen rapidly, most governments have paid down their accumulated public debts and have built up new reserves in the oil savings funds. The Saudi public debt is estimated to have been paid down to approximately 20% of GDP at the end of 2007 from over 100% at the end of 1999. The Gulf oil funds, the biggest of which is the UAE's Adia with $875 billion of assets (Maslakovic

1 This and following data are from the Institute of International Finance (2007a).

2008), have once again become a major channel though which petro-dollars are recycled back into investments in the oil-importing economies. Current financial problems in the European Union and the United States emanating from the American subprime crisis have opened new avenues to investment by the Gulf-based sovereign wealth funds, especially in US investment banks, largely dissipating earlier political resistance.

Social and political objectives are more in the forefront of how Gulf governments are directing their oil funds this time around. There is a bigger emphasis on education, with over 25% of federal budgets now being spent on education and skills training so as to overcome the skills mismatch and to speed up the rate of employment of GCC nationals. The Saudi regime plans to construct six new cities including some located in poor and isolated parts of the country (such as Jizan on the Yemen border) in an effort to create jobs. Part of its plans for improving the national transport infrastructure and thereby overcoming the geographical fragmentation of the economy is a rail line linking Jeddah on the Red Sea with the Gulf coast.

The private sector: a bigger role

Today's oil boom is different from that of the 1970s in real price terms: the oil price rise that accompanied the 1970s boom was much bigger (although if prices rise beyond recent levels of $140/barrel and stay there, this will not hold). Also, the economic, educational and infrastructural starting point of the Gulf economies was much lower in the early 1970s. For example, adult literacy in Saudi Arabia stood at 15% for men and 2% for women in 1970. By 1990, this had risen to 73% and 48% respectively (World Bank 2006). Today the GCC economies have a greater capacity to absorb the oil windfall than in the 1970s, with more developed domestic financial markets and a more extensive private sector. Private investment in the non-oil sector has grown rapidly, driven by strong credit and domestic demand growth. In 2005, private-sector credit grew by about 20% in both Bahrain and Kuwait and by some 40% in the UAE and Saudi Arabia (Institute of International Finance 2006), although there was a sharp contraction in Saudi Arabia in 2006 as a result of the stock market correction. According to data from the central bank of the UAE, total bank assets nearly tripled in 2004–07. This has boosted diversification from hydrocarbons and enabled non-hydrocarbon GDP to grow steadily since 2001, but not as spectacularly compared with the fluctuating oil GDP growth rate (see Figure 5.2).

The huge projects in petrochemicals, aluminium and mining are led mostly by state entities. But the private sector, already well established in the

Figure 5.2: GCC non-hydrocarbon GDP outpacing oil GDP growth, 1994–2007

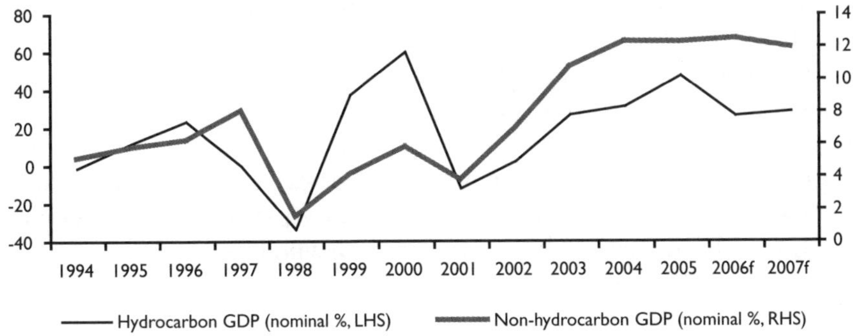

Source: IIF (2007a).

construction and building materials sectors from the 1970s and including steel, cement, glass, etc., is now a major driver of this phase of industrialization. Dynamic GCC multinationals such as Dubai Ports World, Emaar (real estate) and Etisalat (telecoms) have emerged with wide regional and international holdings in mainly real estate, finance, telecoms and tourism. The growth of the private sector has been boosted by the accession to the World Trade Organization (WTO) of Bahrain and Kuwait in 2005, UAE and Qatar in 1996, Oman in 2000 and, last but not least, Saudi Arabia in 2005. The patent protection rules that come with WTO membership have significantly helped local software firms and indigenous pharmaceutical companies in the UAE, reducing the supply of pirated products from Asia. Also, the pace of privatization has picked up. In Saudi Arabia, 2005–06 saw 49 new licences granted to financial institutions; and two private airlines, NAS Air and Sama Air, were launched in early 2007.

Existing monopolies in telecoms are being broken up. In the late 1990s, the big state monopolies such as the Saudi Telecom were corporatized. A telecom regulator, the Communications and Information Technology Commission, was set up and there were sales of state shares to the public. In the past few years, mobile phone licences have been sold throughout the region. In Saudi Arabia, 20 sectors have been identified for privatization. In addition to telecoms, water, transport, mining and government shares in domestic banks and refineries are up for sale. It is expected that the decades-old monopoly of the Saudi Arabian Transport Company will be terminated when its licence expires at the end of 2008, opening intercity bus transport to private-sector operators.

In addition, FDI is being courted more actively. In Saudi Arabia, a one-stop-shop organization has been established, the Saudi Arabian General Investment Authority. The legal and institutional frameworks in the region have been improving rapidly. Saudi Arabia is ranked at 38 (followed closely by Kuwait) in the World Bank's competitiveness index, up from 70 in the 1990s. Progress in Saudi Arabia has speeded up since accession to the WTO. There have been reforms of its commercial laws, and the plan to introduce a secular 10-man supreme court as the highest legal body is also moving forward. Further legislation to improve the business environment, such as reducing red tape and obstacles to start-up capital, are expected to be passed, although the connection of the legal system with the civil and Sharia courts complicates this process.

Diversification: progress and problems

The diversification of the Gulf economies, led by the UAE, has come a long way. The proportion of non-hydrocarbon exports to total merchandise exports in the UAE is estimated to have reached 53% by the end of 2007 (Institute of International Finance 2007b), although about two-thirds of this is re-exports (of precious metals and stones and electrical goods). The share of non-hydrocarbon exports would be higher if total export receipts were considered, including exports of services from the financial, tourism and transport sectors. On the other hand, Saudi Arabia is laying the basis for an indigenous car components industry centred in the King Abdulaziz City for Science and Technology, and plans were announced in 2007 for setting up an assembly plant in Dammam (Economist Intelligence Unit 2008).

These developments would have been unthinkable in the 1960s and 1970s. At that time, the domestic markets of the Gulf were considered to be too small to pursue import-substituting industrialization as a form of diversification (Davidson 2005). Broadly, three different approaches were pursued. First, some countries, Kuwait for example, pursued an investment strategy of overseas expansion in downstream oil and oil distribution. The idea behind this, along with investment in overseas financial assets, was that returns on the overseas investments would continue to furnish income in a post-oil era. Indeed, with the decline in oil prices in the 1980s Kuwait's overseas investment income was bigger than its oil-export revenues.

The second approach has consisted of moving into non-oil but energy-intensive industries in which the region has a comparative economic advantage. Saudi Arabia has made a big investment in petrochemicals, and Bahrain and the UAE have invested in large aluminium projects. The Dubai Aluminium Company has become the seventh-largest producer in the world. Dubai and Abu Dhabi are currently cooperating to establish the biggest aluminium plant in the world. Current plans in Saudi Arabia envisage that by 2020, the country will supply 15% of the global market for both aluminium and plastics. By 2010, the share of Saudi petrochemical output is expected to reach 13% of the world total. The next stage for Saudi Arabia is to tap its non-oil mineral resources. Its plans for the mining sector represent the biggest industrial expansion since the petrochemicals programme started back in the 1970s. Mining is to become the third pillar of the Saudi economy after oil and petrochemicals.

The third approach has been to focus on historical advantages. The UAE pursued its comparative advantage in the lower Gulf of being the best positioned to develop its infrastructure as a logistics hub, enhanced recently by the financial, tourism and real estate sectors (in addition to the focus on heavy industry). The UAE has adopted a combination of all three models. Its diversification strategy has been the most successful in the Gulf: the non-hydrocarbon sectors account for just under three-quarters of real economic output. Others, such as Qatar with its tiny population and vast reserves of gas, have simply continued to develop the hydrocarbon sector while cleverly presenting themselves as an alternative regional financial centre – better regulated, more liberal and independent.

Diversification of the Gulf economies became difficult in the 1980s and 1990s, as falling oil revenues and increased spending on rearmament slowed investments in industrial and agricultural projects significantly. And where there was progress, such as in petrochemicals, Gulf producers had difficulty in overcoming barriers in the nearest markets, such as the EU, because of overcapacity in the petrochemicals industry (Toksoz 1993). This experience revealed the heavy reliance of the GCC economies on global demand, which is closely correlated with the global demand for energy and with oil prices. Despite providing an alternative to oil, diversification into heavy industry, trade and tourism does not reduce external dependence. The Dubai aluminium company referred to above is typical in that it exports 98% of total production, mostly to Asia. The GCC countries continue to face several external dependences: on oil demand, on overseas demand for non-oil, heavy industry exports, tourism and transport services, on technology and, last but not least, on overseas workers at the high and low ends of skills. Although all economies in this globalized world are sensitive to international developments, the reinforcing multiplicity of the Gulf's external dependences is unique.

The cyclical nature of the GCC economies raises further problems. The management of big projects with long gestation periods becomes more difficult to manage. It is not possible to cut back immediately on big projects in response to a drop in the oil price and a related fall in budget revenues, as was shown in the 1980s (International Monetary Fund 2004).

Also, there is the problem of unrealistic expectations from grand plans. For example, the Jizan economic city in Saudi Arabia on the southern Red Sea coast, until now an isolated backwater, is expected to generate 500,000 jobs. But there is some scepticism about this figure, as the industrial city of Jubail, which has the largest concentration of heavy industry in the region, employs only about 100,000 after 30 years of successful growth (Oxford Analytica 2007a).

Economic liberalization: early stages

Economic liberalization is still in its early stages. The royal families and traditional business groups are reluctant to give up their monopoly positions and protectionist privileges. Despite its increased integration with the global economy, the UAE still maintains a 49% restriction on foreign ownership (outside the special zones), and many of the region's stock markets give restricted access to foreigners. 'Agency laws', which give UAE firms monopoly rights to import foreign brands, still remain. Although there have been many improvements in the business environment of several GCC countries, Saudi Arabia is still ranked poorly in contract enforcement and investor protection. The continued lack of transparency of the public sector and of government procurement processes remains a major issue. It is expected that free trade agreements with the EU, the US and other countries should increase transparency, but in the light of experience elsewhere, this is likely to be a slow process under the current political structures.

The banking sector is highly concentrated, mostly in the hands of government and a few leading families. In the UAE, only one bank (Mashreqbank, owned by the Al-Ghurair family) among the top five has no government or ruling family ownership. The GCC governments and regulators stepped in and extended their control over the banking sector as the region's banks were hit by a series of crises between the mid-1980s and the early 1990s. These included the Suq Al-Manakh crisis in Kuwait in the early 1980s, the severe banking crisis in the UAE in the mid-1980s, the impact of the 1990–91 Gulf war on banking-sector liquidity regionally, the débâcle and eventual closure of the Bank of Credit and Commerce International in 1991 and the collapse of the National Commercial Bank in Saudi Arabia. Recent years have seen financial-sector regulation tightened significantly and banks recapitalized. But concentration risk (especially the concentration of banking assets on the construction and real estate sector) and high non-performing loan ratios of 15–30% continue to be problems (Standard & Poor's 2007a).

The public sector: still the main employer of Gulf nationals

One area where diversification has been difficult is the labour market. There are a number of issues here: the high levels of unemployment among Gulf nationals, the concentration of employment of Gulf nationals in the public sector, skills mismatch between education and job opportunities, low levels of backward linkages and employment-creation from the very capital-intensive heavy industries and also the cyclical nature of the jobs created. Despite the rapid growth of the private sector, the public sector remains the largest employer, accounting for 60–70% of indigenous employment in the GCC. In Kuwait and Saudi Arabia, the top two countries by population, nationals make up only about 20% of the total labour force; and of this group, 87% and 53% respectively are employed in the public sector (Oxford Analytica 2007b). The only country that bucks this trend is Bahrain, where 68% of Bahraini nationals work in the private sector. It is unique in taking a market-based approach to reforming the labour market and taxing the employment of expatriates, in contrast with the rest of the GCC, where this is addressed by administrative measures and quotas.

Not surprisingly, there has been a fast pace of job creation in recent years. A World Bank study put the annual rate of job creation in the wider MENA region at 4.5% in 2000–05, outpacing the rate of new entrants into the labour market (World Bank 2007). However, many of the new jobs were in construction and public works programmes, both of which are quite cyclical. Despite the current oil boom, indigenous unemployment in Saudi Arabia rose from 9.7% in 2002 to 12% in early 2007, with the jobless rate among Saudis in their twenties at least double that (Khalaf 2007). To address the skills mismatch, education budgets in the GCC have expanded rapidly since 2002. Approximately 25% of the government budget is now allocated to education in the UAE and Saudi Arabia, aiming to deal with the problem of the skills deficit among the Gulf nationals.

The GCC economies: still oil-driven

Notwithstanding the fiscal buffers built up over the past four years and progress with diversification, the region remains vulnerable to falls in the price of oil. As a share of nominal GDP, hydrocarbons rose from 39% in 2000 to 49% in 2006, even though the non-oil sector has grown rapidly. With the exception of the UAE, hydrocarbon exports as a share of total GCC exports has not fallen, despite the diversification achieved so far. It remains at about 80% of total combined exports (see Figure 5.3). The GCC

Figure 5.3: GCC states' hydrocarbon exports: value and percentage of total exports, 1993–2007

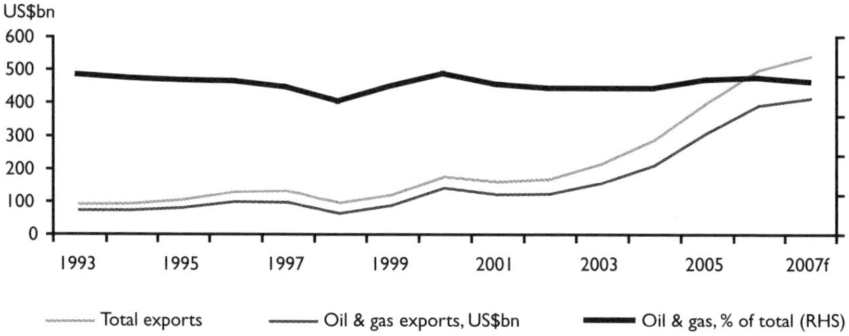

Source: IIF (2007a).

states' share of world oil supplies came down from 40% in the 1970s to 28% in 2006 (Energy Information Administration 2007). However, as the GCC countries have 50% of the world's oil reserves, their share of the world oil supply should still rise over time, keeping oil (and gas) as the mainstay of their economies for the foreseeable future.

The GCC states' budgets remain heavily dependent on hydrocarbon revenues (see Figure 5.4 below). Diversification of budget revenues, such as by introducing income tax, has been a major political challenge, and it has eluded them, even in the depths of the oil price collapse in the late 1990s. There are plans for a GCC-wide value added tax that are being led by the UAE, where it is expected to be in place in early 2009. But extension to the GCC is not expected until 2012. Even then, the introduction of VAT (expected to be no more than 3%) is mostly to replace customs duties as

Figure 5.4: Hydrocarbons as percentage of total GCC budget revenues, 1999–2007

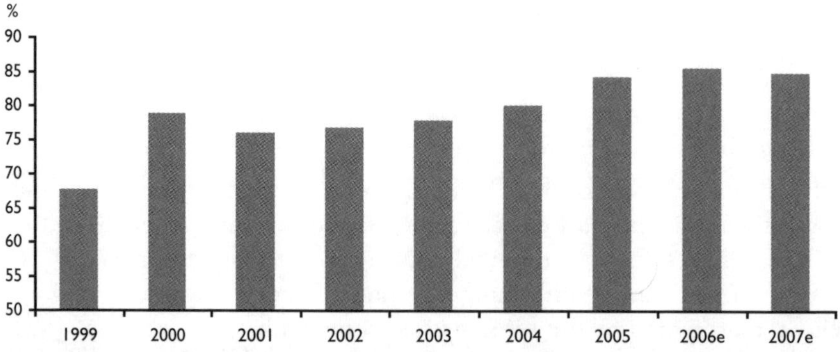

Source: IIF (2007a).

part of the free trade agreements being signed with the US and EU; the tax is unlikely to contribute much more than 5% of fiscal revenues.

So far in the present boom, budget spending has been kept well below budget revenues in the region. However, there is a new challenge to this discipline in the form of fiscal support to cap the effects on consumers of rising inflation. With little leeway to control monetary policy owing to the dollar peg, most governments have resorted to ad hoc administrative measures to fight inflation, most of which involve some form of fiscal subsidy. For example, in January 2008 Saudi Arabia introduced subsidies on rice and other staples, cut tariffs on food imports and awarded a 5% cost-of-living allowance to state employees and pensioners. The government stepped in to pay commercial fees such as port handling, passport issuance, etc. in order to reduce the cost of imports of food and construction materials and the pressure on wages. Although budget surpluses are not threatened in the short term, these subsidies, if not retracted, will become a problem in the longer term.

Weak regional integration and coordination

The GCC needs further regional integration in order to develop its own internal market and cushion against fluctuations in external demand. The GCC was formed in 1981, initially with a political and strategic mission. But the sobering experience of falling oil prices in the 1990s generated more interest in economic integration, and a GCC customs union with a common (5%) external tariff was established in 2003 (two years ahead of the original target). There has been gradual progress towards a harmonized legal and institutional framework. Barriers to the movement of goods, services, labour and capital have largely been lifted and GCC nationals can own property in any member country and invest in each other's equity markets (Fasano and Iqbal 2003).

On 1 January 2008, the GCC common market was launched. But in practice, different regulations on FDI, foreign ownership, participation in capital markets and slow integration with the global banking system continue to restrict the emergence of a regional common market. One sign of low economic integration is the low level of intraregional trade that typifies most of the Arab world. Although the combined GDP of the GCC at the end of 2007 was an estimated $800 billion and combined merchandise exports totalled some $550 billion, intraregional trade accounted for only an estimated $25 billion to $30 billion. Intra-GCC trade has remained at 5–6% of total trade for decades. The recent increase in intra-GCC FDI is a step in the right direction, but there is a long way to go when compared with intraregional trade in emerging Asia, which is just under 50% of total trade (Standard & Poor's 2007b).

The low level of intraregional trade, as shown by Figure 5.5, reflects the lack of complementarity of the GCC economies. This is a consequence of the 'me-too' approach of the GCC countries' development plans. It is not clear that the region has the capacity for four financial centres: Bahrain, Dubai, Qatar and the planned King Abdallah financial district in Riyadh. Similarly, the energy-intensive heavy industry plans now pursued by all the GCC countries depend on the availability of gas and ample feedstocks. Although the GCC is thought to have 24% of the world's total proven gas reserves, Kuwait and Bahrain are already net importers of gas. Saudi Arabia has had to ban the export of gas to channel production to its petrochemicals industry. The UAE is expected to be in deficit by 2012, leaving only Qatar and Oman with net surpluses. But the regional supply of Qatari gas has been held back by disputes over borders, routes for the building of pipelines and pricing. The construction of new cities will exponentially increase the urban demand for gas to produce electricity, leaving less for industry. These are early signs that the region's resources may not suffice to cover all the heavy industry projects. The lack of complementarity of the economies, establishing the same sectors as they compete for external market share, is a serious problem for the region. A more complementary approach to diversification would allow more specialization and intra-industry linkages across the region, ensuring more competitive and soundly based developments (Noland and Pack 2007).

A single currency would give a big push to regional integration. But the

Figure 5.5: Value of intra-GCC trade and total GCC trade, 1993–2005

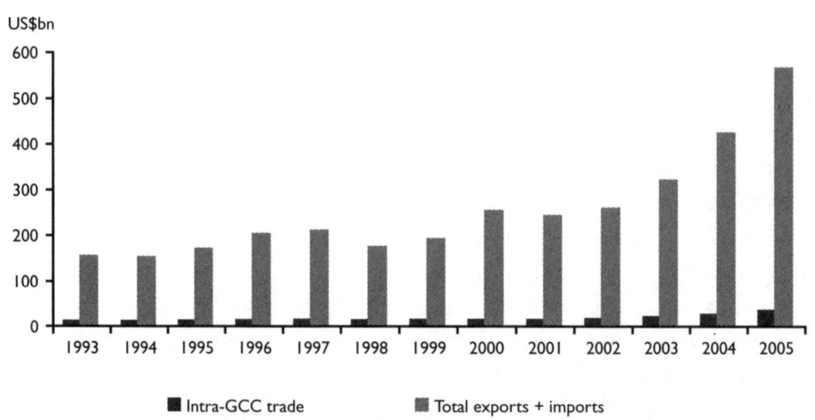

Source: GCC Secretariat.

plan to have a common currency, the Khaleeji, by 2010 that would pave the way for a single GCC market is unlikely to be met. In June 2008, a meeting of GCC central bankers agreed to create a regional 'monetary council' which some have hailed as the nucleus of a joint central bank, as the European Monetary Institute was. Once ratified by each state, the council could come into being in 2010. But it will not have monetary policy decision-making powers. Official statements suggest that the GCC common currency will be a looser arrangement than the euro – more of a common currency area than the monetary union of the Eurozone. A monetary union would require not only a common central bank and currency but also coordinated fiscal policy conduct, transparency in fiscal accounts and jointly defined public statistics, none of which appear to be likely any time soon. The current oil boom has in some ways made regional coordination more difficult, with inflationary trends and the monetary policies of the GCC countries diverging rather than converging. The dominance of Saudi Arabia in the GCC – it has about 60% of combined GDP – is another factor that complicates moves towards regional integration, as evident from current disagreements over the future course of the dollar pegs. The acceleration of inflation and the persistent decline in the value of the dollar have increased pressure on the Gulf currencies for a revaluation or for dropping the peg to the dollar. Kuwait unilaterally revalued in 2007 and dropped its dollar peg, and Oman announced that it would not be ready for a common currency by 2010. Recent statements from the UAE, where inflation is a major problem, suggest that it would like to move towards a more flexible currency regime. Although inflation also hit 10% in April 2008 in Saudi Arabia, the political pressures there do not appear as great as in Qatar and the UAE, where immigrant workers have been protesting against double-digit rates of inflation. Also, the GCC cannot easily break with the dollar peg, not least because the bulk of the region's exports is denominated in dollars. Although a revaluation is possible, the Saudis are likely to remain reluctant to break the peg, no doubt because of the global political and strategic ramifications of the Gulf currencies unpegging from the US currency. But this is not as big an issue for, say, Qatar, which already follows a more independent foreign and strategic policy.

The GCC hinterland: an unstable region

The GCC's population is just under 40 million. There is a hinterland of 300 million in the Middle East and North Africa (MENA), but the region has been beset by political instability and low growth. As with the GCC, intraregional exports in the wider MENA remain low, at under 10% of total exports. More acute political instability exists in the Horn of Africa. The growth dynamic in Egypt, Turkey and India has to some extent helped to offset the weakness of the GCC's immediate periphery in the Levant, the upper Gulf and the Horn of Africa. All this contrasts with the success of the finance and logistics activities of the Asian financial centres of Hong Kong and Singapore in tapping their hinterland for labour, resources and now increasingly as markets as the Asian economies trade more with each other.

There is some movement, however. Intra-Arab trade has picked up since the signing of the Greater Arab Free Trade Agreement and the elimination of intra-Arab tariffs in 2005 (Lawrence 2006). Part of the problem with low intra-Arab trade has been the Euro-Med Association agreements with the EU, which liberalized trade only according to single-country-of-origin rules, discouraging Mediterranean countries from using inputs from each other. This too was changed in 2005: new free trade agreements (FTAs) with the EU allow producers to cumulate processing from different countries in the region that also have FTAs with the EU. There is a goal, although it is not clear whether the deadline will be met, to create a pan-EuroMed FTA by 2010, the same target date for the EU–GCC FTA.

Institutional structures: slow in adapting to change

The onset of a new oil price boom since 2003 has reduced the pressure for economic and political reform. This is seen not just in the Gulf but also in other oil exporters such as Russia. Although the traditional ruling elites in the Gulf have shown considerable capacity to survive and evolve, they have also tended to postpone real political change, preventing a significant loosening of their political and economic control.

The slow pace of economic reform in the region has been seen to be related mostly to Islam and, particularly in Saudi Arabia, to opposition from the conservative Wahhabi clergy. Although this is the case with some reforms, such as the lifting of restrictions on women playing a full social and economic role, it is not the whole story. More careful observation (Aarts and Nonneman (eds) 2005) shows convincingly that reform and liberalization are held back mainly by the traditional patrimonial structures. For example in Saudi Arabia, the number of princes in the royal family has increased over time, generating demand for new avenues of personal entitlement. This has brought an increase in royal administrators and a proliferation of administrative structures, all establishing their own segmented fiefdoms. And once established, they resist change.

The private sector should be one of the key drivers of political and economic reform as the GCC economies diversify. Indeed, as the private sector has become stronger and gained some autonomy, it has voiced its business demands through institutions such as chambers of commerce for less intervention by government, a reduction of red tape, greater openness to FDI and regional integration. But the private sector has desisted from putting forward formal political demands, as long as the regimes refrain from taxing private-sector profits. Hence most private businessmen still operate through their connections to the royal family and the systems of perquisites and favours that is bestowed on them. This keeps the growing business elite segmented and prevents it from functioning as a coherent social force for change. This has left the ruling families themselves as the main effective force for change. This is why most political reforms in the region have been instituted from the top down by benevolent rulers, and have remained for the most part extremely limited.

However, several forces are likely to become stronger in pushing for change in the region today. Regional integration to establish a regional internal market has not been a priority. But this could speed up now that the GCC common market has been launched. With increased regional and global integration (WTO membership, FTAs with the United States and a planned one with the European Union), economic diversification, liberalization and further expansion of the private sector, the traditional political structures of the GCC, which depend on personal and family loyalties, are likely to weaken. The vast bureaucracies and administrations, as they become more complex and are forced to operate more transparently, are likely to become less amenable to political control though kinship networks (Crystal 1995). As we saw in the 1980s, the decline in oil revenues could force a rationalization of welfare services and a reduction of public sector jobs and could require the imposition of taxes, thus threatening the social pact that maintains social peace. With a small domestic market unable to cushion a decline in external demand, these regimes could be exposed to acute future instability unless they allow for real change and develop institutions with flexibility that can generate appropriate policies in response to changing conditions and external shocks.

References

Aarts, Paul and Gerd Nonneman (eds) (2005), *Saudi Arabia in the Balance* (London: Hurst & Co.).

Crystal, Jill (1995), *Oil and Politics in the Gulf: Rulers and Merchants in Kuwait and Qatar* (New York: Cambridge University Press).

Davidson, Christopher M. (2005), *The United Arab Emirates: A Study in Survival* (London: Lynne Rienner).

Economist Intelligence Unit (2008), *Business Middle East*, London, 16 February.

Energy Information Administration, Country Analysis Briefs, 'Persian Gulf Oil and Gas Exports Fact Sheet', September 2004, www.eia.doe.gov; and 2007 data.

Fasano, Ugo and Zubair Iqbal (2003), GCC *Countries: From Oil Dependence to Diversification* (Washington, DC: International Monetary Fund).

Graz, Liesl (1990), *The Turbulent Gulf* (London: I.B. Tauris).

IMF (2001), Article IV Consultation with Saudi Arabia, 7 November.

IMF (2004), Managing Oil Wealth – The Case of Azerbaijan, Washington, DC.

Institute of International Finance (2006), *Country Report:* GCC, Washington, DC, August.

Institute of International Finance (2007a), 'Tracking the GCC Petrodollars', GCC Regional Briefing, 31 May.

Institute of International Finance (2007b), *UAE Report*, Washington, DC, November.

Khalaf, Roula (2007), 'Gulf States Struggle to Narrow National's Jobless Gap', *Financial Times*, 26 April.

Lackner, Helen (1978), *A House Built on Sand: A Political Economy of Saudi Arabia* (London: Ithaca Press).

Lawrence, Robert Z. (2006), *A US-Middle East Trade Agreement: A Circle of Opportunity?* (Washington, DC: Peterson Institute for International Economics).

Maslakovic, Marko (2008), *Sovereign Wealth Funds 2008* (London: International Financial Services).

Noland, Marcus and Howard Pack (2007), *The Arab Economies in a Changing World* (Washington, DC: Peterson Institute for International Economics). See pp. 103–4 for a discussion of the low level of inter-industry linkages across the Arab world. The UAE stands out as an exception.

Oxford Analytica (2007a), 'Economic Cities Require Adjustments', Oxford, 2 March.

Oxford Analytica (2007b), 'Gulf States: Labour Rigidities Create Bottlenecks', Oxford, 5 October.

Standard & Poor's (2007a), 'Bank Industry Risk Analysis: UAE', London, 16 January.

Standard & Poor's (2007b), 'Steady As We Go: The Asia-Pacific Weathers Global Turbulence', Mumbai, 5 November.

Toksoz, Mina (1993), *Pockets of Influence: The EU's Faltering Impact on the Arab Economies*, Middle East Programme Report (London: Royal Institute of International Affairs).

World Bank (2006), World Development Indicators, Washington, DC.

World Bank (2007), The Environment for Women's Entrepreneurship in the MENA Region, Washington, DC.

Part 3

Building an international financial centre

6 The role and functions of an international financial centre

John Nugée

Introduction

One of the hallmarks of the past 30 years has been the increasing globalization and reintegration of the world economy. National economies are now much more linked, and in turn much more interdependent, than they have been since at least the previous golden age of globalization over a century ago; and today very few countries, even among the least developed parts of the world, still seek to remain isolated from the global economy.

Hand in hand with this globalization of the world economy has been an internationalization of the world's financial systems. Exchange controls have been dismantled in both current and capital account sectors, and more and more countries are permitting – indeed actively encouraging – the involvement of the international community in their economies and markets. As a consequence, the business of international finance has grown at an exponential rate. While world trade has grown at a rate that is a multiple of world GDP over the past two decades, cross-border financial flows and financial activities have grown at rate that is a multiple even of that.

For those involved in the rapidly growing business of international finance, major advantages accrue in concentrating their activities and conducting them in one place. Wherever a combination of a critical mass of business, a sufficiently large and skilled workforce and appropriate levels of supervision and regulation have been in place, international financiers have flocked there to do business. This has led to the rise of a small number of international financial centres (IFCs), and these 'centres of excellence' have become a major feature of the international financial environment.

IFCs are not attractive just to the financiers who work in them or to the clients who use their services. Host governments across the globe have welcomed the contribution that international finance, with its high valued-added business and high-quality employment opportunities, can add to the local economy. As a result, the list of governments and countries that would like to host an IFC is ever-growing. In the era of decolonization and 'end of empire' in the 1960s and 1970s, every new country wanted its own flag, currency and national airline. Now many smaller and newer economies consider their national development plan incomplete without a financial sector, and preferably an international one, to attract international financiers, who can add so much to the national exchequer.

In few places is this truer than in the Gulf. As the countries of the GCC modernize and upgrade their economies, they are seeking to position themselves not only as major *users* of financial services as they reinvest their sovereign wealth but also as natural *hosts* to the service providers they employ. In effect, their business proposition is that they can provide the capital both to build the required infrastructure for an IFC and to seed its business and get it up and running.

The ambitions of the GCC countries are clear. The question is, will the business proposition just outlined be enough, and do those countries have a winning hand? The chapters of this section seek to answer this question, and between them they cover all aspects of what it takes to build an IFC and address whether the GCC states have the ability to fulfil their ambitions. But first, it will be valuable to examine exactly what the functions of an IFC are. And to do this, we should start with the role that a financial system plays in a monetary economy.

The role of a financial system

In their classic study,[1] Robert Merton and Zvi Bodie identify five main functions of a modern financial system. They are:

1) A mechanism to amalgamate and combine economic resources, thus generating large pools of capital. The importance of capital to economic development has long been understood. If economic agents had to rely entirely on their own capital resources to fund their activities, they would be unable to make large-scale capital investments and develop successful enterprises. A modern financial system enables a small number of large borrowers to access and put to work the assets of a large number of small savers.
2) A mechanism to transfer economic resources across time and space. This enables individuals to separate the lifetime pattern of income

1 See Robert C. Merton and Zvi Bodie, 'A Conceptual Framework for Analyzing the Financial Environment', in Dwight B. Crane et al., *The Global Financial System: A Functional Perspective* (Boston, MA: Harvard Business School Press, 1995).

(typically highest from the age of 40 to 60) from that of expenditure (typically highest when they are young and establishing themselves and when they are old and drawing down their savings). It also enables a society as a whole to allocate resources so that savings flow to the most productive industry or region of the economy.

3) A mechanism to share risk. Risk-sharing benefits both investors, who can spread their investments across many enterprises, and borrowers, who can obtain finance for projects that would be too risky for a single investor but become acceptable when the risk is borne by many. Diversifying investments, and also insurance and hedging, are classic examples of risk-sharing.

4) A mechanism to reduce the cost of information. A modern financial system is a huge information exchange – on the price of assets, on the creditworthiness of economic agents and on the prospects of success for an economic venture. The financial sector processes and analyses this information and makes it widely and cheaply available to market participants, an essential element of ensuring that society channels its resources into their most efficient use.

5) Underpinning all the above, a mechanism for the clearing and settlement of payments and financial claims, without which the exchange of goods and services would be impossible.

Most of these functions involve bringing people together: enabling creditors to meet debtors, investors to meet borrowers, and risk-takers to meet those providing risk opportunities. These are the classic functions of a market-place, and financial activity has gravitated to meeting places for centuries – whether at Gresham's magnificent Royal Exchange building in the City of London, the coffee houses of Amsterdam or even the souks of the Middle East. And despite the huge advances in communications in the past few years, there is no sign that mankind's preference for gathering together to do business is weakening. In fact, the reverse is true: peripheral financial markets find that their business is inexorably moving away from them and becoming concentrated in fewer, larger financial centres. And these days, few countries can maintain more than one stock market. (Fifty years ago, Britain had several vibrant regional stock markets; and even as recently as the late 1980s, the Federal Republic of Germany had half a dozen regional financial centres alongside the one in Frankfurt.)

Merton and Bodie analysed mainly the national sphere, but what is true of a national financial system is equally true of the international economy. The international financial system performs the same five functions for the international economy that they identified for a national financial system in a national economy. Moreover, because the flows of cross-border finance are larger and its complexities are greater, there is an even greater tendency for the international financial system to converge on a small number of major financial centres. And once such a financial centre has established itself in the international market-place and become a genuine IFC, the advantages of having a critical mass of expertise are enormous. It is no real surprise therefore that the established IFCs have increased their dominant role in the past decade.

The components of an IFC

What are the essential components of an IFC? One of the most basic is a strong, fair and relatively constant legal and regulatory framework. Market participants need to be certain of their rights and obligations, of their ownership of property and intellectual capital and of their ability to plan and conduct their business in an orderly way without undue change or interference from the authorities. This is not the same as *no* interference from them: regulators need to be proactive in generating the required legal environment, and a free-for-all in which anything is permitted is not conducive to international business. It means that the authorities should set out the rules for business and then, as much as possible, refrain from making unnecessary changes to them.[2] International financiers are well used to taking and managing *financial* risk – it is their core business. But they are less able to manage *regulatory* risk, and if a government constantly changes the rules under which they operate, international business will quickly find another jurisdiction that offers more certainty.

The second main ingredient of a successful IFC is a wide range of skills and professions. As well as the core financial skills of commercial and investment banking, asset management and insurance, market-making and brokerage, there are a host of ancillary but equally necessary professions. Prominent among them are the accounting and actuarial professions, legal and compliance specialists and information systems and the media. This is where the advantages of critical mass in a successful IFC are at their strongest: despite all the advances in electronic communications, there is still

2 The same arguments can be made about taxation, both corporate and personal. Many people assume that an IFC will flourish only in an environment of low or even no tax. But this is not necessarily true, as the examples of London and New York show. What is true is that sudden and unexpected changes in corporate or personal taxation can quickly render the plans of financial companies (and their employees) invalid, and those changes will be a very strong disincentive to anyone seeking to establish or maintain their business in that centre.

no substitute for physical proximity to others and for physical meetings to discuss and to further business.

Other components an IFC needs in order to succeed are good communications to the outside world, both electronic, for information flow, and physical, such as air and other transport services; an open capital account and current account to facilitate the movement of international funds; and a liberal policy on the employment of expatriates so that the IFC can attract and employ the best financial minds regardless of nationality or passport. It is seldom enough for a putative IFC merely to enable expatriates to live and work there legally. The infrastructure to support them – a certain lifestyle, international schools for their children and so on – must also be available.

One issue that arises in the discussion on what makes an IFC succeed is whether it is necessary for the host country to have a vibrant domestic market for the IFC to interact with. On the surface, it might seem logical that an active domestic market can only be a positive: at the least, it will provide a basic financial infrastructure and a financially aware workforce for the proposed IFC to use and build on. Yet it does seem that a lively domestic market is neither necessary (one thinks of the success of Hong Kong and Singapore, which have built highly successful IFCs without having an extensive domestic market first) nor sufficient (as the evidence from Japan and Germany demonstrates: Tokyo has long been the largest domestic market in Asia but has failed to attract much international business, and Frankfurt dominates the Eurozone without seriously challenging London as Europe's premier IFC).

It is striking that even with all the above components in place, a financial centre is not guaranteed to succeed. The experience of Malaysia's Labuan Offshore Financial Centre shows that the authorities can create the appropriate opportunities, infrastructure and regulatory environment but cannot compel the world's international financiers to come. It is perhaps easier to suggest which conditions might hinder the development of an IFC than to indicate which will guarantee success. Three in particular stand out, and we might call them 'the three -ics'.

1) It is hard for a market to become an IFC if it is too *domestic*. Domestic activities will dominate and will mean that the imperative to develop the international side of the market is always muted.
2) It is hard for a market to become an IFC if it is too *bureaucratic*. International financiers have very little appetite for battling with national bureaucracies.

3) It is hard for a market to become an IFC if it is too *idiosyncratic*. The closer a market conforms to international norms in its customs and practices, the lower the barrier to entry and the less an international company must change its working methods to fit in.

The GCC states would be well advised to take these lessons to heart as they develop and internationalize their financial centres.

7 The Gulf's changing financial landscape: from capital source to destination and emerging hub

Daniel Hanna

Introduction

The role of the Gulf[1] as a source of capital and as an investor in global financial markets is a well-known, and often controversial, one. In the past, the region's excess petrodollars were tied to the emerging debt crisis of the 1980s; now the focus is on the rising power of its sovereign wealth funds. However, less has been written about the Gulf's changing internal financial landscape. Since 2000, a combination of reform, high oil prices and changing capital flows has turned it into one of the fastest-growing capital markets in the world.

Despite record oil revenues, and in striking contrast to previous oil booms, the Gulf has become a destination for investment as well as a source. The region became a net recipient of foreign direct investment in 2000 and foreign investors are increasingly active in its domestic capital markets, attracted by high returns and relatively low correlations with other markets. Given its large current account surpluses, the Gulf will remain a net exporter of capital for the foreseeable future. However, these countries can no longer be characterized as passive, one-way investors. Instead, a burgeoning financial sector is emerging at the centre of reciprocal capital flows that combines international institutions with growing domestic players.

The Gulf's financial institutions are becoming more important actors in global markets and investment decisions are increasingly tied to the region's broader strategic aims. Domestic job-creation through the financial sector is one aim. Building stronger ties to Asia is another. Regional governments are using their surplus capital to build new financial links with South, Central and East Asia. The search for attractive returns remains critical, but there is an explicit hope that stronger investment links can create a hinterland for the region's financial sector and turn the Gulf into a financial hub that can match Hong Kong, Singapore and even London.

1 The Gulf is understood to mean the six members of the Gulf Cooperation Council (GCC): Bahrain, Kuwait, Oman, Qatar, Saudi Arabia and the United Arab Emirates. The Gulf and GCC will be used interchangeably.

Challenges remain, and the region's aspirations outstrip its current capabilities. Competition among the Gulf states to be the principal regional financial centre has spurred reform and the spread of best practice; but it has also hampered effective government coordination, which may hinder further growth. Regulatory differences have widened rather than narrowed and a single regional capital market appears to be a distant prospect. The current uncertainty over the potential single GCC currency is a symptom of the situation.

Nonetheless, the progress of the Gulf's financial sector has been remarkable. Ambitious governments, backed by large petrodollar surpluses, will ensure that their financial institutions play an even more active role in the global financial markets in the years ahead.

The Gulf's economic prospects transformed

In less than 10 years, the Gulf has been transformed from a region in economic turmoil to a financial powerhouse. At the end of the 1990s, it suffered from high unemployment, spiralling public deficits and downward pressure on its currencies. Since 2000, a combination of rising oil revenues, government reform and soaring investor confidence has turned around the GCC's economic prospects. In less than seven years, the regional economies have doubled in size. Those economies combined ended 2007 as the world's sixth-largest emerging economy, with a GDP of $790 billion. An average

Figure 7.1: Gulf oil revenues, 1980–2006

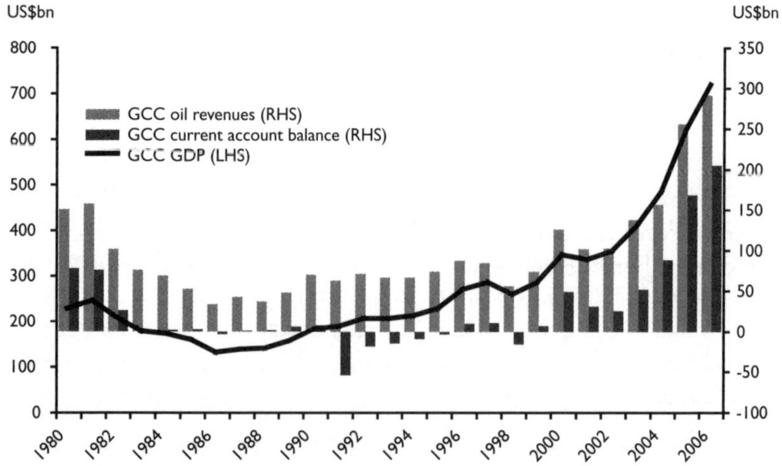

Sources: IEA, IMF and author's estimates.

per capita income of $33,000 now outstrips that of any other non-OECD country (IMF *WEO*, author's estimates).

Oil has been at the heart of this renaissance, as Figure 7.1 indicates. Record oil prices have brought $1.4 trillion flowing into the Gulf since 2000. Annual oil revenues are running at twice the level of the 1980s and 1990s in current terms (IMF *WEO*, author's estimates). In real terms, Gulf oil revenues in 2008 are likely to be record highs. However, oil has not been the only factor in the region's changing fortunes. All GCC governments have embarked on a path of economic reform, albeit at varying speeds: they have liberalized markets, privatized companies and opened their economies to foreign competition. Even Saudi Arabia, traditionally the most conservative of the Gulf states, has embraced change, as highlighted by its accession to the World Trade Organization in 2005.

The combination of strong oil revenues and state-driven reforms has had a tremendous impact on the regional economies in both the energy and the non-energy sectors. Average annual growth has been 14% in current dollar terms since 2000; while Qatar's nominal growth rate, for example, has averaged 24% per annum, almost quadrupling the size of the economy during the past seven years. The region's economic boom has spread well beyond the energy sector. GCC corporate earnings have averaged 35% per annum between 2004 and 2007 (author's estimates, Zawya various).

The regional financial sector: a major beneficiary

The Gulf's financial sector has been one of the biggest beneficiaries of the regional boom. Despite increased competition from international institutions, domestic banks continue to dominate their local markets, enjoying preferential regulatory treatment and government business. As the Gulf economies have grown, so have the local institutions. Gulf banks' assets doubled between 2001 and 2006 to $500 billion. The sector's return on equity rose from 16% in 2002 to 30% in 2006, while its non-performing loans fell to under 2% of total loans (Standard and Poor's 2007).

Economic conditions have ensured that the regional banking sector has benefited from better asset quality as well as from easier access to capital. As the economies have grown, so have deposits and demand for retail and corporate financial services. Figure 7.2 highlights the increased financial activity in Saudi Arabia, the region's biggest economy, and also how the majority of lending is now being directed towards the private sector. International rating agencies have lifted their assessment of the Gulf countries and their major institutions, which has allowed greater access to international

Figure 7.2: Private-sector lending to Saudi banks, 1988–2007

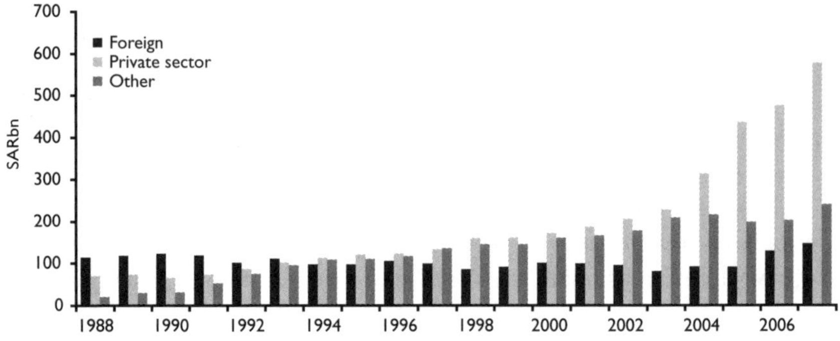

Source: Saudi Arabian Monetary Authority (SAMA).

capital markets. Despite the backdrop of tightening global credit conditions, the region's banks remain liquid and often over-capitalized.

Prudent government policy has also forced banks to innovate. Several regional governments initially used the unexpected rise in oil revenues to retire public debt. Since 2000, Saudi local currency debt has fallen from SAR610 billion, equivalent to 100% of GDP, to SAR300 billion, 25% of GDP in 2007 (SAMA various, author's estimates). As a result, financial institutions, the majority debt-holders, saw a simultaneous increase in liquidity and a shrinking of available domestic assets. In a bid to maintain return on investment, the local banking sectors in all Gulf countries pushed aggressively into retail products for the first time, leading to a rapid increase in the amount of personal loans, credit cards and mortgages.

Figure 7.3: The rising value of regional equity markets, 2001–07

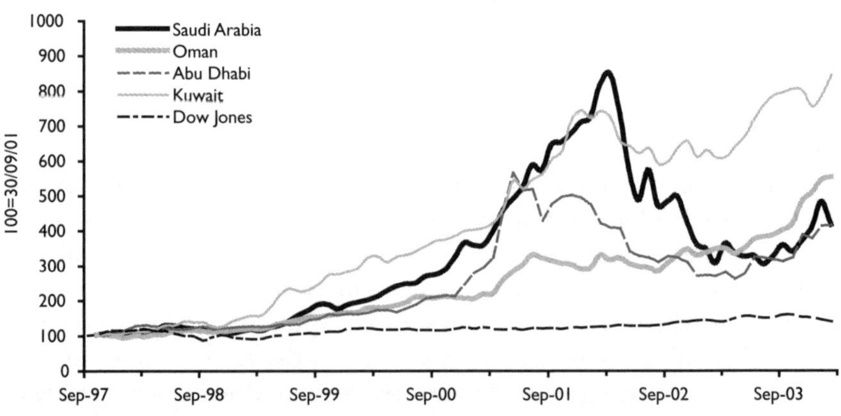

Source: Bloomberg and author's estimates.

Financial institutions have also benefited from the region's soaring capital markets, with brokers' fees becoming a major source of income. Between 2001 and the end of 2007, local equity markets grew sixfold, reaching a total capitalization of $1.116 trillion. In Saudi Arabia, average daily trade volumes on the Tadawul exchange grew from $72 million in 2003 to $2.9 billion in 2007. Even small markets, such as Oman, have seen strong growth in volumes. Oman's average daily trade volumes rose from $3.4 million to $34 million over the same period. As Figure 7.3 shows, the region's equity markets have significantly outpaced the major market indices, such as the Dow Jones Industrials (AMF various, Datastream, author's estimates).

Government reform: new opportunities

Economic growth has created a conducive environment for the banking sector, but recent government reforms have catalysed real change. A consensus among Gulf policy-makers on government reform has emerged on three themes: asset market liberalization, privatization through initial public offerings (IPOs) and increased investment in infrastructure.

The recent wave of liberalization of the Gulf markets began with real estate. At the turn of the century, every GCC country had restrictions on the ownership of real estate, even for nationals. This has now changed, and the liberalization of markets has led to the investment of $1 trillion in regional real estate and infrastructure projects. Dubai, which took the first steps to open up ownership to GCC nationals, to foreign residents and, finally, to international investors, exemplifies the impact that opening up markets can have. A quarter of its GDP in 2006 was related to the real estate sector, with local estimates suggesting that foreigners account for up to 50% of purchases of property. Restrictions on real estate investment remain, particularly for international investors in Saudi Arabia and Kuwait, but there is momentum behind further liberalization.

Naturally, the real estate boom has offered financial opportunities and scope for financial innovation. Alongside project finance and increased corporate lending to the construction sector, there has been a knock-on effect in retail banking. Before 2003, mortgage markets did not exist in the Gulf. In 2006, residential mortgages touched $3.1 billion in Dubai alone. As projects have become more ambitious and financing terms more onerous, financial institutions have been forced to innovate. For example, the region's first asset-backed securitization was backed by Dubai mortgages in 2005. Qatar's first corporate *sukuk* (Islamic bond) was based on a real estate project.

Government sponsorship, either direct or indirect, of real estate and infrastructure projects has played a large role in their viability. Government involvement also represents a new desire to invest in local economies. In the past, the small size of the local non-energy economy compared to oil revenue inflows limited the capacity to absorb large domestic investment. The growth of the Gulf economies, reform and a need to create attractive employment for the growing local workforce has led to a reassessment of this policy. Regional governments are now sponsoring over $1.5 trillion in projects over the next seven years (see Table 7.1).

Another policy embraced by all regional governments has been the partial privatization of state-owned companies through IPOs in order to redistribute state wealth and to encourage a shareholder class to emerge. Offerings have been priced typically at regulatory par value, well below the book value of the company, which has ensured unusually high returns. As a result, the Gulf has seen a rapid expansion of shareholding among the local population. By 2005, local newspapers reported that half the population of Saudi Arabia owned stocks.

The positive response of investors to privatizations has supported the emergence of private-sector IPOs. In total, between 1995 and 2003, the Gulf had nine IPOs, which raised a total of $0.4 billion. By comparison, 31 IPOs raised over $11 billion in 2007 (see Figure 7.4). This included the DP World IPO, listed on the new Dubai International Financial Exchange (DIFC), which was the world's fourth largest that year. A further 80 offerings had been publicly announced by the end of 2007. Buoyant economic conditions, high liquidity and strong investor confidence have given companies a real alternative to bank financing.

In addition to stimulating greater local involvement, regional regulators have gradually opened equity markets to foreign investors. Markets across the board are now accessible to non-national investors. However,

Table 7.1: GCC projects (US$bn) scheduled by 2015

	Infrastructure	*Industry*	*Energy*	*Petrochemicals*	*Utilities*	*Total*
Bahrain	21	3	1	0	3	28
Kuwait	182	2	48	4	12	248
Oman	20	4	8	11	4	47
Qatar	59	4	55	15	17	150
Saudi Arabia	168	16	35	79	83	381
UAE	580	22	29	54	13	698
Total	1,030	51	176	163	132	1,552

Source: MEED (September 2007).

Figure 7.4: Initial public offerings in the GCC states, 1995–2007

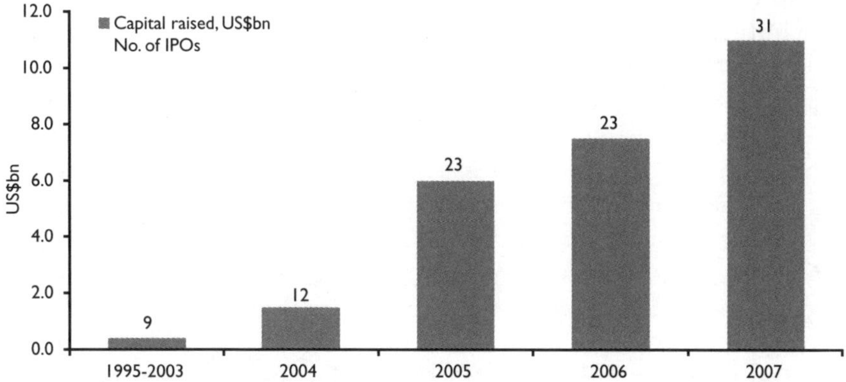

Source: Reuters, Gulf Capital and author's estimates.

restrictions do remain: for example, international investors in Saudi Arabia can gain access to equities only through mutual funds. All other Gulf countries are open to direct investment, subject to ownership ceilings of between 25% and 70%.

The Gulf: destination as well as source of capital

One distinctive feature of this period of high growth in the region has been the increased level of capital inflows from international investors. Foreign involvement in the Gulf's real estate sector has been noted above, but the change has been much wider. In 2006, all GCC countries except Kuwait were net recipients of FDI, despite record oil revenues. The positive trend started in 2000, when combined GCC net FDI turned positive for the first time in 20 years. As Figure 7.5 shows inward FDI reached a record high in 2006 (the most recent available data), marking the sixth successive year of positive net inflows – the longest stretch since records began in 1970. From 2000 to 2006, the region had already attracted levels of FDI inflows that were three times higher in current terms than for the whole of the 1980s.

Another marked change from the 1980s is that FDI has been spread more widely across the region. Between 1980 and 1989, Saudi Arabia accounted for 92% of all inward FDI to the Gulf; but between 2000 and 2006, despite attracting $10 billion more in investment, it accounted for just 40%. All GCC countries have seen more inflows, but the UAE's success has been the most notable. During this time, the Emirates attracted $34.3 billion, compared to just $500 million during the 1980s (UNCTAD).

Figure 7.5: Changing capital flows: the GCC states' FDI, 1970–2005

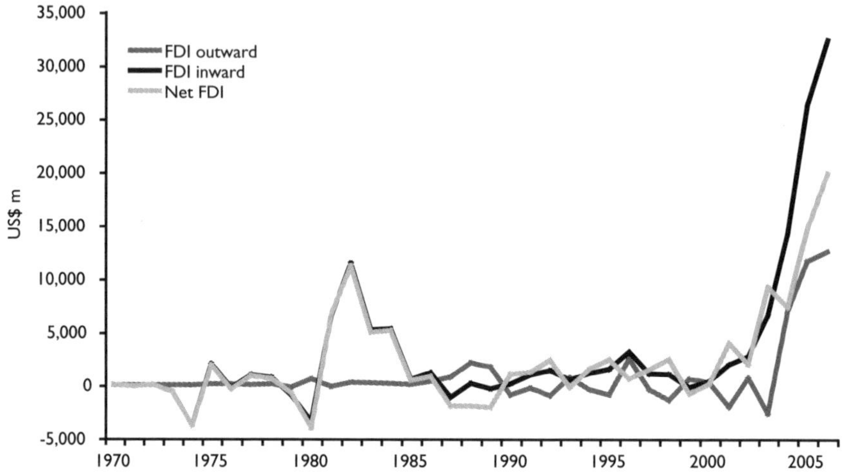

Source: UNCTAD.

Portfolio funds are harder to track, but where data are available they tell a similar story to the FDI data. In 2000, GCC and international investors owned less than 1% of the quoted shares on the Dubai financial market. By 2007, this had reached 14%, with more than half of foreign investors coming from outside the Gulf (DFM various). Moreover, more than one-third of all transactions in 2007 were carried out on behalf of foreign investors according to the exchange. International interest in the region's new equity and debt issuances is another indicator. According to a DP World press release, 60% of allocated shares from its 2007 IPO went to investors from outside the Gulf. Market participants estimate that European investors accounted for 50% and 70% respectively of Nakheel's $750 million and Aldar's $1.4 billion 2007 convertible *sukuk* issuances (Zawya 2007). With the launch in 2007 of the MSCI Frontiers Index, which contains all GCC markets except Saudi Arabia, international interest is likely to increase further.

Aspirations to be a new financial hub

As the Gulf's economies and capital flows have grown, so has ambition for its financial sector. GCC governments and bankers are hoping to build on increased domestic financial needs and growing investment links with the rest of the world to develop a financial centre spanning the time zones not covered by New York, London and Hong Kong. The Gulf hopes to use its capital to support the financial development of its wider neighbourhood of the Middle East, North Africa and Central and South Asia in a way similar to how Singapore has supported the financial needs of South-East Asia. Given high oil prices and the size of its current account surplus, ($205 billion in 2007, which is likely to rise to over $300 billion in 2008), the Gulf has significant resources with which to pursue this aim (author's estimates).

Regional governments are already using their wealth to strengthen their access to financial infrastructure. For example, Dubai and Qatar are investing in leading financial institutions so as to acquire the technology, relationships and influence that support their ambitions. Dubai has purchased stakes in the London Stock Exchange (LSE), NASDAQ and the Swedish stock exchange OMX. Qatar has taken a large stake in the LSE for similar reasons and, jointly with Kuwait, it purchased $925 million of equities in the IPO of the Industrial and Commercial Bank of China (ICBC).

Public diplomacy is being used to build stronger bilateral ties with Asia as well. The GCC has increased the number of official delegations to key countries. It has recently signed a free trade agreement (FTA) with Singapore and is currently negotiating FTAs with India, Pakistan, Japan and Turkey. The private sector is also shifting its investment focus towards emerging markets. Recently, Saudi Telecom purchased $3.1 billion in Malaysia's Maxis Communications; the Dubai-based real estate developer Emaar plans to invest up to $7 billion in Morocco; and Kuwait's MTC has announced the creation of a $10.3 billion African investment fund.

New regulatory foundations

All GCC countries have revamped their legal and supervisory frameworks in the past seven years. Dubai and Qatar have gone one step further and established entirely new and independent financial zones. This overhaul has underpinned the recent success of the region's financial sector. The Dubai International Financial Centre and the Qatar Financial Centre (QFC), set up in 2004 and 2005 respectively, have established a legal framework and a set of institutions that operate independently of local jurisprudence. Based on international best practice and with English as their legal language, these onshore financial centres are redefining how local and foreign investors and institutions interact. From an international perspective, they offer foreign institutions entry into local markets with 100% ownership and no tax liability.

The DIFC and the QFC hope to become regional benchmarks, to catalyse domestic financial development and to draw in international firms. Both have already attracted many of the major international investment banks. By early 2008, the DIFC had attracted over 190 financial institutions and had 536 firms operating within its jurisdiction. The QFC is also growing quickly, and by the end of 2007 had issued licences to 42 banks and insurance companies, reinvigorating competition in the domestic financial sector.

The Gulf's financial sector has grown and opened up even outside the new zones. In 2004, Saudi Arabia established the new independent Capital Markets Authority (CMA), which has since reformed the regulation of all aspects of the domestic financial sector. It has also issued 11 new licences to wholly foreign-owned financial institutions, the first such issuance in 20 years. Broadly, the changes have been welcomed by Saudi bankers, but, in a blow to regional integration, the CMA has also placed new restrictions on offshore banking, including from GCC jurisdictions. Bahrain substantially revised its banking regulations in 2006 and, in another move against the regional trend, unified its banking regulations and supervision under the central bank.

Regional strength in Islamic finance

The one area where the Gulf is indisputably becoming a centre of financial innovation is Islamic finance. This is a market that it increasingly dominates given its religious ties and the strength of its Islamic financial institutions. Total Islamic assets worldwide are estimated to exceed $900 billion and are growing at 15% a year (IMF 2005). The Gulf's financial institutions alone account for one-third of this amount. The Gulf's Islamic banks now compete with conventional banks across the spectrum of retail, corporate and investment products.

In the field of Islamic capital markets, the Gulf, and Bahrain in particular, is leading innovation and development. In 1999, Bahrain launched the Dow Jones Islamic Market, to provide a benchmark for equity prices for Islamic institutions. There are now an estimated 125 Islamic equity funds in the region. Bahrain has also pushed ahead with reforms – through the creation of the Liquidity Management Centre and the International Islamic Financial Market – to provide same-day liquidity and to avoid reliance on conventional banks. In the debt markets, the Gulf has set a series of benchmarks, including the longest-dated *sukuk*, from SABIC, the first hybrid structure from the Saudi-based Islamic Development Bank (IDB) and the first pre-IPO convertible *sukuk*[2] from DP World.

2 This allows investors to convert a non-equity ownership interest into shares of equity at a set conversion date.

Further challenges

Competition between the Gulf countries has been, in a broad sense, positive for financial development, as it has spurred improvements to the regulatory and investment environment. However, with Bahrain, Qatar and Dubai all focused on positioning their national financial sector as a regional financial hub, there can be negative consequences.

The most immediate challenge is to improve coordination between regulators and financial supervisors, particularly between the national bodies and the authorities of the new financial zones in Qatar and Dubai, in order to avoid regulatory arbitrage. There has been recent success in establishing formal procedural lines of communication but much remains to be done. Greater effort is needed to ensure more systematic coordination and consolidated supervision at the national level and, ideally, at the regional level too.

The growing role of Islamic finance complicates the regulators' task further. Supervisors across the Gulf are under pressure to re-examine the treatment of Islamic finance as institutions expand and push against what are regarded as excessively restrictive controls. There are no firm regional, or indeed international, standards, and Gulf regulators vary significantly in their approach. Islamic institutions are kept under the same central bank supervision regime as conventional banks in Bahrain and Qatar, with only slight modifications, which have been formalized in ad hoc central bank circulars. The other Gulf countries have adopted different approaches, and the QFC and the DIFC have yet to finalize their approach.

Regulatory reform has also made the creation of a single Gulf capital market harder to achieve. Recent changes have increased national differences and multiplied the number of national supervisors. The markets remain fractured on national lines, and those changes have perhaps made regional integration a more distant proposition.

Regional capital markets: still underdeveloped

Despite recent progress and surging liquidity, Gulf financial markets remain underdeveloped. Local currency debt markets are shallow and shrinking. One unintended consequence of the Gulf's prudent current fiscal policies has been the rapid repayment of local currency debt. Although these policies may be prudent, the repayment of debt has left all the Gulf countries, with the partial exception of Saudi Arabia, without a meaningful yield curve beyond one year. In Qatar's case, its domestic yield curve is not liquid beyond three months.

As a result, the local currency bond and derivative markets remain nascent. The first local currency corporate bond was launched in Saudi Arabia, the largest capital market, only in 2003; and currency and interest rate swaps, for example, are available only in the Saudi riyal and the UAE dirham. Local demand for these products has remained modest, given easy access to international capital and strong currency pegs. However, this may change as companies and investors become more concerned about the likelihood of currency reform.

A lack of financial tools further complicates the task of dealing with the current economic boom. The traditional policy-making levers are not available to governments in the region. The currency peg to the dollar means that local domestic interest rates are set externally, and central banks lack other monetary tools. This policy dilemma has led to an increase in speculation about whether the Gulf states will abandon their 20-year-old currency pegs to the dollar, which in turn has raised concern about the likelihood of a single Gulf currency, officially scheduled for 2010.

Most of these challenges are solvable. As Singapore has demonstrated, budget surpluses do not prevent the development of a local bond market or of management tools for local currency financial risk. The International Monetary Fund and the European Central Bank have been consulted on the practicalities of a single currency and the sustainability of the Gulf states' currency peg to the dollar. Options for both are known, and could be implemented. Moreover, the regional economies, and companies and individuals, have shown in the past that they are able to deal with unexpected volatility, and the macro-economy is likely to be able to absorb a change in foreign exchange policy without significant disruption.

The biggest obstacle to the region's financial emergence is a lack of consensus and coordination among Gulf policy-makers. With a clear direction, the region could use its considerable financial clout to build a thriving international financial hub. But without one, and without a unified regional capital market, it is a more daunting challenge. A regional strategy may yet evolve naturally, with each country developing a complementary niche that builds on its respective strengths – perhaps with one focusing on Islamic banking and another concentrating on international finance or energy finance.

Despite these challenges, the Gulf will play a much more active role in global markets in the future. Its development is, perhaps, more evidence of the shift eastward in the global financial balance of power. However, not until regional policy-makers and financial players can reach a consensus on further reform will the Gulf truly emerge as a new financial hub.

References

AFP (2007), 'Islamic Finance Expands as Wealth Grows in Gulf', March.
Arab Monetary Fund, *Quarterly Bulletin* (AMF various), various issues.
DFSA, press releases, various.
DP World (2007), 'DP Lists on DIFX' (press release), November.
Dubai Financial Markets (DFM various), annual reports, various.
Gulf Capital (2007), 'IPOs in 2007'.
Higgins, M., T. Klitgaard and R. Lerman (2006), *Recycling Petrodollars*, Federal Reserve Bank of New York Research Paper Series – Current Issues in Economics and Finance (12) 9 (December): 2–8.
Federal Reserve Bank of New York Research Paper Series – Current Issues in Economics and Finance (12) 9.
IMF (2005), 'Islamic Finance Gears Up', *Finance and Development*, December.
IMF (2006), 'UAE Article IV'.
IMF (2007a), 'Saudi Arabia Financial Stability Report'.
IMF (2007b), 'UAE Financial Stability Report'.
IMF, *World Economic Outlook* (IMF *WEO*), statistics.
Middle East Economic Digest (*MEED*), MEED.com.
Nsoul, Saleh M. (2006), 'Petrodollar Recycling and Global Imbalances', IMF.
QFC, press releases, various.
Reuters, EMEA IPO quarterly reports, various years.
SAMA, annual reports, various.
Standard and Poor's (2007), 'Facing Challenges from a Position of Strength', Emmanuel Volland.
UAE Central Bank, annual reports, various.
UNCTAD, FDI statistics.
Zawya (2007), 'The Evolution and Rise of the Convertible Sukuk', Zawya.com, August.
Zawya.com, various years.

8 GCC financial centres: a global competitiveness perspective

Ghaleb O. Faidi

Introduction

Several GCC financial centres are vying for a sustainable position among the globally recognized hubs, and much financial coverage has focused on the competition among these emerging players. The spotlight has been on recent high-profile overseas acquisitions. The GCC centres will no doubt compete over the coming years to consolidate their regional position, attract financial institutions, create global linkages and add depth to their markets. However, to achieve a long-term position as a globally recognized financial hub, each GCC centre must constantly assess its current competitive position in relation to the established international financial centres. Each must also define a target position based on its competitive advantages and exploit those advantages in order to reach and maintain its target position. In the process, the GCC centres will need to address some key imperatives if they are to secure a lasting position on the financial centres map.

Competitive positioning

In order to understand how the GCC centres fit in among the globally recognized financial hubs, a comparative benchmarking study is needed. In March 2007, the City of London published the first edition of the Global Financial Centres Index (GFCI-1). The Index ranked 46 financial centres in terms of competitiveness in five essential areas: people, business environment, market access, infrastructure and general competitiveness. It is essential to keep in mind that the GFCI rankings may not reflect the current scale and impact of a financial centre, especially when it comes to emerging hubs. At the same time, centres that maintain a high competitiveness ranking over an extended time are likely to be, or to eventually become, significant in terms of scale and impact as well. Some may question the Index's potential bias based on the participant pool and the methodology, especially the predictive approach to answers not supplied by the survey's participants. Generally, however, GFCI-1 contained very useful findings.

GFCI-1 categorized London and New York as the only *global* centres, with the ability to connect participants directly a main determining criterion. London had a slight edge over New York as the world's most competitive centre. Hong Kong and Singapore ranked third and fourth respectively and were classified as *international* financial centres, where a significant volume of cross-border transactions is conducted. It is important to note that *niche* players, such as Zurich and Geneva, ranked high among the world's most competitive financial centres. Although unlikely to become global players on the scale of London and New York, they are worldwide leaders in their specialist area. Dubai, the only GCC centre covered, was ranked 25th out of 46 centres. It was regarded as an evolving city that, as 'financial services broaden and deepen', is expected to join the 'leaders' box' (centres with strong sub-sectors and strong domestic markets).

The second edition of the Index (GFCI-2) was published in September 2007, and ranked the top 50 financial centres worldwide. The top ten listed the same centres as GFCI-1, with three of them changing position. Dubai moved up three places to 22nd. When participants were asked which centre was likely to become significantly more important and which centres' institutions were likely to begin operations in the next two to three years, Dubai was mentioned more than any other. Bahrain and Qatar were added, and were ranked 44th and 47th respectively. The study did not offer detailed responses of participants in relation to those two centres.

In GFCI-3, published in March 2008, the number of centres assessed jumped to 66. The eight most competitive ones in GFCI-2 sustained their ranking: London and New York were again recognized as the top two global centres, holding a significant lead over Hong Kong and Singapore. The three GCC centres benefited from substantial investment in financial infrastructure, and as a result their ratings rose strongly. Dubai was again identified as 'a key and growing regional hub' and the centre most likely to increase in importance over the next two to three years. Bahrain and Qatar experienced the biggest increase in the ratings from GFCI-2, by 59 and 51 points respectively. Bahrain improved on its 44th GFCI-2 rank by five positions, Qatar's rank remained unchanged and Dubai's declined by two positions. However, the ranking changes are somewhat less informative than the rating changes for centres ranked 16th or higher in GFCI-3 owing to the division of the Channel Islands into two separate rankings (Jersey and Guernsey are ranked 16th and 19th respectively) and the addition of five new centres.

Table 8.1: Ranking/ratings of GFCI-4 financial centre competitiveness: the top 10 and the GCC, 2008

GFCI-4 rank	*GFCI-4 rating*	*Financial centre*	*Study comments*
1	791	London	Global
2	774	New York	Global
3	701	Singapore	International
4	700	Hong Kong	International
5	676	Zurich	Niche
6	645	Geneva	Niche
7	642	Tokyo	National
8	641	Chicago	International and regional
9	636	Frankfurt	National
10	630	Sydney	National; also international and regional
23	597	Dubai	Evolving (centres with high ratings/susceptible to change)
43	529	Bahrain	Volatile*
45	525	Qatar	Volatile*

* Centres that are not rated as highly [relative to the leading centres as per the study] might be able to move upwards rapidly with improvement in some respects [owing to high sensitivity to some of the 57 'instrumental factors' used in the study].
Source: The Global Financial Centres Index 4, and earlier editions. www.zyen.com/Activities/On-line%20surveys/GFCI.htm

Published in September 2008, GFCI-4 ranked 59 financial centres, with nine additional centres not receiving sufficient assessments to be ranked. In GFCI-4, London and New York retained their respective rankings and their designation as the only truly *global* centres (see Table 8.1). However, the knock-on effect from the 'credit crunch' significantly reduced their lead over other centres, especially in Asia and the GCC. In addition to the real damage caused by the crisis, the survey cited reputational damage as a key factor in the decline. In Asia, Singapore claimed the third position, surpassing Hong Kong. In terms of rating, both Asian centres are closing the gap with New York. Two niche centres, Zurich and Geneva, continued to feature strongly among the top ten centres.

All three GCC centres improved their own competitiveness in GFCI-4, as is evident from their higher ratings. In terms of ranking relative to other centres, Dubai moved up one position to 23rd and continued to be identified by the survey participants as the centre most likely to increase in significance over the next few years. Perhaps a more telling leading indicator is that Dubai also continued to be mentioned as the centre where more respondents' institutions were likely to open offices. Qatar, which has shown a sharp rating increase since it was added to the index in GFCI-2, has seen its GFCI-4 numerical rank improve two positions to 45th. Bahrain dropped four positions relative to other centres and ranked 43rd.

The Index has yet to include Kuwait and Saudi Arabia. In view of the relative size of the latter's economy, recent moves to open it up, if sustained, could lead to significant growth in its financial services industry and affect the long-term outlook for the Gulf region's financial centres.

The above findings are very relevant to the aspiring GCC centres. As London and New York are categorized as the only global centres and well-regarded hubs such as Singapore and Hong Kong trail behind, the GCC centres must decide on their long-term target position.

Dubai's overall value proposition as a trading and business hub supports its multi-sector financial services aspirations. With limited hydrocarbon resources, it has been motivated to diversify as a matter of necessity, and over the past 20 years it has taken solid measures to build up its physical and regulatory infrastructure to meet the demands of international participants. At the same time, traction (i.e. the extent and speed of establishment) will vary among the various financial services sectors that Dubai has been working to attract and develop. It will depend on various factors, such as the strength of the sector-specific value proposition, market conditions and cross-border regulatory constraints. Thus Dubai may become a global player in some sectors and a regional leader in others and could serve primarily national needs in still others. Overall, it has a sizeable business momentum and appears to be well positioned to become a regional financial services hub.

Although Qatar has regional aspirations, its efforts seem to be focused for the time being on the needs of its hydrocarbon and industrial sectors. Bahrain has similar motives for developing its economy, and has established itself over the past three decades as a regional banking centre. With more limited resources than Qatar, Bahrain is working to upgrade its physical and regulatory infrastructure to the level required to attract more international participants. One of its strengths is Sharia-compliant finance. In fact, Sharia-compliant finance is a thread that goes through all sectors, and, at a regional level, it could give the GCC as a whole a distinct advantage.

Until recently, the focus of the GCC centres has been on developing a general multi-sector value proposition and attracting a critical mass of institutions. This focus is beginning to shift, especially in Dubai, to the creation of depth of scale and impact. A critical requirement for creating depth is that the GCC governments take some counter-intuitive steps. For example, in order to establish a yield curve and to deepen the capital market, they must issue bonds of various maturities at a time of significant current account surpluses. Dubai, with limited petroleum revenues, is proceeding with such an issuance, including a UAE dirham (AED)-denominated issue under its recently established AED15 billion ($4.08 billion) medium-term note programme. In addition to funding the local infrastructure needs of the Dubai government, the issuance aims to contribute to the development of the domestic bond market. The GCC governments must also privatize profitable businesses, require them to offer shares to the public for the first time, and allow further participation by foreign investors.

As specializations develop, unhealthy competition, leading to pressure on an already limited talent pool, may give way to 'coopetition' between the Gulf centres. This would translate into a healthy balance between cooperation and competition that allows for efficiencies to be maintained as a result of competitive forces and, at the same time, for region-wide strengths in areas such as Sharia-compliant finance to emerge.

Imperatives

In order to secure a sustainable position on the regional and international level, the GCC centres must fulfil four imperatives.

The people factor Along with regulations, the availability of qualified labour has consistently ranked in various studies as a leading success factor for any financial centre. This is especially true for the GCC, where institutional finance is relatively new and the financial services talent pool is limited. The challenge for the GCC centres in the short term is to attract world-class talent from other centres and retain it. In parallel, they must develop a national/resident talent pool so as to address long-term needs.

Regulation Confidence in the system is a key success factor for any financial centre, and a solid regulatory framework goes a long way towards building that confidence. The aspiring GCC centres realized this early on and have been working to ensure that they adopt, as required for their environment, the best of breed in terms of regulation. But the design of a world-class regulatory framework is not enough; establishing a regulatory track record is a further key requirement. Thus even though the region's more recent financial services regulatory bodies were modelled on international best practice, a longer track record is needed to demonstrate effectively their ability to anticipate, avert and manage potential crises.

Regulators in the region will also need to carry out a balancing act in order to remain credible but at the same time responsive to commercial needs. The subprime crisis in the United States has raised questions as to whether the regulators should have anticipated and moved in to prevent or to contain the impending crisis. However, in many cases it is difficult for a regulator to anticipate risk associated with a fast-growth activity. An overly risk-averse approach can stifle an emerging opportunity and delayed action can lead to sizeable damages in terms of money and reputation. This is a challenge for all regulators. For the aspiring centres, however, effective achievement of this balance can mean the difference between success and failure in global positioning.

Another debate in the Gulf region has been about whether the new world-class regulations the GCC centres are implementing to attract international/institutional players should be ring-fenced from the existing local regulatory environment or should be a replacement for it. But the debate seems to be more about timing, as there is a consensus that the standard outside the centres must also be raised eventually. There also seems to be a consensus that a unitary regulator is the approach to take. In the case of Dubai, ring-fencing the Dubai International Financial Centre (DIFC) made sense at the time of establishment in view of the peculiarities of the federal system and the focus on attracting institutional business, which was largely absent from the UAE. That approach allowed for the rapid development of the DIFC and secured Dubai a sizeable advantage in business momentum. Qatar, on the other hand, has announced plans for a single national regulatory system by early 2009, and local institutions have been given three years to meet its standards. Considering the size of the Qatari economy, the conversion should be feasible within that time frame. Regardless of how a regulatory framework is launched initially, all aspiring centres must raise regulatory standards throughout their economy in order to facilitate the development of deep capital markets and financial services activities.

Governance Effective governance, both at country and corporate levels, is another essential confidence-building factor. The countries of the region, like most emerging economies, still have a long way to go in this area. At the same time, there are very positive developments. There appears to be increased awareness of the need to improve governance. Initiatives such as Hawkamah, the Institute for Corporate Governance, set up by the DIFC with the participation of the Organisation for Economic Co-operation and Development, the International Finance Corporation, the Center for International Private Enterprise, the International Institute for Management Development and others, are working to increase awareness and to improve the implementation of corporate governance on a regional basis.

Many regional companies still do not understand the direct benefits of effective governance; they see its requirements simply as a matter of regulatory compliance. However, several studies in the West have shown that well-governed companies command higher market value. For unlisted and family-owned businesses, effective governance can gain them the respect and loyalty of investors, suppliers and customers. As cases in the West and the region have shown, the perception of improper governance can be as important as the reality of it. Therefore, transparency and effective communication are important elements of building confidence.

Self-assessment Availability of timely quality data is the backbone of effective analysis and decision-making. For the aspiring centres to understand their position and to effectively set their targets, accurate benchmarks must be established. Such benchmarks would allow them to establish a baseline and to measure progress as well as to provide investors and institutions with the information they require in order to assess and exploit emerging opportunities. Unfortunately, the availability of reliable data remains an issue in many parts of the region. For benchmarking purposes, there is a further issue: the availability of data on a national rather than a centre level, leading to ineffective evaluation relative to other centres.

Conclusion

The success of the various GCC centres should be judged according to the targets that they have set, not a single finishing line. In the development stage, the GCC centres are likely to identify the same opportunities, but long-term sustainability will require some of them to develop specializations based on identified competitive advantages. This need not be viewed as a zero-sum game. If one looks at the financial map of Europe or the United States, it is evident that multiple centres within a single region can establish themselves as globally recognized centres, even if their focus is limited to a specific niche. With the GCC at the heart of a region with over 2.1 billion people whose demand is growing rapidly, there are ample opportunities for the growth of the financial services industry. However, only the GCC centres that have a well-defined position based on long-term competitive advantages followed up by effective execution are likely to sustain a position in the global financial services sector.

9 Institutional arrangements for financial regulation and supervision: OECD experience and emerging practice in the Gulf region*

Alexander Böhmer

Introduction

Global governance of financial markets is back on the international agenda. The current global credit crunch caused by the subprime crisis in the United States raises issues of transparency, market integrity, regulation and institutional supervision. As the search for yield has led market participants to move into alternative, less regulated instruments and products, regulators and supervisors face new challenges. The question of adequate regulatory and supervisory models for the financial markets of newly emerging players, such as those in the Gulf region, has thus become even more relevant. Recent debates in the wake of the banking crisis have put into question any notion of 'best practice' or 'superior model/legal tradition' for financial sector supervision and regulation.

Over more than the past decade, several member countries of the Organisation for Economic Co-operation and Development (OECD) have introduced changes in the regulatory or legal frameworks governing their financial services sectors and other countries have considered such reforms. In a few cases, these reforms in the structure of financial-sector regulation have been made in response to a financial crisis. More frequently, however, changes have reflected efforts to realign organizational structures with changing market realities. Already in 2002, an OECD study showed that two major new trends have led countries to question the adequacy of the earlier arrangements (Lumpkin 2002).

Two major new trends

First, new financial products have emerged that do not fit into existing categories. This has also led to a convergence of products and services

* The views expressed in this chapter are personal and cannot be attributed to the OECD.

across the various categories of financial service provider. As an example of product innovation and convergence, a money market mutual fund has many characteristics in common with a short-term bank deposit, and these instruments effectively compete for the same pool of savings. However, each product is typically offered by different kinds of institutions, which are subject to different regulatory regimes. These developments have increasingly blurred the traditional lines of demarcation among the different pillars of the financial system (i.e. banks, insurance companies and securities firms) as institutions have sought opportunities to cross-sell products, to expand across borders and to achieve economies of scale. Financial institutions of all types are more and more offering products and services (directly or through affiliates) that compete not only against those offered by similar types of institutions but also against those offered by other categories of service providers.

Secondly, the choice of an appropriate supervisory framework is made even more difficult by the formation of complex financial services groups that provide a wide range of financial services. As financial groups and conglomerates centralize their internal controls and risk management, it becomes more difficult to oversee them on a consolidated legal entity basis owing to the increased complexity of the corporate structure and the related risks.

Institutional arrangements for supervision

According to evidence drawn together by the study mentioned above, OECD countries have responded by a) redefining the responsibilities of existing oversight agencies and improving communications among oversight bodies and/or b) creating new institutions to engage in financial supervision.

A common way of redistributing responsibilities among oversight bodies is by the creation of a single body responsible for the supervision of financial services. Those jurisdictions adopting this model believe that it is the best means to deal with the emergence of innovative financial products and to improve communication among supervisors. As of 2007, 13 OECD countries (out of a total 30 members) have introduced unified regulators.

The remaining OECD countries have decided either that a) existing institutional arrangements are satisfactory and the solution is to define responsibilities more clearly and to improve communication among supervisory bodies or that b) supervisory responsibilities should be redistributed in some way other than the creation of a unified regulator.

The range of supervisory regimes in practice suggests that there is no consensus as to the existence of a single 'best' approach to, and organizational structure for, adapting financial supervision to changing market realities. Some countries have reorganized their regulatory agencies and, in some cases, established a single unified supervisory agency. Still, the majority of OECD countries have separate supervisory agencies. Many alternative models exist, and they can be made to work effectively. But until there is a longer track record of experience, especially with unified agencies, it will be difficult to make definite recommendations. The interconnectedness of the various financial-sector components has been mentioned as an important argument in favour of a single unified regulator. However, a year into the banking crisis which started in summer 2007, the single unified regulator concept is facing some critical appraisal.

One remaining contentious issue is the role of the central bank in supervision. Most OECD countries that have formed unified regulators have decided to remove the central bank from the supervision of individual institutions. But most other countries have generally decided that the central bank should have an active role in the supervision of individual institutions.

Evolving practice in OECD countries

Before the approaches to financial supervision in the Gulf region are looked at, it is important to examine the relevance of the OECD countries' supervisory and regulatory approaches that have informed practice in the Gulf region. It will also be of interest to examine several case studies from the Asia-Pacific region.

The *United Kingdom* and Ireland, which are important centres in which institutions from other countries conduct cross-border transactions, have adopted an integrated structure for financial supervision. The British authorities have seen it as essential to pursue the highest-quality financial supervision and regulation in order to strengthen their country's position as a global market-place. Thus a major overhaul of financial supervision was undertaken in 1986 as part of a programme aimed at modernizing financial markets under the Financial Services Law. In May 1997, the Chancellor of the Exchequer announced a policy of reforming financial services regulation: a new regulator would be created that would merge banking supervision and investment services regulation into the existing Securities and Investments Board (SIB). The SIB formally changed its name to the Financial Services Authority (FSA) in October 1997. A memorandum of understanding (MoU) was signed in late 1997 between the Bank of England (Bank), the FSA and the Treasury. It spells out the responsibilities of each and it stipulates the main ways in which these bodies would cooperate, including provisions on clear accountability, transparency, no duplication of effort and regular information exchange. The first stage of the reform of financial services regulation was completed in June 1998, when responsibility for banking supervision was transferred to the FSA from the Bank. In May 2000, the FSA took over the role of UK listing authority from the London Stock Exchange. The Financial Services and Markets Act, which was implemented on 1 December 2001, transferred to the FSA the responsibilities of several other organizations.

Using a single handbook of rules and guidance for the firms it supervises, the FSA has developed an integrated and risk-based approach. In this system, financial institutions are assigned to one of three business units – Retail Markets, Wholesale and Institutional Markets, and Regulatory Services – and are headed by managing directors who sit on the FSA board. Each of these business units is further divided into firm-specific divisions. For example, regulation of the major banks, building societies, investment banks and insurance companies rests with the Wholesale Firms Division and is under the aegis of the Wholesale and Institutional Markets Unit. The FSA also has nine sector-specific groups, headed by a sector leader, which fulfil cross-organizational responsibilities.

Strengthening consumer protection was partly the motive for the decision to create a new single regulatory authority for financial services in Ireland. The Irish Financial Services Authority reports now to the minister of finance and is responsible for prudential regulation of financial service providers as well as for consumer protection.

In Japan and South Korea, the decision to move to a unified supervisor was spurred in large part by financial crises. In Japan it was the malaise of the banking system that persisted through the 1990s. In South Korea it was the post-1997 Asian financial crisis. Both countries decided that an upgrading of supervisory skills and increased supervisory independence from the government would advance the cause of sound supervision.

In *Japan*, the government agency responsible for the regulation and supervision of banks, securities houses and insurance companies is the Financial Services Agency (FSA). The FSA was established in 2000 under the jurisdiction of the Financial Reconstruction Commission (FRC). The FSA became responsible for planning the financial system, of which the Ministry of Finance had previously been in charge. In January 2001, the FSA became an external organ of the Cabinet Office; and with the concurrent abolition of the FRC, its responsibilities were enlarged, including the disposition of failed financial institutions. The involvement of the Ministry of Finance in financial regulation is now limited, for the most part, to the resolution of failed financial institutions, to financial crisis-management and to supervising the Deposit Insurance Corporation and the Insurance Policy Holder Protection Corporation. Although the FSA is the single regulator, the Bank of Japan still undertakes on-site inspections of major banks (i.e. those that are its counterparties in the payments system).

South Korea hosts a consolidated financial supervisory agency named the Financial Supervisory Service (FSS), which was created by the Act Concerning Establishment of Financial Supervision Organizations. Although the FSS is a specialized government-affiliated agency, it is independent in the conduct of its responsibilities. In consultation with the Financial Supervisory Commission, the Ministry of Finance and Economy (MOFE) regulates matters concerning the financial system. Under this regulatory framework, the FSS supervises the operations of financial institutions and coordinates policy with relevant authorities (e.g. MOFE, the central bank, etc.).

Singapore, although not an OECD member country, has established the Monetary Authority of Singapore, which is a fully integrated financial supervisor. This seems to be an emerging model for smaller countries, whereby all sectoral supervisors are housed under the same structural roof and the institution also acts as the central bank. Although separate laws govern the activities of different financial service providers and supervision has been conducted largely on an institutional/sectoral basis, staff in the various units work closely together and there is cross-sectoral cooperation.

Gulf countries' supervisory systems

In the Gulf's nascent financial markets, where financial regulation did not exist before, financial centres started to emerge using and emulating models from OECD member countries. These models, however, were adapted to develop a set of new regulations and institutions catering to the specific needs of the region. Generally, in Middle Eastern and North African (MENA) countries, unlike in OECD member countries, there has been less of a trend towards a single-regulator model.

Bahrain embodies, to the largest extent in the MENA region, the unified regulator approach. It follows the logic that in countries with small populations a unified supervisory model might be beneficial given issues such as the relatively small pool of qualified and experienced personnel. Consolidation of the regulatory framework for the financial sector followed a decision in 2002 to move all financial-sector regulation to the Bahrain Monetary Agency (BMA). Prior to the creation of the Central Bank of Bahrain (CBB) in September 2006, the BMA had acted as the sole regulatory authority for the country's financial sector. The CBB's mandate is prescribed in the Central Bank of Bahrain and Financial Institutions Law 2006, which defines its objectives broadly. The CBB's responsibilities include the licensing, regulation and supervision of persons undertaking regulated financial services; the provision of banking services to the government; and the licensing and supervision of banks (conventional and Islamic), as well as of the providers of insurance services (including insurance firms and brokers), investment business licensees (including investment firms, Bahrain Stock Exchange brokers, money brokers and investment advisers) and other financial service providers (including money-changers, representative offices, finance companies and ancillary service providers). The CBB also regulates the Bahrain Stock Exchange (BSE) and acts as the listing authority for companies and financial instruments listed on the BSE. It is responsible in addition for regulating conduct in Bahrain's capital markets. The CBB has been successful in issuing a number of regulations ranging from regulating the investment sector to launching an integrated licence framework. Nonetheless, the Financial Sector Assessment Programme noted the challenge 'to oversee a large and growing number of institutions while integrating supervision across the financial sector' (FSAP 2006: 13). The recently launched Bahrain Financial Harbour (May 2007) is to be supervised by the CBB too.

Qatar has recently announced that it will unify its regulators into one supervisory body. The new regulator will combine the central bank's supervisory department, the Qatar Financial Markets Authority (the newly formed regulator of Doha's stock market and brokers), and the Qatar Financial Centre Regulatory Authority (QFCRA). Further, it will create a new supervisory regime for insurance in the state. It is now expected to begin work in 2009. Since the intention to create a single regulator was first proposed, the Qatari government has also announced that it will consider expanding the QFCRA's British common law legal system, to cover the whole of the country's commercial law.

The QFCRA is an independent statutory body that reports directly to the Council of Ministers. It regulates and supervises the full spectrum of financial services activities conducted in or from the Qatar Financial Centre (QFC) itself – a special financial services zone. These include all types of banking, insurance, asset management, financial advisory services, securities and derivatives dealing and Islamic finance. As a combined banking, insurance and markets regulator, the QFCRA has powers of authorization, supervision and enforcement consistent with those available in major world financial markets. Authorized firms (i.e. those authorized to conduct relevant financial services activities) are supervised by the QFCRA. It can take enforcement or disciplinary action for non-compliance with applicable laws and rules. An independent appeals body has been established under the QFC Law to hear appeals against its decisions. The QFCRA has signed MoUs with other regulatory authorities worldwide, including the Island of Jersey's Financial Services Commission; the Bahrain Monetary Agency; the Isle of Man Financial Supervision Commission and the Isle of Man Insurance and Pensions Authority; the Financial Supervisory Commission of the Republic of Korea; the China Banking Regulatory Commission; and the Department of Insurance of the State of Delaware in the United States.

In *Saudi Arabia,* the Saudi Arabian Monetary Agency (SAMA) is in charge of banking supervision, and responsibility for regulating the capital market lies with the Capital Market Authority (CMA). The King Abdullah Financial District (currently under construction) is projected to accommodate the CMA, the stock exchange (currently known as the *tadawul,* it will be renamed the Saudi Arabian Financial Exchange) and financial institutions and other service providers such as accountants, auditors, lawyers, analysts, rating agencies, consultants and information technology providers. Although a formal depositor insurance scheme as in some OECD countries (e.g. the UK, the US and Germany) does not exist, banking supervision has proved to be effective so far. The few cases in which banks have faced financial difficulties have been resolved either by partial government acquisition of the banks in question or by merging them with other, sounder financial institutions. Generally, Saudi banks are among the highest capitalized in the world, with capitalization much exceeding the Basel capital adequacy requirements. Regulation of the capital market, of the general financial market and of financial transparency still needs to be enhanced. The continuing problems of the Saudi capital market can be attributed at least partly to public concern about the lack of transparency of listed companies and to the need for stricter penalties for financial misconduct. In particular, the modest upper limits of potential penalties curb the effectiveness of capital market supervision.

In September 2004, *Dubai* opened the Dubai International Financial Centre (DIFC), seeking to gain the same stature as the leading financial centres in New York, London and Hong Kong. It covers several sectors of financial activity, such as banking services; capital markets; asset management and fund registration; insurance and reinsurance; and Islamic finance. Since September 2005, it has also accommodated the Dubai International

Financial Exchange. Financial services in the DIFC are regulated by the Dubai Financial Services Authority (DFSA). This institution is committed to integrity, transparency and efficiency and has supported the Hawkamah, the first institute for corporate governance in the region. It has formulated its regulatory and legal framework along the lines of best practices of jurisdictions in Europe, North Africa and the Far East. The DFSA has signed MoUs with other regulatory authorities worldwide, among them the China Banking Regulatory Commission, the British FSA and the US Commodity Futures Trading Commission.

Outside the jurisdiction of the DIFC and the DFSA, the *United Arab Emirates* retains its own independent financial regulatory system, without a single financial services regulator. The supervisory regime is overseen by the Central Bank of the UAE, the Emirates Securities and Commodities Authority (ESCA) and the Ministry of Economy and Planning (MEP). The Central Bank regulates the banking and investment business; ESCA administers certain categories of investment and securities business, such as exchange operations and brokerage businesses. The insurance business is regulated separately, by the MEP.

The *Kuwaiti* banking system is regulated mainly by the Central Bank of Kuwait. Licensing new entrants or closing banks is conducted in cooperation with the Ministry of Finance and Economy. Banking regulations are formulated and supervision is implemented relatively transparently, and banking supervision practices are being brought into line with international standards.

The Kuwait Stock Exchange (KSE) was created in 1983, following a first stock exchange, which was already established in 1977. It is regulated not by an independent capital markets regulatory authority but by its market committee, which is responsible for supervision, enforcement and regulation of the equity market. The KSE does not have powers to penalize financial malpractice. A draft capital market authority law, to establish an independent, single and accountable authority, is currently under discussion in Parliament.

Investment companies are supervised by the Central Bank of Kuwait and also by the Kuwait Stock Exchange if they are listed. The insurance sector is supervised by the insurance department of the Ministry of Commerce and Industry, but the long-standing governing law is criticized as lacking key elements of a modern insurance supervision regime.

References

Financial Sector Assessment Program (FSAP, 2006), International Monetary Fund, April, p. 13.

Goodhart, C. A. E. (2000), 'The Organisational Structure of Banking Supervision', Occasional Papers No. 1, Financial Stability Institute, Bank for International Settlements, Basel, November.

Hainsworth, Antony and Andrew Henderson (2007), 'Financial Regulation in the UAE', *International Financial Law Review*, Supplement – The IFLR Guide to the United Arab Emirates, 147: 12–14.

Institute of International Finance (IIF) Confidential (2007), Kuwait Country Report, August.

Islam, Mazhar M. (2003), 'Regulations and Supervision of Financial Institutions in GCC Countries', *Managerial Finance*, 29 (7): 17–42.

Kingdom of Bahrain: Financial System Stability Assessment, including Reports on the Observance of Standards and Codes on the following topics, Banking Supervision, Insurance Supervision, Securities Regulation, and Anti-Money Laundering and Combating the Financing of Terrorism, International Monetary Fund, IMF Country Report No. 06/91, March 2006.

Kuwait: Article IV Consultation – Staff Report; Staff Statement; Public Information Notice on the Executive Board Discussion ; and Statement by the Executive Director for Kuwait, International Monetary Fund, IMF Country Report No. 06/132, April 2006.

Lumpkin, Stephen A. (2002), 'Supervision of Financial Services in the OECD Area', in *Financial Market Trends* (Paris: OECD).

Mwenda, Kenneth Kaoma (2006), 'Legal Aspects of Financial Services Regulation and the Concept of a Unified Regulator', Law, Justice and Development Series, World Bank.

Singer, David Andrew (2007), *Regulating Capital: Setting Standards for the International Financial System* (Ithaca, NY: Cornell University Press).

Web pages of:

Dubai International Financial Centre (DIFC): www.difc.ae

Dubai Financial Services Authority: www.dfsa.ae

Central Bank of Kuwait: www.cbk.gov.kw

Kuwait Stock Exchange: www.kuwaitse.com

Qatar Financial Centre Regulatory Authority: www.qfcra.com

Appendix 9.1: Organization of financial supervision by sector: OECD member countries and selected others

	Banking	*Securities*	*Insurance*	*Pension funds*
Australia	Australian Prudential Regulation Authority	Australian Securities and Investments Commission	Australian Prudential Regulation Authority	Australian Prudential Regulation Authority
Austria	Financial Market Authority	Financial Market Authority	Financial Market Authority	Financial Market Authority
Bahrain	Central Bank of Bahrain	Central Bank of Bahrain	Central Bank of Bahrain	Central Bank of Bahrain
Belgium	Banking, Finance and Insurance Commission	Banking, Finance and Insurance Commission	Banking, Finance and Insurance Commission	Banking, Finance and Insurance Commission
Canada	Office of the Superintendent of Financial Institutions	Provincial Securities Commissions	Office of the Superintendent of Financial Institutions & Provincial Government	Office of the Superintendent of Financial Institutions & Provincial Government
China	China Banking Regulatory Commission	China Securities Regulatory Commission	China Insurance Regulatory Commission	Ministry of Labour and Social Security
Czech Republic	Czech National Bank	Czech National Bank	Czech National Bank	Czech National Bank
Denmark	Danish Financial Supervisory Authority	Danish Financial Supervisory Authority	Danish Financial Supervisory Authority	Danish Financial Supervisory Authority
Finland	Financial Supervision Authority	Financial Supervision Authority	Insurance Supervisory Authority	Insurance Supervisory Authority
France	Banking Commission	Financial Markets Authority	The controlling authority of the insurance and mutual insurance companies	The controlling authority of the insurance and mutual insurance companies
Germany	Federal Financial Supervisory Authority	Federal Financial Supervisory Authority	Federal Financial Supervisory Authority	Federal Financial Supervisory Authority
Greece	Bank of Greece (Supervision of Credit and Financial Institutions Department)	Capital Market Commission	Ministry of Development (Insurance Supervisory Authority)	Social Insurance Institute
Hong Kong	Hong Kong Monetary Authority	Securities and Futures Commission	The Office of the Commissioner of Insurance	Mandatory Provident Fund Schemes Authority

	Banking	*Securities*	*Insurance*	*Pension funds*
Hungary	Hungarian Financial Supervisory Authority	Hungarian Financial Supervisory Authority	Hungarian Financial Supervisory Authority	Hungarian Financial Supervisory Authority
Iceland	Financial Supervisory Authority	Financial Supervisory Authority	Financial Supervisory Authority	Financial Supervisory Authority
Ireland	Financial Services Regulatory Authority	Financial Services Regulatory Authority	Financial Services Regulatory Authority	Financial Services Regulatory Authority
Italy	Banca d'Italia	Commissione nazionale per le società e la borsa (CONSOB)	Agency for Private Insurance Companies and Companies of Public Interest Supervision (ISVAP)	Commissione di Vigilanza sui Fondi Pensione (COVIP)
Japan	Financial Service Agency	Financial Service Agency	Financial Service Agency	Ministry of Health, Labour and Welfare
Korea	Financial Supervisory Commission	Financial Supervisory Commission	Financial Supervisory Commission	Financial Supervisory Commission
Kuwait	Central Bank of Kuwait	Kuwait Stock Exchange (market committee)	Ministry of Commerce and Industry (insurance department)	Kuwait's Public Institute for Social Security (PIFSS)
Luxembourg	Financial Supervision Commission	Financial Supervision Commission	Insurance Commission	Financial Supervision Commission
Mexico	National Banking and Securities Commission	National Banking and Securities Commission	National Insurance Commission	National Commission for the Retirement Savings System
Netherlands	Banking Supervision Department, Nederlandsche Bank	Netherlands Authority for the Financial Markets	Banking Supervision Department, Nederlandsche Bank	Banking Supervision Department, the Nederlandsche Bank
New Zealand	Reserve Bank of New Zealand	Securities Commission	Insurance and Superannuation Unit (part of the Ministry of Economic Development)	Insurance and Superannuation Unit (part of the Ministry of Economic Development)
Norway	Financial Services Agency of Norway	Financial Services Agency of Norway	Financial Services Agency of Norway	Financial Services Agency of Norway

	Banking	*Securities*	*Insurance*	*Pension funds*
Oman	Central Bank of Oman	Capital Market Authority	Capital Market Authority	Public Authority for Social Insurance
Poland	Commission for Banking Supervision	Polish Securities and Exchange Commission	Insurance and Pension Funds Supervisory Commission	Insurance and Pension Funds Supervisory Commission
Portugal	Bank of Portugal	Portuguese Securities Market Commission	Portuguese Insurance Institute	Portuguese Insurance Institute
Qatar*	Qatar Central Bank The Qatar Financial Centre Regulatory Authority (QFCRA) for banks within QFC	Doha Securities Market QFCRA (for activities within the QFC)	Ministry of Economy and Commerce QFCRA (for activities within the QFC)	General Retirement and **Pension** Authority (GRPA)
Saudi Arabia	Saudi Arabian Monetary Agency	Capital Market Authority	Saudi Arabian Monetary Agency (Insurance Supervision Directorate); health: also Council of Cooperative Health Insurance	General Organization for Social Insurance (GOSI) and Retirement **Pension** Agency
Singapore	Monetary Authority of Singapore	Monetary Authority of Singapore	Monetary Authority of Singapore	Central Provident Fund Board
Slovenia	Bank of Slovenia	Financial Market Authority	Slovenia Insurance Supervision Agency	Slovenia Insurance Supervision Agency
Spain	Bank of Spain	National Commission of the Securities Market	General Directorate of Insurance and Pension Funds (within the Ministry of Economy and Finance)	General Directorate of Insurance and Pension Funds (within the Ministry of Economy and Finance)
Sweden	Swedish Financial Supervisory Agency	Swedish Financial Supervisory Agency	Swedish Financial Supervisory Agency	Swedish Financial Supervisory Agency
Switzerland	Federal Banking Commission	Federal Banking Commission	Federal Office of Private Insurance	Federal Social Insurance Office

	Banking	*Securities*	*Insurance*	*Pension funds*
Turkey	Banking Regulation and Supervision Agency	Capital Market Board	Turkish Treasury	Turkish Treasury
UAE	Central Bank of the UAE, Banking Supervision and Examination Department	Securities and Commodities Authority	Ministry of Economy (Insurance Companies Division); Insurance Commission (recently established)	**General Pension and Social Security Authority (GPSSA)**
UAE/Dubai	Dubai Financial Services Authority (for activities within the Dubai International Financial Centre (DIFC)	Dubai Financial Services Authority (for activities within the DIFC)	Dubai Financial Services Authority (for activities within the DIFC)	Dubai Financial Services Authority (for activities within the DIFC)
UK	Financial Services Authority	Financial Services Authority	Financial Services Authority	Pensions Regulator
USA	Office of the Comptroller of the Currency (OCC), Federal Reserve Bank (FRB), State Bank Supervisors, Federal Deposit Insurance Corporation (FDIC)	Securities and Exchange Commission	State Insurance Commission	Department of Labor

* It has been announced that in 2008, Qatar's financial sector supervision structure will be reformed with the establishment of a single integrated financial regulatory body combining the resources of a number of existing authorities including the Qatar Central Bank (QCB), the Qatar Financial Markets Authority (QFMA), the Qatar Financial Centre Regulatory Authority (QFCRA) and the Ministry of Economy and Commerce.

10 Expatriate life in the GCC countries

Tarek Fadlallah and Ruth Davis

Introduction

The GCC countries are undergoing a dizzying transformation and modernization: economies, skylines and demographics are all in flux. Financial services are hoped to be the 'new oil', the new driver of growth. The 1960s and 1970s also saw sweeping changes, linked with development of the oilfields, but today the focus is on building the real estate, infrastructure and policy environment needed to sustain large and successful financial centres.

Once they are built, how many people will come? Bahrain, Qatar and the UAE are all seeking to recruit financial expertise. Competition is intense, as barriers to movement by the global labour force have fallen significantly. Therefore many countries are seeking to lure skilled financial workers from the same global pool by offering ever-increasing wages and an attractive lifestyle. As the scale of financial operations becomes larger and the need for staff increases, the ability to attract and retain these skilled and mobile workers is emerging as a major challenge for the GCC.

The March 2008 City of London Corporation *Global Financial Centres Index* quotes an employer as saying that the availability of skilled staff and government support in bringing them into a jurisdiction is 'the single greatest multiplier in all other aspects of successful business'.[1] A deep pool of human talent helps to attract a critical mass of banks, companies and financial institutions to a city. This, in turn, leads to agglomeration effects, positive spillovers, knowledge transfer and economies of scale. Emerging hubs are fighting over a finite pool of qualified and experienced financial, legal and accounting professionals; and although wages are high everywhere, the lifestyles on offer in competing cities vary greatly. London and New York, the biggest international financial centres by scale of operations, are two of the most cosmopolitan and dynamic cities in the world. Ensuring

1 Mark Yeandle, Alexander Knapp, Michael Mainelli and Ian Harris, *The Global Financial Centres Index* 3, City of London, March 2008, p. 5.

Figure 10.1: Lifestyle cluster

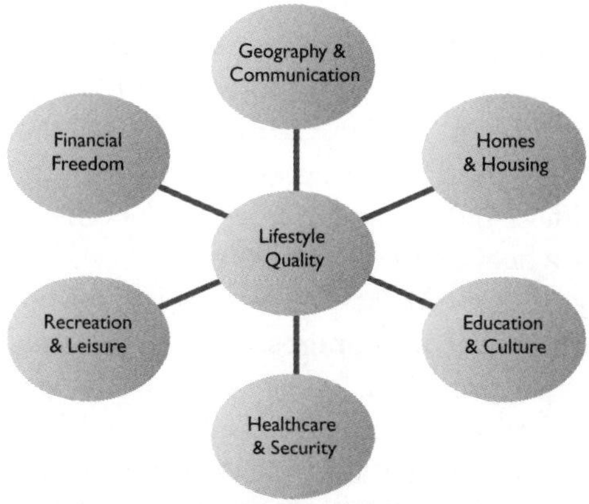

that a cluster of small desert states in the Middle East are as habitable and desirable as the world's most vibrant cities is no easy task. It demands not only large-scale government investment but also significant adjustments by the domestic populations and potentially difficult compromises.

Although committed governments can pump investment into transport, housing and the general living environment to ensure that these are world-class, they cannot directly legislate for or create 'cosmopolitanism' or vibrancy. As Mercer notes, 'A city with a high Quality of Living index is a safe and stable one, but it may be lacking the dynamic *je ne sais quoi* that makes people want to live [there].'[2] Quantifying this *je ne sais quoi* may not be possible, but there are several components to the 'lifestyle cluster' (see Figure 10.1), and this chapter aims to explore them.

Recreation, leisure and culture and financial freedom

Dubai already has a great allure and high quality of life for expatriates in the financial sector. As one commentator puts it, 'the perception of Dubai is based on the Burj, the Palm trilogy and sunshine 365 days a year. So far, you could call it a successful marketing campaign.'[3] It is a five-star environment of top-end hotels, restaurants, serviced apartments, golf courses and spotless beaches. Migrants make up as much as 90% of the population in Dubai. This suggests that, so far, the incentives are strong enough and the

2 Highlights from the 2007 *Mercer Quality of Living Survey*, at http://www.mercer.com/referencecontent.jhtml?idContent=1128060#le fe.

3 Quote by Martin Kohlhase, Moody's Dubai, in Margaret Coker, 'Scandals in Dubai Cast a Cloud', *The Wall Street Journal*, 28 April 2008.

marketing campaign is working (although many of these migrants are temporary guest workers rather than financiers). A recent HSBC survey confirmed this, revealing that the UAE ranked as the second-best location in the world for expatriates after Singapore.[4] Its criteria included earnings, accommodation and luxury. The UAE scored highest in the luxury category: expatriates in Dubai typically have access to private hospitals and schools, take frequent holidays and enjoy the services of domestic staff, and they own property, cars, a boat and a swimming pool.

The availability of domestic staff has served to free up more time for leisure. Concessions and compromises have been made in most GCC countries in order to provide a range of nightlife and entertainment options without violating local customs. Dubai and Bahrain can now offer restaurants that compare favourably with those in Hong Kong and even Paris, and there has been a steady stream of concert performances from world-class musicians. Cinemas are numerous and Dubai now hosts an annual film festival. There are a large number of luxury malls, one with an indoor ski slope. And the Gulf has established its name as a destination for major sporting events, for example the FIA Formula 1 Grand Prix, the ATP Tennis championships and the Asian Games. Universal Studios is building a theme park in Dubai, and Ferrari is building a branded theme park in Abu Dhabi that will include a race track and numerous rides and attractions.

Time magazine has asked, 'It is spectacular, but is it anything more than mere spectacle?'[5] In part as a response to this kind of question and to a perceived image of Dubai as showy or unsophisticated (for instance, theatre and opera have not yet taken off there), Abu Dhabi is seeking to carve a nuanced reputation as a cultural destination. It is building its own versions of the Louvre and the Guggenheim Museum. Buying up big brands in the art business can be seen as merely another form of consumerism ('cultural engineering', as cynics call it), but these states are at the beginning of a journey and are undergoing very rapid change. With such a diverse mix of nationalities (over 150 in the UAE alone), home-grown creativity and cultural achievements have already begun and are sure to flourish further.

The high level of luxury and numerous leisure options are made possible by the Gulf's high salaries and low taxes – these continue to be among the biggest incentives for expatriate workers. There is no individual income tax, and the region is one of the few in the world with no sales tax or VAT. Investors have a high degree of freedom regarding what they do with their money because free movement of capital and currency convertibility

4 *Expat Existence*, HSBC report, July 2008. The sample size was 2,155, compared with the total global expatriate population of 17.1 million (OECD estimate).

5 Rami Khouri, 'City Limits', *Time*, 14 May 2008, p. 56.

Table 10.1: Economic freedom of the GCC states

World ranking	Country	Economic Freedom	Business Freedom	Trade Freedom	Fiscal Freedom	Gov't Size	Monetary Freedom	Investment Freedom	Financial Freedom	Property Rights	Freedom from Corruption	Labour Freedom
19	Bahrain	72.2	80.0	80.8	99.7	80.3	74.3	60	90	60	57	40.0
39	Kuwait	68.3	68.5	81.0	99.9	74.6	73.8	50	50	55	48	82.1
42	Oman	67.4	55.8	83.6	98.5	60.7	74.7	60	60	50	54	77.2
66	Qatar	62.2	60.0	70.8	99.8	72.1	69.4	30	50	50	60	60.0
60	Saudi Arabia	62.8	72.5	76.8	99.7	69.1	76.7	30	40	50	33	80.6
63	United Arab Emirates	62.8	47.9	80.4	99.9	80.2	70.9	30	40	40	62	76.2

Source: Edwin J. Feulner, Kim R. Holmes and Mary Anastasia O'Grady, 2008 Index of Economic Freedom (Washington DC; The Heritage Foundation and Dow Jones & Company, 2008) at www.heritage.org./index.

are permitted, with no foreign exchange restrictions. Weak spots include investment freedom, financial freedom and property rights (see Table 10.1), but deregulation is under way. The launch of the Gulf Cooperation Council common market on 1 January 2008 and other efforts at market liberalization should improve future levels of economic freedom. Access to capital markets for non-nationals is opening up and multiple free zones are being established, notably in Saudi Arabia and Dubai.

These highly desirable fiscal conditions are being tempered by recent surges in inflation (a problem in the West too). Qatar and the UAE are the worst affected, with double-digit inflation. Dubai will have an introductory VAT rate of about 5% in 2009, and other GCC countries are expected to follow suit. However, for now the region has some of the most attractive fiscal conditions in the world, and economists speculate that it will take several years for any significant personal taxation plans to develop.[6]

Housing, education and healthcare

In 1994, May Seikaly wrote that 'the system has created superficially modern-looking societies without solving the dilemmas that rapid Western

6 'UAE plans VAT in 2009' *International Tax Review*, Euromoney Institutional Investor PLC, July–August 2008.

modernisation has brought.'[7] There was tension between financial and material emancipation (some say 'excessive consumerism') and the lack of complementary progress in the political and civic sphere: the education, healthcare and entertainment sectors were all underdeveloped. This restrictive social environment encouraged expatriates to see their assignments as temporary and solitary, a means of saving money and earning promotion while their families often remained at home. This is still the case in some places, where expatriate oil and finance workers may be housed in gated communities and there are restrictions on the movement of women. However, the smaller GCC states have opened up and developed much more, resulting in fairly liberal societies and good provision for expatriates' needs in housing, health, education and so on. Qatar, Kuwait and Bahrain host several churches for their Christian expatriate population.

As mentioned, housing standards are high: private gyms and swimming pools are common and tennis courts are often provided in compounds of apartments. However, the shortage in the supply of housing (for example in Dubai) and delays in the delivery of new projects mean that rents are soaring. They rose by 30% in 2006 and 17% in 2007. Abu Dhabi too had a shortage – nearly 8,000 homes in 2007, creating long delays in the rental process and feeding inflation and fears of an eventual real estate crash. According to a survey by the Abu Dhabi Department of Planning and Economy, expatriates spend over 40% of their income on rent and utilities while nationals spend only 28%.[8]

Despite recent and short-term problems, prices remain competitive and good value for the quality of accommodation, as shown by Figure 10.2. With an average monthly rent of around $3,000, Dubai rental prices rank only 14th in a list of the most expensive cities in 2008. This makes it cheaper than most large financial centres, and prime real estate is still only about a quarter of the price of similar properties in London.

In the long term, the question of property rights has greater significance than current price rises. Property rights are a weak spot (see Table 10.1). But since 2002, restrictions on non-GCC nationals owning real estate have been eased, in recognition that offering property rights to foreigners fosters a sense of ownership and belonging, encouraging loyalty and long-term residency.

The UAE was the first to reform property ownership rules, and allow foreigners to buy and rent out real estate in certain areas of Dubai with long

7 May Seikaly, 'Women and Social Change in Bahrain', *International Journal of Middle East Studies*, vol. 26, no.3 (August 1994), 415–26, at p. 416.
8 H. Michael Jalili, 'Expats Spend 41% of Earnings on Housing', *The National* (Abu Dhabi), 23 June 2008.

Figure 10.2: Sale and rental prices

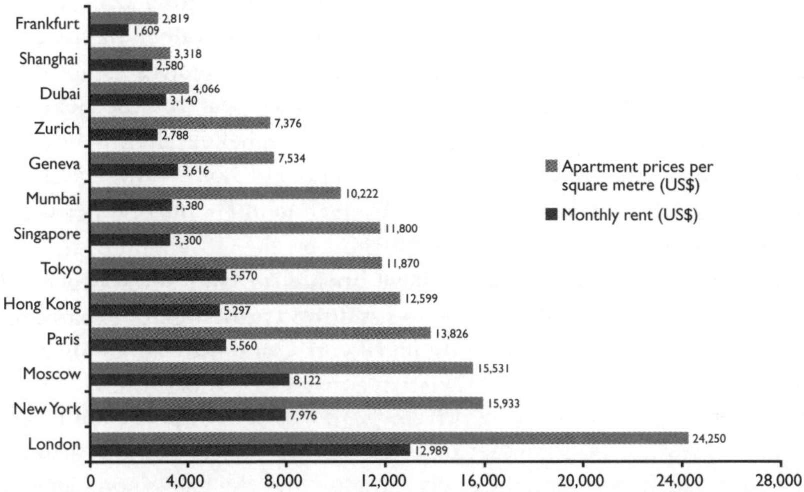

Source: *www.globalpropertyguide.com* (2008)

leases. Similarly in Bahrain, foreigners can buy property in selected parts of Manama, and in Qatar and Oman a limited amount of real estate has been designated for foreign purchase. The rapid development of domestic mortgage lending markets – lending almost doubled in 2007 in the UAE[9] – reflects the fact that many foreigners are taking up these opportunities, encouraged by high inflation and low interest rates.

Buying real estate often comes with residency benefits, depending on the jurisdiction. Foreigners have been promised 10-year residency visas on the purchase of certain properties in Dubai, although recent indications from the government have raised doubts about the authority of developers to make such promises. In some developments in Qatar, buyers are automatically given residency rights for themselves and their family that expire only when the property is sold. Otherwise, owners can bequeath property to their heirs. This kind of stability is an important factor in securing the commitment of expatriate workers and their families to the region.

The growth of the education sector has been another key factor in attracting expatriates on a long-term basis. State schools have traditionally taught in Arabic and relied on rote learning. Generally expatriates have used private international schools that follow US or UK curricula and teach in English, or they have even educated their children abroad. However, GCC leaders have made the schooling sector a priority, forging links with and importing the best educational 'branding' and institutions from abroad.

9 Daliah Merzaban, 'UAE Mortgage Lending Soars', 9 July 2008, at Arabianbusiness.com.

In Abu Dhabi, the Sorbonne has sanctioned its first branch outside France, and negotiations are in progress with a number of leading US universities for more 'franchises'. Qatar's Supreme Education Council has recently begun the 'Outstanding Schools Initiative', which involves establishing 2–3 private international schools in Qatar every year for the next five years, starting with the American Michael E. DeBakey High School for Health Professions and the International School of London in September 2008. The Qatar Foundation has brought five major US universities to the country, offering degrees at US standards.

Government provides basic universal healthcare for GCC citizens, but more complicated procedures have sometimes required specialist equipment or medical skills unavailable locally. Migrant worker healthcare is generally paid for through company insurance schemes, and governments are actively encouraging private providers to set up. In Abu Dhabi, Mubadala Healthcare is partnering with leading international healthcare institutions such as Imperial College London and the Cleveland Clinic to bring experience and expertise to the region. Dubai Healthcare City, a new 'centre of excellence', has secured a franchise of the Harvard Medical School. As set out in its 2008 budget, the Saudi government plans to finance the building of eight new hospitals and 250 primary care centres, in addition to the 79 hospitals/clinics currently under construction and the expansion of existing healthcare facilities. And in Qatar, Hamad Medical City will provide an extensive network of healthcare facilities.

Crime and security

Levels of serious crime are very low in the Gulf by international standards. For instance, in Bahrain there is one homicide per 100,000 people (see Table 10.2). This compares favourably to the UK and the US.[10]

There is some concern about the threat of terrorism, however. In June 2008, the British Foreign Office revised their risk assessment of the UAE. The website stated that 'there is a high threat from terrorism. We believe terrorists may be planning to carry out attacks in the UAE.'[11] Attacks, if carried out, would probably strike at popular expatriate and tourist spots. Saudi Arabia experienced a spate of terrorist attacks in 2003, but the smaller GCC states have not been targeted in the same way. Even so, the official level of the terrorist threat does have implications for people considering

10 UNDP, *United Nations Human Development Report* 2007/2008, pp. 322–5.

11 Foreign Office website, http://www.fco.gov.uk/en/travelling-and-living-overseas/travel-advice-by-country/middle-east-north-africa/united-arab-emirates.

Table 10.2: Crime rates: an international comparison

Country	*Intentional homicides (per 100,000 people)* 2000–2004	*Prison population (per 100,000 people)* 2007
Singapore	0.5	350
Hong Kong	0.6	168
United Arab Emirates	0.6	288
Qatar	0.8	55
Saudi Arabia	0.9	132
Luxembourg	0.9	167
Bahrain	1.0	95
United Kingdom	2.1	124
United States	5.6	738

Source: UNDP, *Human Development Report 2007/2008*.

relocation with their families, and it will be watched carefully. There are also, of course, long-standing geopolitical concerns: the GCC is near Iran and its uncertain nuclear ambitions; there is continued unrest in Iraq, Lebanon and Afghanistan; and the Arab-Israeli conflict remains volatile.

Geography and communications

Geographical position and accessibility are crucial for the financial industry in view of the international character of the talent pool and the global nature of modern portfolio investments. The Gulf region is helped by its convenient location as a hub between the Western world and booming Asia: it is a few hours from Europe, three hours from Mumbai and seven hours from Hong Kong and Shanghai. Connectivity has been substantially improved by the rise of the Gulf's national airline carriers: Emirates (the fastest-growing carrier worldwide), Gulf Air, Etihad and Qatar Airways. Frequent flights to a growing number of destinations have enabled some degree of international commuting and a good deal of conference-hopping. These airlines have also been very successful in securing international visibility, branding the Gulf as a mainstream stopover and holiday destination. Emirates has helped to secure Dubai's place at the heart of global passenger traffic, and Dubai International Airport has been expanding rapidly. Its capacity has reached 60 million passengers a year.

Improved telecommunications and connectivity have complemented this increasing geographical accessibility. Digital satellite services and broadband Internet are available as standard, allowing people to trade foreign exchange on the beach, for instance, or to see television programmes in their own language. Being able to stay in touch with family and developments at home (for instance by watching Premiership football games) has made relocation to the Gulf seem much less remote and much more appealing than it was for the first wave of migrants.

Conclusion

The first wave of the construction boom in the Gulf was aimed at capturing the upper end of the tourist market by building five-star resorts and developing 'luxury' leisure activity, including sport and shopping options. The Gulf has entered the second wave of development: it is now addressing the deficits in civil society, housing, education and healthcare. Much progress has already been made, although this is a difficult and long-term challenge. Although hotels, shopping centres and sports centres can seemingly be built almost overnight, the building of a world-class civil society takes years and can be riddled with problems and delays. And the sheer pace of change threatens to bring its own troubles: overcrowded cities, inadequate infrastructure for burgeoning populations, traffic congestion and deteriorating air quality. The domestic population are nostalgic for the empty roads and clean air of the past, and in conservative circles there is concern about growing demographic imbalances and widening inequality, and fears that local customs are being compromised and that the Arabic language is being marginalized. New developments must be reconciled with traditional values in order not to alienate and disenfranchise GCC citizens.

The GCC states are dynamic and forward-looking. They are diligently fulfilling the practical and less tangible requirements and creating the infrastructure necessary for a good, even luxurious, 'quality of living'. Gulf governments' investments will not only encourage an increased inflow of skilled professionals but also materially improve conditions for their own citizens. They may be helped in their recruitment drive by current economic downturns elsewhere in the world. Gulf businesses should be able to lure talent and experience from London and New York to help build that critical mass of people and activity that will ensure genuinely self-sustaining, innovative financial centres. With continued investment in infrastructure and culture, and a diverse workforce, a distinctive and cosmopolitan lifestyle is materializing, along with that elusive *je ne sais quoi.*

Part 4

GCC sovereign wealth funds: impact, risks and implications

11 Asian and Gulf sovereign wealth funds: a tale of two continents

Paola Subacchi*

Introduction

Concern about the growth and activities of sovereign wealth funds first came to prominence in mid-2007.[1] China's acquisition of a $3 billion stake in Blackstone, a US private equity fund, focused a spotlight on the immense amount of capital that countries with large balance of payments surpluses had accumulated in less than a decade. Then, in summer 2007, the China Development Bank (CDB) and Singapore's Temasek Holdings acquired a 3.1% and 2.1% stake respectively in Barclays, one of the biggest banks in Europe by market capitalization. Investing $3 billion and $2 billion respectively, CDB and Temasek Holdings also acquired a seat on Barclays' board.[2]

These deals drew the attention of public opinion to the sheer size of the two funds and to their 'sovereign' nature: they belong to a sovereign state even if, more often than not, the chain of management and accountability is quite complicated, which gives much autonomy to the fund managers. SWFs are estimated to have almost $4 trillion[3] worth of assets under management. Although significant, this is still a fraction of the value of funds in other investment categories.[4] It is not so much the total size of SWFs as the dynamics of their growth – many of them originate from high commodity prices – and the cross-border nature of their asset holdings

* This chapter is part of a joint project between Chatham House and FEEM (Fondazione Eni Enrico Mattei. The author thanks Andrea Goldstein, John Nugée, Vanessa Rossi and an anonymous reviewer for comments and suggestions.

1 The first disquiet was over the Dubai Ports deal in early 2006. The Dubai Ports saga was very big news in the United States, but at the time it seemed like an isolated episode.

2 The acquisition of a seat on the board of the target company depends on how the deal is structured and the objectives of the acquirer. For instance, China Investment Corporation did not acquire a seat on Blackstone's board.

3 This figure, and those in Table 11.1, are perhaps top-end estimates. As evidence of how estimates may differ from each other, see the other chapters in Part 4 of this volume.

4 According to the estimates by IFSL (International Financial Services London), at the end of 2007 total assets under management in pension funds and in mutual funds were estimated at $28.5 trillion and $27.3 trillion respectively.

that raise operational, institutional and policy issues. According to the IMF (2008), the value of SWF holdings could soar to $6–10 trillion by 2013. Other projections indicate that it could be as much as $12 trillion by 2015 (Jen 2007a; Chatham House 2008).

Even though SWFs played a critical role as major investors in big banks and financial institutions during the early stages of the credit crisis, they are still regarded with suspicion. As summarized by the IMF (2007: 50), there is concern about the limited publicly available information on most funds, the multiplicity of their objectives and the lack of clarity about their institutional structures and investment management. Similarly, there are worries that an absence of transparency over strategies and operations makes it difficult to assess SWFs' asset management activities and their impact on capital markets and the wider global economy. Finally, it is feared that without more public accountability, funds could alter their governance structures, which, in turn, could lead to sudden changes in their investment policy. Public ownership of SWFs also raises concern that recipient countries could place restrictions on their capital accounts in order to avoid certain types of foreign direct investment.

As recent research[5] has begun to show, SWFs are not all the same; more often than not, they present more differences than similarities. It is crucial to be able to differentiate between funds and to pick up on their differences based on source of funding, goals and management style as they inform each fund's activities. To bundle all of them together risks incompleteness and an over-simplified analysis. This is a notable danger for countries with assets that are increasingly targets for SWFs because their governments must respond with an appropriate policy.

In this chapter, I shall use still scarce anecdotal evidence and also tables to sketch the differences between SWFs from the GCC and those from Asia. I shall focus in particular on the economics of SWFs and shall discuss whether Asian funds, because of the nature of their funding, are forced to pursue a more aggressive investment approach than the commodity funds, thereby becoming less welcome investors in host countries.

A problem of definition

Although SWFs have existed since the 1950s, there is little anecdotal evidence and almost no statistical information to support a deep understanding of them. We even lack a generally accepted definition, so that they are often confused with sovereign pension funds and official FX

5 One of the most recent surveys on SWFs is in State Street (2008).

reserves.[6] The closest to a commonly shared definition – and surely the one most referred to – is that given by Clay Lowery, US Acting Treasury Under Secretary for International Affairs, who recently defined an SWF as 'a government investment vehicle which is funded by foreign exchange assets and which manages these assets separately from official reserves (US Treasury 2007). On this basis, most observers agree that SWFs have the following elements in common:[7] 1) they are state-owned; 2) they are investment funds, although they may invest in productive companies; 3) they have no significant liabilities, unlike sovereign pension funds; 4) they have a high foreign exchange assets exposure but are managed separately from the rest of the central bank's reserves; and 5) they have a long investment horizon and low leverage (Beck and Fidora 2008: 6).

Looking at how SWFs are financed – by receipts from energy and commodities exports[8] or by transfers from official foreign exchange reserves[9] – provides a critical distinction, between commodity funds and non-commodity funds. The former are often an instrument used by commodity-dependent economies to smooth their revenue over a long time and use that revenue in order to diversify their economy.[10] External surpluses are therefore channelled into government investment funds and held usually in the form of stocks, bonds or property. A real asset is replaced by a financial asset.[11]

Non-commodity funds are used to diversify FX assets and to earn a higher return by investing in a broad range of asset classes, including longer-term government bonds, asset-backed securities, corporate bonds, equities, commodities, real estate, derivatives, alternative investments and FDI. For them the goal is the preservation and enhancement of the international purchasing power of their reserves.[12]

6 One of the consequences of this lack of a uniform definition is that different tables of SWFs and their assets seldom agree precisely on totals of assets under management or even on which funds to include.

7 For a discussion of how to define SWFs, see Jen (2007c).

8 These receipts, in turn, can either be owned or taxed by the government.

9 Large balance of payments surpluses have enabled non-commodity exporters to transfer 'excess' FX reserves to stand-alone investment funds, to be managed for higher returns.

10 For example, Russia's Oil Stabilization Fund (OSF) was established in January 2004 with the aim of stabilizing the monetary impact of changes in oil prices. Tax proceeds above the threshold of $27 a barrel were saved in the OSF. It formed a part of the total official reserves of $357 billion, which made Russia the world's third-largest holder of official reserves. As of 1 April 2007, the OSF had $109 billion invested in sovereign bonds of the US (45% of the total), euro (45% of the total) and the UK (10% of the total). In that month the Duma approved the split of the OSF into the Reserve Fund and the National Wealth Fund. This structural change came into effect on 1 February 2008. See Jen (2007b).

11 On this, see Chapter 12 in this book, by Stephen Jen.

12 In this regard, Temasek Holdings does not completely fit the definition of an SWF. The source of its funding is from investment income and fiscal surplus rather than FX reserves. But as it

Table 11.1: SWFs with assets of more than $100 billion

Fund	*Country*	*Launch year*	*Type*	*Assets ($bn)*
Abu Dhabi Investment Authority and Corporation (ADIA)	UAE (Abu Dhabi)	1976	Commodity	875.0
Government Pension Fund – Global (GPF)	Norway	1990	Commodity	396.5
Saudi Arabia Monetary Agency Foreign Holdings*	Saudi Arabia	n.a.	Commodity	365.2
Government of Singapore Investment Corporation (GIC)	Singapore	1981	Non-commodity	330.0
SAFE Investment Authority	China	n.a.	Non-commodity	311.6
Kuwait Investment Authority (KIA)	Kuwait	1953	Commodity	264.4
China Investment Corporation (CIC)	China	2007	Non-commodity	200.0
Hong Kong Monetary Authority Investment Portfolio**	China	1998	Non-commodity	173.0
National Welfare Fund	Russia	2008	Commodity	162.5
Temasek Holdings	Singapore	1974	Non-commodity	159.0

* Not strictly an SWF as over half of it is straightforward FX reserves and held in fixed income.
** HKMA do not split out their investment portfolio. $173bn is the whole of their Exchange Fund (FX reserves).
Source: SWF Institute (http://www.swfinstitute.org/funds.php, accessed on 26 August 2008).

Commodity and non-commodity funds can be distinguished from one another according to two criteria. The first criterion is geographical: commodity funds belong mainly, although not exclusively, to countries in the Gulf region – with the notable exceptions of Russia and Norway. Non-commodity funds belong chiefly to Asian countries (see Table 11.1). The second criterion is the number of years that these funds have existed. For the most part, commodity funds have been around for longer than non-commodity ones. The first SWF to be established (although not sovereign), in 1953, was Kuwait Investment Authority (KIA). With the exception of the Singaporean funds, large Asian SWFs have been created only recently. China Investment Corporation (CIC), the youngest, was incorporated in 2007. This reflects the source of Asian funds and the fact that

shares some features with SWFs and is commonly included among them, I follow the usual practice here. On Temasek Holdings, see Goldstein (2008).

Table 11.2: Funds' share of total SWF sector assets, 2007

Country	*Assets ($bn)*	*% share*
United Arab Emirates	875.0	22.7
Singapore	489.0	12.7
Norway	396.5	10.3
China	684.6	17.8
Saudi Arabia	365.2	9.5
Kuwait	264.4	6.9
Russia	162.5	4.2
Others	616.8	16.0
Total	3,854.0	100

Sources: SWF Institute (http://www.swfinstitute.org/funds.php, accessed on 26 August 2008) and author's calculations.

for some time Asian countries have preferred a policy of exchange rate management which has led to accumulations of large surpluses in their FX reserves.

Asia and the GCC countries play by far the biggest roles in the SWF sector with approximately 30% and 40% respectively of all assets (see Table 11.2). The GCC countries are also very prominent in individual country rankings: the United Arab Emirates has about 23% of the global total; China has almost 18%; Singapore almost 13%; and Saudi Arabia about 10%.

The divide between commodity funds and non-commodity funds is clear – and one can even broadly conclude that there is a regional split between Asia and the Gulf region according to where one type of fund is more common. It is thus interesting to examine whether different sources of funding of the two types of SWF fundamentally influence investment strategies and, if so, what are the policy implications.

'Coming of age'

Commodity and non-commodity funds share a need for diversification. To use expressions by Stephen Jen in this book, GCC countries need to diversify their asset base from '100% oil',[13] and this diversification needs to be multi-generational. Asian central banks need to diversify their assets

13 They need to diversify their financial assets as well, in the same way as Asia. This is a two-tier process for the Gulf SWFs but not for the Asian ones, for which the diversification of financial assets is the main issue.

from '100% sovereign bonds', away from the dollar and from fixed income. To do this they both must look for long-term returns and thus more risky assets instead of acting solely with regard to short-term liquidity considerations.

Trends in capital flows observed since early 2007 leave little doubt about the intention of countries with a large accumulation of capital to take a more professional and dynamic investment approach. This shift occurred roughly around the time when the oil price rose above $50 a barrel and held steady in the $50–70 range from late 2005 to September 2007 (when it began to climb again[14]). Previously, government wealth funds were mainly a vehicle for accumulating low-risk and low-return securities, mirroring to some extent the official reserves, but with the added function of stabilizing government revenues and protecting them from volatile commodity prices. But as export revenues were generating large capital inflows, so the opportunity cost of following the same strategy of seeking low-risk low-return investments was also increasing. Moreover, both existing stocks and new capital inflows were losing value because of the depreciation of the dollar. As a result, investment strategies and attitude to risk have become more adventurous, as have asset and currency diversifications. The shift towards a more professional and energetic approach has huge implications – in terms of both economic and market dynamics and international and domestic politics. Still too little is known about SWFs' investment policies, making it hard to analyse in detail their likely implications. Not surprisingly, then, the SWFs have become a major political issue. Their sheer size, their prospective growth rate, their potentially strategic nature[15] and their lack of transparency and poor governance have recently caused worry that they could become a source of financial[16] as well as geopolitical instability.

Too big for their economy?

A common feature of commodity and non-commodity sovereign wealth funds is that their underlying economies have a limited capacity to absorb export revenues. This is due to the size of those economies (especially in the case of the GCC countries), the rapid speed with which extra export revenues have emerged, the limited depth and development of domestic financial markets and their institutional and legal set-up. With the

14 It was on average about $90 a barrel in the last quarter of 2007, up from an average of $75 a barrel in the third quarter.
15 Some commentators refer to SWFs as an aspect of 'state capitalism' (Lyons 2007).
16 But SWFs would claim that they are the ultimate force for stability, being long-term cash-funded investors.

Table 11.3: Leading Asian and Gulf SWFs: their value relative to their national economy, 2007

Fund	*Country*	*Type of fund*	*Fund value as % of 2007 GDP*
Abu Dhabi Investment Authority and Corporation (ADIA)	UAE (Abu Dhabi)	Commodity	730.0
Government of Singapore Investment Corporation (GIC)	Singapore	Non-commodity	243.0
Saudi Arabia Monetary Agency Foreign Holdings	Saudi Arabia	Commodity	25.5
Kuwait Investment Authority (KIA)	Kuwait	Commodity	813.0
China Investment Corporation (CIC)	China	Non-commodity	0.8
Hong Kong Monetary Authority Investment Portfolio	China	Non-commodity	10.0
Temasek Holdings	Singapore	Non-commodity	65.0

Sources: SWF Institute, IMF and author's calculations.

exception of CIC, the size of all the main Asian and GCC funds is disproportionate to that of their national economy, as shown by Table 11.3.

A comparison of the size of these funds and the market capitalization of the principal stock exchanges shows that the total assets of the main Gulf SWFs exceed the market capitalization of the GCC stock exchanges, which is estimated to be about $1 trillion (Chatham House 2008). The assets of the two Singaporean funds almost equal the market capitalization of their domestic stock exchange. By contrast, the assets of CIC are only approximately 25% of the market capitalization of the Shanghai stock exchange, although China's total FX holdings correspond to some 65–70% of that market's capitalization.

Because of their large size relative to their national economy and partly because, like FX reserves, they must be held outside as the counterpart to the balance of payments, SWFs need to focus on acquiring some of their assets in international markets. Given the projected growth of SWFs, future deal flows might face increased competition for investment opportunities and thus more constraints on finalizing deals or managing acquisitions.

Each fund is different

What do we know about the sovereign wealth funds? Singapore's GIC and Temasek Holdings have existed for more than 25 years, and their investment policies and allocation of assets are broadly understood.[17] The GIC, for instance, invests in 40 markets, with a long-term focus through systematic diversification across equities, fixed-income securities, foreign exchange, commodities, money markets, alternative investments, real estate and private equity. Temasek Holdings operates under commercial principles so as to maximize long-term returns. Its geographical asset mix is broadly as follows: 33% domestic, 41% rest of Asia, 23% OECD countries (except South Korea) and 3% the rest of the world.

The Abu Dhabi Investment Authority and Corporation (ADIA), which has been around since the 1970s, invests mainly in equities, fixed-income securities and real estate, but it is increasingly looking at alternative investments. KIA, the oldest SWF, takes both minority stakes and co-investments, showing broad sectoral preferences, from industry to real estate. Its General Reserve Fund is invested in the local, Arab and international financial markets; the Future Generation Fund is invested in global assets.

The China Investment Corporation is the 'new kid on the block'. It came into prominence in June 2007 when, despite not yet being fully operational, it agreed to acquire a stake of $3 billion (almost 10%) of the initial public stock offering of the Blackstone Group, one of the largest US private equity firms. The CIC fund was then officially established in September 2007 with $200 billion drawn from the official FX reserves. This SWF has the potential for rapid growth thanks not only to the Chinese economy's rate of expansion but also to its consolidation with other investment bodies. Indeed, an additional $200 billion is expected to be added as a result of the merging of the Central Huijin Company into CIC.[18] CIC is also expected to buy out the investments held by the People's Bank of China, the central bank, which has holdings in most state-run banks.

CIC's investment policy and asset allocation have not been disclosed, but it looks to have a larger mandate than the Central Huijin Company, including a large array of assets from several major financial institutions. China's leadership is involved in shaping CIC's strategy for it. Vice Premier

17 It is worth stressing here that openness and transparency are not a function of age. For instance ADIA is older than both GIC and Temasek but still pretty much a black box.

18 The Central Huijin Investment Company (CHIC) is an investment company controlled by the People's Bank of China (PBoC). CHIC in turn controls three of China's biggest state banks. In November 2007, the newly formed CIC assumed responsibility for the assets and liabilities of CHIC. It is reported that the PBoC obtained about 500 billion yuan ($67 billion) in compensation for CHIC.

Table 11.4: The 10 largest SWF transactions, 2007–08

	Acquirer	*Target*	*Sector*	*Acquired stake (%)*	*Value ($mn)*
Dec. 2007	GIC	UBS	Financial	9.0	9,750
March 2007	Dubai Holding	Emaar Properties	Real estate	28.0	7,597
Nov. 2007	ADIA	Citigroup	Financial	4.9	7,500
January 2008	GIC	Citigroup	Financial	4.4	6,880
January 2008	Korea Investment Corp., KIA, Mizuho Corporate Bank, TPG-Axon, NJ Division of Investments and others	Merrill Lynch	Financial	15.0	6,600
April 2007	Saad Group	HSBC	Financial	3.1	6,553
Dec. 2007	Temasek Holdings, Davis Selected Advisors	Merrill Lynch	Financial	15.0	6,200
January 2008	KIA, Prince Alwaleed bin Talal, and others	Citigroup	Financial	3.3	5,620
Dec. 2007	CIC	Morgan Stanley	Financial	9.9	5,000
August 2007	Istithmaar	MGM Mirage	Consumer–retail	9.5	5,000
Total					66,700

Source: Newton (2008).

Zeng Peiyan has suggested that China should invest in natural resources in order to increase its strategic reserves. Other high-ranking party officials prefer that the country should acquire shares in high-tech companies, to help close more rapidly the gap with leading industrialized countries. Lou Jiwei, a former vice minister of finance and now CIC's chairman, has said that the fund will operate on the principle of 'commercial operation' and will abide by the local laws of the countries where it invests.

Of the ten largest SWF deals in 2007–08, their sectoral distribution is clearly skewed towards the banking and financial sector (see Table 11.4). And, as Table 11.5 shows, the sovereign wealth infusion for this sector is dominated by funds from the Gulf, China and Singapore. In terms of investment size, the acquisition of significant stakes seems to be a preference of the Asian funds. All the Gulf funds have kept their stakes below 5%. Is

Table 11.5: Principal SWF infusions for banks, March 2007–April 2008

Company	*Investor*	*% stake*	*Investment value ($bn)*	*Security type*
Citigroup	ADIA	4.9	7.5	New convertible units
Citigroup	GIC	3.7	6.88	New convertible units
Citigroup	KIA	1.6	3.0	New convertible units
Merrill Lynch	KIA	3.0	2.0	New convertible units
Merrill Lynch	Temasek Holdings	9.4	4.4	New common stock
Morgan Stanley	CIC	9.9	5.0	New convertible units
Barclays plc	Temasek Holdings	1.8	2.0	Common stock
UBS	GIC	9.8	9.75	New convertible units
UBS	Saudi Arabia Monetary Agency Foreign Holdings	2.0	1.8	New convertible units

Sources: SWF Institute and official press releases.

this significant information that suggests different investment strategies by commodity funds and non-commodity funds? It is a well-known fact that Temasek Holdings tends to both acquire significant stakes and play an active role in the target company,[19] but what about CIC and, to some extent, GIC?

The economics of SWFs

To address the above questions we now turn to the sources of the funds. A useful approach, by Rozanov (2008), looks at funds' liabilities and separates equity-based funds from debt-based funds. The former are commodity funds that represent an equity-like claim on the underlying assets. The latter are non-commodity funds that are funded by the issuance of local currency-denominated debt. This approach emphasizes the additional constraints and complications that non-commodity funds tend to face compared to the simpler – from both institutional and accounting points of view – commodity funds. The best example of this is China's CIC. The decision to separate this new SWF from PBoC has important implications not only in terms of governance – the removal of the potential conflict of interest between low-risk foreign reserves and the higher-risk management fund – but also for the balance sheet. In simplified accounting terms, one can

19 This is because Temasek Holdings is not a proper SWF (see note 12).

understand CIC's funding as being assets borrowed from SAFE (the State Administration of Foreign Exchange) and funded by issuing short-term yuan-denominated bonds. This has two important consequences. First, the new fund is debt-based. Second, there is a currency mismatch between dollar-denominated assets and renminbi-denominated liabilities.

These two factors combined have huge implications for the economics of CIC and for its investment strategies. Not only do the US-denominated assets have to earn a dollar return, but they also have to compensate for any further strengthening of China's currency that reflects the strength of the Chinese economy. In the past three years the renminbi has appreciated in real terms by an average annual rate of 5%. This is the return that CIC must guarantee in order to retain the value of its assets. To this must be added another 5%, which is the interbank rate. On the whole, the fund needs to generate a 10% return just to break even.[20] What does this mean for investment strategies?

The evidence available so far is too patchy to allow any firm and plausible conclusion.[21] However, to strengthen the suggestion that SWFs' economics can have a significant impact on their investment strategies – and to indicate future lines of research – it is worth comparing CIC with Norway's Government Pension Fund-Global (GPF). This is an equity-like fund that seeks returns in foreign currency and does not have a liability-driven hurdle rate in local currency (Rozanov 2008: 40). The GPF's objective is to gain 'high return subject to moderate risk'. Since 1997, the return on the fund, once adjusted for inflation, has been 4.67%; the net real annual return, i.e. after management costs, has been 4.58%.[22] Between 1998 and 2007, the fund manager's average excess return relative to the benchmark per annum amounted to 0.4 percentage points. This is a respectable performance, but it would be far from acceptable for the CIC in view of its 'hurdle' rate.

Since 1998, the GPF has invested mainly in fixed-income securities (50–70% its portfolio) and 30–50% in equities – previously, it had invested only in government securities. Of the equity portfolio, 40–60% is invested in currencies and markets in Europe, 25–45% in the Americas and Africa and 5–25% in Asia and Oceania. Of the fixed-income securities, 50–70% has been invested in currencies and markets in Europe, 25–45% in the Americas and Africa and 0–15% in Asia and Oceania. The portfolio's country distribution within the respective regions is based on the market

20 This rate depends on how fast the renminbi appreciates on the back of inflationary pressures.
21 For an empirical analysis of the financial impact of SWF investments in the stock of listed companies, see Fotak et al. (2008).
22 The average nominal annual returns on the equity portfolio and the fixed-income portfolios for 1998–2006 have been 5.37% and 7.02% respectively.

size of individual countries. The fund tends to hold less than a 1% stake in individual companies.

The GPF's strategy seems to be consistent with the goals of the Gulf SWFs, but would clearly not suit a fund with the objectives of CIC. To gain higher returns, CIC cannot structure its portfolio like the GPF or the other equity-based commodity funds. It must adopt a more aggressive style. The result is a fully diversified portfolio that includes higher risk-higher return assets along with more liquid, less volatile and lower-return assets. Therefore, the portfolio is likely to include a relatively larger proportion of emerging-market equities, private equity funds, hedge funds, infrastructure funds, etc. Indeed, after CIC acquired a stake in Blackstone, it was disclosed that it would continue to invest in private equity funds and hedge funds and to provide financial support to state-owned enterprises in overseas investment and financing. It is also likely that CIC will make some strategic investments, i.e. a 5–10% stake in a company, or try to achieve corporate control.

This is the thorniest issue arising from the establishment of China's SWF. The economics of CIC suggest that it would make sense for the fund to follow the same value-creation model as private equity funds. This means turning round underperforming companies and creating value in them. Would this work? Perhaps it would work in Asia, but it hardly seems to be a viable and efficient model to apply to investments in more remote countries. Moreover, CIC would have to rely on foreign professionals with the relevant skills, as Chinese institutions tend to lack global experience, both in investing overseas and in running enterprises in foreign countries.

Finally, and more importantly, would this strategy be consistent with China's overall development targets? It has been suggested, particularly by the press, that investments by SWFs could satisfy China's quest for energy, commodities and knowledge: they could be acquired by direct investments in key companies. Rather than following the classic private equity model of value-creation, CIC's acquisition strategy would be directed by goals of technology transfer, skill acquisition and access to commodities. But this seems to confuse the role of CIC as a portfolio assets manager with the remit of 'beating' the central bank in foreign reserves management. Moving in the less familiar territory of direct, 'strategic' investments would be a risky strategy in both financial and political terms.

Not surprisingly, then, three of CIC's first four international equity mandates for foreign fund managers issued at the end of 2007 featured an emerging-market component, with two benchmarked against the MSCI emerging market index and the MSCI Europe, Australia and the Far East. Even more significant is the call for managers to outperform those indexes by 300 and 200 basis points respectively. The mandate for Asian (except Japanese) equities invites fund managers to propose benchmarks and performance targets. The fourth mandate has the target of outperforming the MSCI All Country Index by 300 basis points (*Institutional Investor* 2008).

Like all sovereign wealth funds, CIC will have to gain and retain political support. This imperative is clear in the words of Chairman Lou Jiwei of CIC. Talking about its potential for expansion through the transfer of China's foreign exchange reserves, he pointed out that this will depend on its profitability. 'If I am making losses every day, how can I face asking the government for more money?' (*China Daily* 2007).

Indeed, as it reports to the State Council[23] and ultimately to Premier Wen Jia Bao, the fund must be consistent with China's long-term economic policy goals. CIC's board of 11 members includes representatives from half a dozen agencies, including the finance ministry, the central bank, the commerce ministry and the National Development and Reform Commission, China's powerful economic planning agency. Although disagreements among the diverse members of the committee could significantly hamper decision-making, empirical evidence has shown that diversity on a board tends to enhance a company's monitoring and performance. Thus even if there is a risk that economically efficient choices could be shunned by politically driven decisions, CIC's governance seems to point in the right direction.

Conclusion: the way forward

The distinction between commodity and non-commodity funds and the way they are funded seems to suggest fundamental differences in the way that Gulf and Asian, especially Chinese, funds are created and operate. Research should concentrate on this area in order to highlight, through a systematic analysis of deals, whether Asian debt-based non-commodity funds are forced to pursue a much more aggressive investment strategy, which makes them less desirable investors for host countries than commodity funds.

Another critical area for research is the use of SWFs in exchange rate policy. In an article in *Foreign Affairs*, Deputy Secretary of the US Treasury Department Robert Kimmitt seems to suggest a role for non-commodity funds to perpetuate 'undesirable underlying policies' (2008: 122) that

23 It is worth noting here differences in corporate governance. Some funds, such as Temasek Holdings, report directly to the head of state.

can undermine financial stability. Although the article does not provide further details, the implicit target seems to be China's exchange rate policy. Would SWFs provide Beijing with further ammunition to 'manipulate' the exchange rate, as the US administration often claims? If so, would equity-based commodity funds from the GCC countries[24] be more welcome than debt-based SWFs, above all those from China? Are Gulf SWFs' investments 'economically rather than politically driven' (Kimmitt 2008: 126)? After all, the extent of their asset accumulation depends on their underlying reserves rather than, as in the case of China, on how successful they are in avoiding shifting to increased exchange rate flexibility. This can be the next line of attack on SWFs, and serious research on the topic is necessary in order to dispel fear, inform good policies and provide accurate information about the 'new power brokers' (Farrell et al. 2007).

References

Beck, Roland and Michael Fidora (2008), *The Impact of Sovereign Wealth Funds on Global Financial Markets*, Occasional Paper 91 (Frankfurt: European Central Bank, July).

China Daily (2007), 'China Wealth Fund Aims for Stability, Openness', 16 October.

Chatham House (2008), *The Gulf as a Global Financial Centre: Growing Opportunities and International Influence*, Chatham House Report (London: Royal Institute of International Affairs, June).

Farrell, Diana, Susan Lund, Eva Gerlemann and Peter Seeburger (2007), *The New Power Brokers: How Oil, Asia, Hedge Funds, and Private Equity are Shaping Global Capital Markets* (San Francisco: McKinsey Global Institute, February).

Fotak, Veljko, Bernardo Bortolotti and William Megginson (2008), 'The Financial Impact of Sovereign Wealth Fund Investments in Listed Companies', Working Paper, University of Oklahoma, June.

Goldstein, Andrea (2008), 'Temasek – Un fondo sovrano o piuttosto una reincarnazione dell'IRI nello Stretto di Malacca?', *Osservatorio Monetario*, 3, forthcoming.

IMF (2007), *Global Financial Stability Report*, Washington, DC, April.

IMF (2008), *Sovereign Wealth Funds – A Work Agenda*, Washington, DC, February.

Institutional Investor (2008), 'CIC Emerges: China's New Fund Sets High Bar on Foreign Mandates', February.

Jen, Stephen (2007a), 'How Big Could Sovereign Wealth Funds Be by 2015?,' Briefing Note, Morgan Stanley Global Research, London, 3 March.

Jen, Stephen (2007b), 'Russia: the Newest Member of the "SWF Club"', Briefing Note, Morgan Stanley Global Research, London, 26 April.

24 These countries are, incidentally, in the United States' sphere of influence.

Jen, Stephen (2007c), 'The Definition of a Sovereign Wealth Fund', Briefing Note, Morgan Stanley Global Research, London, 25 October.

Kimmitt, Robert M. (2008), 'Public Footprints in Private Markets: Sovereign Wealth Funds and the World Economy', *Foreign Affairs*, 87 (1), January–February, 119–30.

Lyons, Gerard (2007), *State Capitalism: The Rise of Sovereign Wealth Funds*, Standard Chartered Global Research, London, 15 October.

Newton, Alastair (2008), *The Politics of Sovereign Wealth: An Overview* (London: Lehman Brothers International).

Rozanov, Andrew (2008), 'A Liability-based Approach to Sovereign Wealth', *Central Banking Journal*, 18 (3), 38–42.

State Street Corporation (2008), *Sovereign Wealth Funds. Assessing the Impact*, Vision, 3 (2) (Boston, MA: State Street Corporation, July).

US Treasury (2007), 'Remarks by Acting Under Secretary for International Affairs Clay Lowery on Sovereign Wealth Funds and the International Financial System', press release, 21 June, San Francisco, http://www.treas.gov/press/releases/hp471.htm.

12 The GCC: transforming oil wealth into financial portfolios

Stephen L. Jen

Introduction

Sovereign wealth funds are the newest and one of the most powerful categories of investor. They are already large in size (close to $3 trillion in assets under management), and they will probably surpass the world's total holdings of official foreign reserves in the next five years.[1] They could potentially grow to about $12 trillion by 2015.[2] Currently, the countries exporting oil and gas control two-thirds of the assets managed by SWFs; Asian countries account for the rest. The future evolution of the 'oil-based' SWFs, in terms of both the size and the balance of their portfolios, will have important implications for the world's risky asset prices.

This chapter makes two points. First, to maximize their investment returns, the members of the Gulf Cooperation Council should aggressively accumulate financial wealth through their SWFs. Based on experience since 1985, vigorously converting wealth underground (oil) into wealth above ground (financial assets or physical assets) could, subject to production constraints, have helped the GCC countries to accumulate total wealth up to three times faster than leaving the oil underground. In addition, this higher investment return would have been accompanied by lower volatility.

Secondly, fully investing the capital by SWFs has powerful implications for the financial markets. Specifically, the emergence of SWFs should, all else being equal, favour equities over bonds. In terms of geographical area, SWFs are likely to be positive for emerging-market (EM) states, at the expense of both dollar and euro assets. The yen and yen assets may also be major beneficiaries. Lastly, SWFs will probably be active in the alternative investments market and exert considerable influence in that relatively less liquid sector.

1 The world's official foreign reserves stood at some $7 trillion as of Q1 2008.
2 Stephen L. Jen (2007), 'How Big Could Sovereign Wealth Funds be by 2015?', Morgan Stanley.

GCC oil reserves: their value and best use

The six members of the GCC (Bahrain, Kuwait, Oman, Qatar, Saudi Arabia and the United Arab Emirates) have close to 500 billion barrels of proven oil reserves. At today's market price, this is worth more than $70 trillion.[3] When its proven natural gas reserves are taken into account too, the total underground wealth of the GCC easily exceeds $75 trillion. At the same time, the financial assets of the sovereign wealth funds of the GCC countries total 'only' around $1.5 trillion, which may have been invested 25:45:30 in bonds, equities and alternative investments. In addition, there are about $80 billion worth of official foreign reserves held by the GCC central banks. Figure 12.1 shows the comparative size of these funds.

For the GCC countries, the ratio of wealth underground to above ground is about 50:1 – significantly above the ratio of 6:1 for Norway, which has been aggressively transforming its oil and natural gas wealth into financial wealth for the past decade.[4] Thus even though the GCC members' SWFs are already among the largest and oldest in the world, they are, in view of the size of their proven oil reserves, still relatively 'young' in the oil-to-financial-assets transformation process. For this reason, they should grow substantially larger over time.

Essentially, the GCC states are faced with the choice of, on the one hand, leaving the oil underground and waiting for it to appreciate in value or, on the other hand, extracting it, selling it and converting it into financial wealth. Extracting and selling their reserves of crude is not the same as 'spending' their wealth; it is instead a transformation of one form of asset holdings to another. The objective question, therefore, rests on the financial benefits and disadvantages of doing so.

From a long-term perspective, returns on equities have far outstripped returns on bonds, money markets and, importantly, unproduced oil. Even though oil prices in the coming years may continue to be squeezed higher, there is considerably greater volatility associated with oil prices than with equity prices. Figure 12.2 shows the cumulative nominal investment returns on various assets since 1985. As can be seen, the performances of these asset classes are extraordinarily diverse. Since 1985, global real estate and global equities have been the best performers, while oil and non-energy commodities have been laggards. If one had invested 100 Special

3 In comparison, the total market capitalization of publicly traded equities in the world is about $45 trillion.

4 Knut Kjaer, 'From Oil to Equities', speech delivered in November 2006. Mr Kjaer is the CEO of Norges Bank Investment Management (NBIM).

Figure 12.1: The wealth of the GCC states, total, oil and by investment, 2007

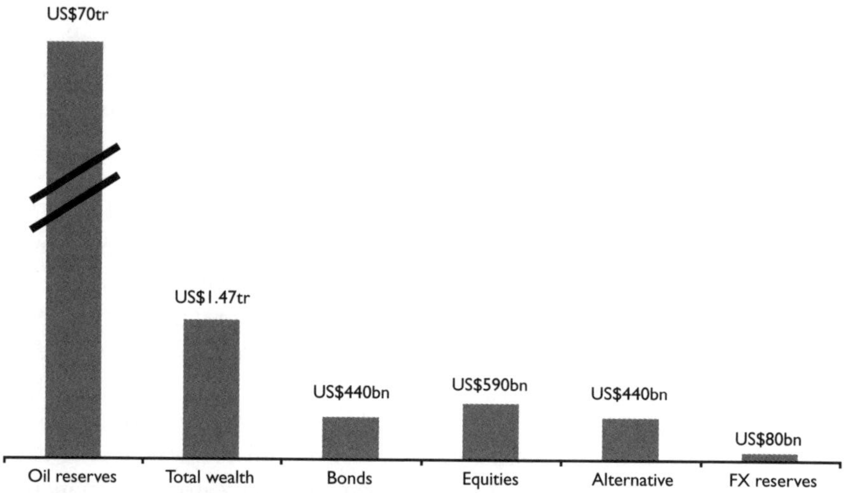

Sources: British Petroleum and Morgan Stanley Research.

Drawing Rights (SDR)[5] in each class of asset in 1985, the investment would now be worth SDR802 for global real estate, SDR635 for energy instruments, SDR546 for global equities, SDR441 for global bonds, SDR293 for non-energy commodities and only SDR227 for crude oil.[6]

Although past performance does not guarantee future performance, equities are likely to outperform oil in the next 25 years, even if, for a while, strong global demand for oil keeps oil prices elevated and undermines equities.[7] The justification for the GCC countries to convert wealth in the form of oil to 'higher-octane' assets such as equities makes much financial sense from the perspective of expected returns.

That the performances of various asset classes can be so diverse should not be news. What is important to the GCC members' sovereign wealth

5 SDRs are international reserve assets created by the IMF, useful for comparison over several years in a 'currency-neutral' manner.

6 These are quarterly data as of end-Q1 008. Since then, oil has risen from around US$100 to US$145 a barrel, and the cumulative return on physical crude oil should be commensurately higher in this chart. At the same time, the cumulative returns on properties and global equities have retreated.

7 There are opposing forces acting on the relative returns on equities and crude oil. On the one hand, strong global demand growth for oil may weigh on potential growth in the world and hurt company margins. Thus equities could be undermined by rising oil prices. On the other hand, high petrodollar receipts enjoyed by oil exporters need to be invested somehow. This chapter is focused on the latter effect, assuming that oil demand destruction will eventually re-equilibrate the oil market, albeit at higher oil prices. In the long run, the latter force is likely to dominate the former, though one could argue it is the former force that contributed to the current bear equity markets.

Figure 12.2: Nominal (SDR) investment returns on classes of asset since 1985

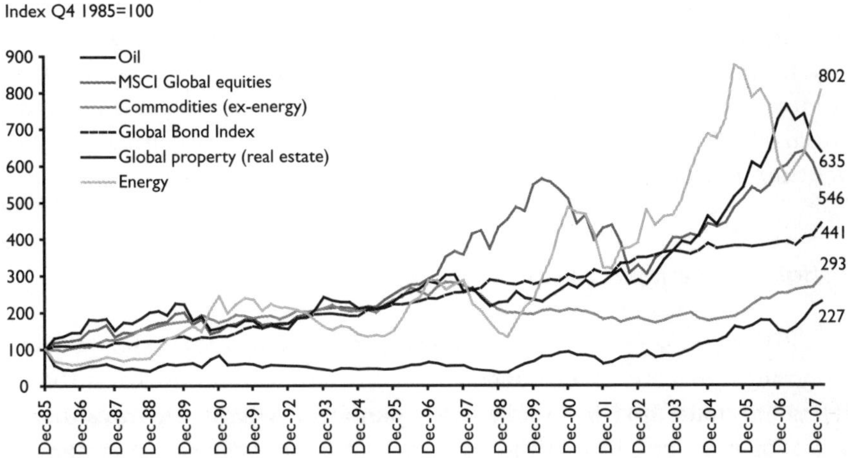

Sources: Haver, GPR Research, Knut Kjaer of the Norges Bank and Morgan Stanley.

Figure 12.3: The efficient frontier confronted by GCC sovereign wealth funds, 1987–97

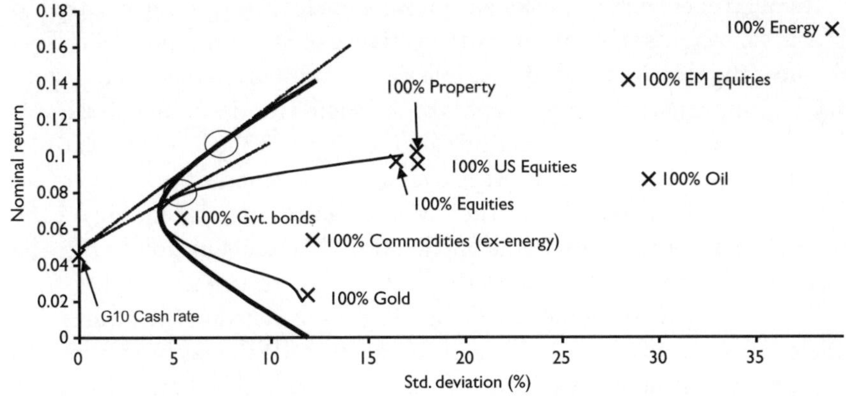

Source: Morgan Stanley Research.

funds, and to investors in general, is not only the investment return but also the associated risk of various investments. Figure 12.3 shows a scatter chart of the return–risk profiles of various asset classes. As can be seen, equities have had a far superior track record in terms of expected returns, and they have also had a much better risk profile.[8]

8 The average annual return for crude oil is higher in this figure mainly because oil prices collapsed in the mid-1980s. To bring into sharp relief the point about oil having higher volatility, data from 1987 to 2007 were used.

In sum, over the past generation, oil has been a relatively low-return but high-volatility asset while equities have been a high-return and high-volatility asset.[9] Thus, from a purely financial perspective, it makes more sense for the GCC countries vigorously to convert oil (underground wealth) into financial assets (above-ground wealth). Given that the value of their proven oil reserves is $70 trillion, their SWFs could grow substantially larger over time, with material implications for the financial markets in general.

Portfolio allocation for GCC sovereign wealth funds

The GCC states' sovereign wealth funds, and SWFs in general, should have important implications for financial markets. But in order to assess these effects one must first form a general opinion on what their investment portfolios may look like. Although different SWFs will almost certainly have different preferences and therefore different investment portfolios, collectively they have some unique traits relative to official reserve portfolios and pension fund portfolios that can help us to understand their strategies.[10]

To construct Figure 12.3, calculations were made for each level of expected return the weights that minimize the variance of the entire portfolio. This produces the 'envelopes' of the feasible asset combinations shown in Figure 12.2. The upper part of the envelope is the efficient frontier, which illustrates the combinations of assets maximizing return given the level of volatility. The riskless cash rate (G-10 average over 3 months) marks the intercept on the vertical axis. Theoretically, the investor can choose, depending on the preferred risk profile, any point on this line. The tangent point with the portfolio efficient frontier shows the highest risk–return trade-off.[11]

There are two schedules in Figure 12.3. One schedule illustrates the efficient frontier of a long-only portfolio, as most SWFs may be confined to long-only investments. A second efficient frontier is also shown, assuming that some SWFs may outsource to fund managers, who can have a short

9 In the coming years, oil prices are likely to remain on a structural uptrend. However, it is likely that equities will continue to outperform them. In terms of Figure 12.3, the bottom part of the efficient frontier curve could shift up, reflecting a higher expected return on oil.

10 Among these traits are a 'liquidity premium' associated with a longer investment horizon and greater risk tolerance.

11 I assume that the typical SWF invests in oil, equities (MSCI Global), bonds (Global Government Bond Index II, Merrill Lynch), non-energy commodities (Goldman Sachs Non Energy Commodities Index) and global property (GPR General Property Securities Index Global). I also assume that these investments are all denominated in Special Drawing Rights, so that implicitly the SWF behaves like global investors, which diversify their holdings across G-4 currencies. On average, the currency composition of their portfolios is 42% in dollars, 32% in euros, 15% in yen and 12% in pounds sterling.

(i.e., a net sell) position on these assets. The flexibility of being able to short/sell assets clearly enhances the investment return at all levels of risk. Thus the relevant portion of the efficient frontier of the second schedule is higher than that of the first.

In addition to the two efficient frontiers, the figure also shows where the portfolios would sit in this return–risk space if 100% of the portfolio were invested in any one asset class. In terms of the efficient frontier of the array of assets available to the GCC countries, energy instruments, equities and bonds could form the constellation described in Figure 12.3, with unproduced oil being an underperformer with high risk. Bonds act as a counterweight to equities, helping to achieve the risk–reward balance that is preferred by the owner of the portfolio. It is possible that the GCC countries may have a 30:40:30 split between bonds, equities and alternative investments, which are the broad portfolio composition of large, established pension funds. If this assumption on the portfolio weighting is incorrect, the chances are that their exposure to bonds may be less than 30% and that their exposure to alternative investments may be more than 30%. In any case, the optimal portfolio, from a financial perspective, is one that has a high exposure to equities.

In short, the GCC countries' portfolios will diversify from the '100% oil' point in Figure 12.3 while Asian exporters' SWFs will diversify their assets from the '100% sovereign bonds' point. In other words, the GCC countries have embarked on a multi-generational diversification from oil while Asia will diversify from the dollar and US Treasury bills.

The implications of SWFs for financial markets

There are several important implications of sovereign wealth funds for financial markets. First, the GCC states' SWFs should favour equities over bonds. As capital is diverted from official reserves into SWFs, risky assets in general and equities in particular should be supported, at the expense of sovereign bonds. All else being equal, the mere formation of SWFs should lead to a 40 basis-point (a basis point is one-hundredth of a percent) rise in long-term sovereign bond yield and a 10% rise in the price-to-earnings ratio of global equities.[12] These are very conservative estimates of their likely impact on bonds and equities. With $50 trillion of wealth underground, the GCCs could be an immense source of support for equities. The market capitalization of the world's equity markets is currently also some

12 S. Jen and D. Miles (2007), 'Sovereign Wealth Funds and Bond and Equity Prices', Morgan Stanley.

Table 12.1: Implications of SWF investment flows for global financial markets

	Currency composition of official reserves (%)		*Market capitalization (% of the world total)*			*25:45:30 Model Portfolio*	*Potential FX flows ($)*
Currency	*World*	*Developing*	*Bonds*	*Equities*	*Alternative*		
	[1]	[2]	[3]	[4]	[5]	[6]	[7]
Dollar	64.8	60.5	48.3	40.0	29.0	**43.0**	−526
Euro	25.6	28.6	22.0	18.3	24.0	**18.3**	−309
Pound sterling	4.7	5.9	2.1	8.5	5.0	**8.5**	78
Yen	2.8	2.6	8.6	12.8	11.0	**12.8**	306
Other	2.1	2.4	19.0	20.4	31.0	**17.4**	451

[1] The currency weights from the IMF's COFER database for the world's reserves.
[2] The currency weights for the developing countries sub-category.
[3] The weighted average market capitalization shares of fixed-income instruments.
[4] The global market share of equities, in terms of market capitalization.
[5] I assume that GDP weights should dictate the broad weights of alternative investments.
[6] These are the blended currency weights assuming a 25:45:30 asset allocation split between bonds, equities, and alternative investments.
[7] Potential FX flows (billions of dollars) associated with portfolio rebalancing, based on $3 trillion in assets under management.
Source: Haver, Datastream, and Morgan Stanley Research.

$50 trillion. This gives some perspective on the likely impact over time of the GCC's oil reserves on risky global asset prices. In essence, owing to the presence of SWFs, global equities in the medium term will probably go up enthusiastically and down grudgingly.

Secondly, full investment of SWFs' capital could hurt both the dollar and the euro and help the currencies of emerging-market states. In many ways, SWFs mark a watershed in financial globalization. These new reservoirs of capital signify the rise of emerging powers, and they will probably be diverted from developed markets into developing markets, with clear implications for currencies. Thus there is likely to be a good deal of emerging market-to-emerging market, or 'South-to-South', investment flows through the SWFs.[13] It is likely that both the dollar and the euro will be sold by SWFs and that many of the EM currencies, as well as the yen and the pound sterling, will be bought.

13 To the extent that some EM central banks maintain exchange rate objectives, the prospective inflows to them from other EM economies will be absorbed in official reserves, which in turn could perpetuate this investment cycle in the EM space. Such a 'multiplier' effect could create 'indigestion' in capital flows.

Table 12.1 illustrates these assumptions. Columns [1] and [2] indicate the currency composition of the world's reserves and the reserve holdings of the world's developing countries. Dollar, euro and pound sterling assets account for approximately 95% of the world's reserve holdings, and central banks have collectively been moving out of dollars and into the other two currencies.[14] On the basis of the available data on the market capitalizations of various bond and equity markets in the world, the percentage share of the bond and equity markets could be broken down into different currencies (columns [3] and [4]). For the world's market shares of 'alternative investments', which include real estate, infrastructure, private equity, commodities and hedge funds, they are assumed to be broadly in line with countries' GDP shares as a percentage of the world's GDP (column [5]). SWFs are likely to adopt, in the long run, a model portfolio that consists of 25% in bonds, 45% in equities and 30% in alternative assets.[15] Using this benchmark, I computed the 'benchmark' currency exposure of SWFs (column [6]): 43% in dollars, 18% in euros, 17% in non-G-4 (mostly EM) currencies, 13% in yen and 9% in pounds sterling. Comparing the currency shares indicated in column [2] to those in column [6], one can see that the portfolio which many SWFs will eventually adopt, however long that process may take, will probably have a very different currency composition from the currency composition of reserve assets. Based on the SWFs' total assets under management of $3 trillion, a full deployment of their capital in line with the long-term benchmark currencies implies large sales of dollars and euros and sizeable purchases of EM currencies and yen.

Thirdly, besides being a key player in bond and equity markets, SWFs will probably have considerable exposure to 'alternative investments', which include infrastructure, private equity, real estate, real estate debt, commodities and hedge funds. (As mentioned above, my guess is that many SWFs could have a long-term model portfolio of 25% in bonds, 45% in equities and 30% in alternative investments.) Although bond and equity markets are very liquid, many alternative investments may not be. Given the long investment horizon of most SWFs, they enjoy a 'liquidity premium' that allows them to be active in these relatively illiquid markets

14 This trend is clear from the IMF's COFER data. However, it should be pointed out that much of this diversification is 'passive diversification', whereby central banks only partially accommodate the movements in exchange rates by buying less of the appreciating currency. In any case, the *value* of the weighting on euros has risen, even though the *quantity* of euros bought has actually declined.

15 The average portfolio allocation for large, established pension funds has, as pointed out earlier, a 30:40:30 split between bonds, equities and alternative investments. However, in most countries with SWFs the official foreign reserves are also large. This is why I have assumed that the SWFs in these countries are likely to have a substantially lower exposure to bonds and a greater focus on asset classes with high expected returns, although with a higher market volatility.

in which traditional real-money investors cannot be. SWFs will, as a result, be a dominant force in the alternative investment markets.

SWFs may be especially interested in four sectors: high-tech, financials, resources and infrastructure. High-tech and resources are two ends of the value-added chain that yield strategic advantages to countries with SWFs. Financials are attractive in view of their ability to capture the rise of wealth in general, and the growth of the middle class in particular, in the globalization process. Infrastructure is essentially a long-duration fixed-income asset with a high yield. If this assumption is correct, there will be large capital flows into these four sectors. Already, we have witnessed numerous high-profile acquisitions by SWFs of distressed financial institutions in the West. This should not come as a surprise, as these highly desirable assets are now being offered at fire-sale prices, and political resistance to these acquisitions is weak, at least for the time being, as those financial institutions are in a compromised position. In any case, the key point here is that given SWFs' size and the relatively low liquidity of the alternative markets, their transactions are likely to attract much public attention, which may affect the sentiment of private investors and policy-makers.

Infrastructural spending

The total population of the GCC countries is a relatively modest 36 million, with Saudi Arabia accounting for 24 million. Infrastructural spending (physical, educational and otherwise), to facilitate the development of the non-oil sector and to push the GCC up the value-added ladder, is essential. Singapore and Switzerland are good models for emulation: these economies with relatively small populations have managed to punch above their weight by being more competitive and productive. The GCC states have a good opportunity to engineer such a great leap forward, with the help of oil and SWF earnings. Clearly, GCC policy-makers will need to come to a view on the ideal level of infrastructural spending, relative to the size of investment in financial assets, through SWFs.[16]

16 Incidentally, Russia faces precisely the same problem. The key difference between the GCC countries' SWFs and Russia's National Welfare Fund (NWF) is that Russia's oil revenues are considerably more modest relative to its infrastructural spending needs. In some scenarios, it is conceivable that the NWF could be depleted within the next decade.

Conclusion

There are compelling reasons for the members of the GCC to continue to accumulate wealth through their SWFs. With $50 trillion in oil wealth underground to be converted into financial wealth, their current SWF holdings of $1.5 trillion of financial wealth reflect a fraction of this multi-generational oil-to-equities transformation. Further, the willingness and ability of SWFs to invest in a broader set of assets than sovereign bonds opens up interesting opportunities for them and has implications for various markets that matter to investors. The full deployment of capital through SWFs should 1) favour equities over bonds, 2) favour non-G-3 assets and currencies over those in G-3, and 3) have great influence in the alternative investment sector.

Appendix 12.1: The size of the SWFs

The assets under management by SWFs now total more than $3 trillion (see Table 12A.1). Given the elevated oil prices and buoyant exports from Asia, most of the funds listed in this table are expected to grow rapidly.

Three funds are worth highlighting. First, although it may take some time for the China Investment Corporation (CIC) to be fully set up and functional, this SWF is likely to become the largest in the world in several years' time. China is accumulating foreign reserves at a rate of $350 billion–$400 billion a year from what is already considered to be an excessive stock of foreign exchange reserves. Additional transfers from the People's Bank of China to CIC are more probable than not.

Secondly, Russia's SWF, with $32 billion, became operational on 1 February 2008. If unmolested by the fiscal authorities, it could grow to $600 billion in 10 years' time. Thirdly, and perhaps most importantly, Japan is contemplating establishing its own SWF. I believe that the arguments in favour of an SWF in Japan are very compelling and that the objections from the Ministry of Finance so far will eventually be overcome. What makes Japan's prospective SWF important is its size: it will probably be drawn from the country's excess official foreign reserves, which could total $700 billion, and also the Government Pension Investment Fund, which now has $1.5 trillion under management. Moreover, part of the Japanese government's real estate holdings (it owns 25% of the country's land) may be securitized and put to work, managed under the SWF.

The likely trajectory of the SWFs over the next decade can also be computed, on the basis of assumptions on how current account balances

GCC sovereign wealth funds

Table 12A.1: The assets of sovereign wealth funds

Country	*Fund name*	*Assets (US$m)*	*Inception year*	*Source of funds*
Total		**3,023,116**		
UAE	ADIA[1]	875,000	1976	Oil
Saudi Arabia	Saudi Arabian funds of various types[1]	400,000	N/A	Oil
Norway	Government Pension Fund – Global	380,000	1996	Oil
Singapore	GIC[1]	330,000	1981	Other
Kuwait	Reserve Fund for Future Generations	250,000	1953	Oil
China	CIC, including Central Hueijin Co.[2]	200,000	2007	Other
Singapore	Temasek Holdings[1]	159,210	1974	Other
Libya	Oil Reserve Fund	70,000	2005	Oil
Qatar	Qatar Investment Authority	60,000	N/A	Oil, gas
Algeria	Fond de régulation des recettes	42,600	2000	Oil
US (Alaska)	Permanent Reserve Fund	39,800	1976	Oil
Russia	National Wealth Fund	32,000	2003	Oil
Brunei	Brunei Investment Authority	30,000	1983	Oil
Malaysia	Khazanah Nasional BHD	25,700	1993	Other
Rep. of Korea	Korea Investment Corporation	20,000	2006	Other
Kazakhstan	National Fund	21,500	2000	Oil, gas
Canada	Alberta Heritage TF	16,600	1976	Oil
Chile	New SWFs based on the Copper Fund[3]	15,500	1985	Copper
ROC (Taiwan)	National Stabilization Fund	15,000	N/A	Other
Iran	Oil Stabilization Fund	15,000	1999	Oil
Nigeria	Excess Crude Account	11,000	2003	Oil
Botswana	Pula Fund	6,900	1966	Diamonds
Oman	State General RF	2,000	1980	Oil, gas
Azerbaijan	State Oil Fund	3,340	1999	Oil
Venezuela	FIEM	756	1998	Oil
Trinidad & Tob.	Revenue SF	460	2000	Oil
Kiribati	Revenue Equalization Fund	400	1956	Phosphates
Uganda	Poverty Action Fund	350	1998	Aid
	Oil- & gas-related funds	2,250,056		
	Non-oil-related funds	773,060		

Notes:

1 My guesstimates as of May 2008.

2 Launched in September 2007. Central Huijin will have $130 billion on its balance sheet.

3 Reserve Pension Fund (FRP), Economic and Social Stabilization Fund (ESSF) and Economic Stabilization Fund (FEES).

Source: various country sources and Morgan Stanley Research.

Figure 12A.1: The potential worth of SWFs by 2015

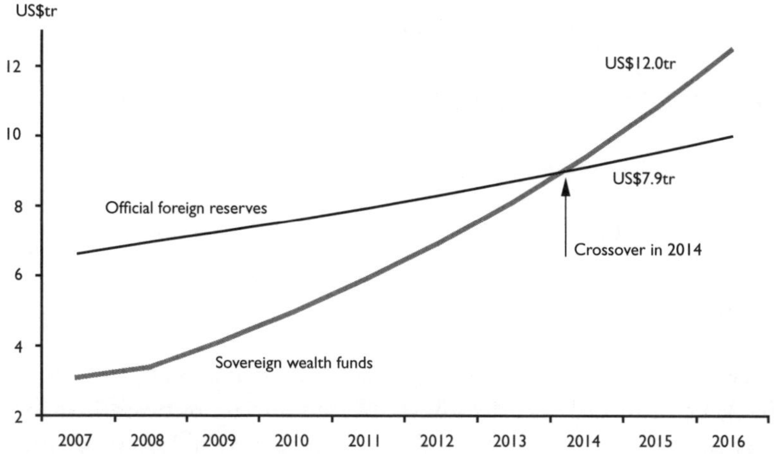

Source: Morgan Stanley Research.

will evolve in the coming years in these countries. Figure 12A.1 shows that with some reasonable assumptions, total assets under management by SWFs could reach $12 trillion by 2015. Official foreign reserves are now close to $6 trillion, about double the value of all SWFs, but the SWFs could surpass the world's reserves in value as soon as 2011.

13 Financial markets under attack? Gulf investors and the rise of economic patriotism in the West*

Andrea Goldstein and Fabio Scacciavillani

Introduction

The massive current account surpluses accumulated by the GCC countries in the wake of record oil prices have spurred intense outward investment activity carried out through a number of vehicles, notably, but not limited to, those commonly defined as sovereign wealth funds. These funds, which until recently attracted little attention except from a few specialized niches in the financial markets, have come to prominence over the past two years owing to a few high-profile acquisitions and because their sheer size has grown dramatically. In fact, their increasing sophistication is shaping some noteworthy trends in global financial markets. Since the start of the subprime crisis in mid-2007, they have provided substantial liquidity to sustain stock valuation while behaving as stable investors focused more on long-term results than on short-term gains.

In this chapter, we first provide an overview of the SWFs from GCC countries and then sketch the contours and motivations of their international activities. We examine three cases that have attracted international attention and generated controversy: the DP World takeover of the UK's Peninsular and Oriental Steam Navigation Company (P&O), the investments by Qatar and Dubai in European stock exchanges and the failed acquisition of Sainsbury's, the UK retailer, by the Qatar Investment Authority (QIA). Finally, we link these episodes to the debate in OECD countries regarding FDI, national security and market transparency.

* The views and opinions expressed in this chapter must be attributed solely to the authors, as they might not coincide with those of the OECD, the Dubai International Financial Centre and/or their respective governments. We thank the editors and an anonymous reviewer for most helpful comments and suggestions.

SWFs: an overview

Sovereign wealth funds have been in operation for some time, at least since 1956, when an investment vehicle was created in the Gilbert Islands to manage the proceeds from the sale of phosphates.[1] The first sovereign country to form an entity entrusted with the management of its export revenues was Kuwait. In 1960, the General Reserve was launched, followed in 1973 by the Future Generations Fund, endowed with 50% of the General Reserve and also 10% of the yearly budget surplus. In 1982, the Kuwaiti government decided to consolidate all the assets of the Ministry of Finance, as well as the General Reserve and the Future Generations Fund, under the Kuwait Investment Authority. The experience of Kuwait inspired others. Among high-income economies, Singapore and Norway have been pioneers in this area, and today a number of large countries and regions (prominent among which are South Korea, Australia, Russia, China, Alberta and Alaska) have accumulated sizeable assets in SWFs. Table 13.1 gives a list of the major SWFs.[2] Also, many developing countries, including Botswana, Chile, Trinidad and Tobago and Uganda, have set up sovereign investment vehicles.

Nonetheless, SWFs remain a distinctively Gulf phenomenon. The Emirate of Abu Dhabi instituted the Abu Dhabi Investment Authority in 1976, and today it holds (according to some estimates) almost $900 billion. Oman created the State General Stabilization Fund in 1980. Its worth today is $8 billion. Another emirate in the UAE, Dubai, controls various funds among which the most active is Dubai International Capital, founded in 2004 with assets estimated at $12 billion. The Dubai Group (established in 2000 and with $7 billion under management) and Isthitmar (owned by Dubai World, it began in 2003 and manages $7 billion) act on behalf of the ruling family and its associates. The Qatari government instituted the Qatar Investment Authority in 2005. Saudi Arabia already has many investment vehicles focusing on domestic projects, such as the Saudi Arabia Government Investment Company, and the government reportedly was considering the creation of a fund to consolidate and manage foreign investments, which could easily become the largest in the world. However, the latest news has cooled down these expectations, as the Saudi authorities have announced that, at least initially, their fund will be endowed with

1 Because the Gilbert Islands were a British colony at that time, the fund could not technically be described as 'sovereign'. Today it is worth about half a billion dollars.

2 The list is not exhaustive, as some countries do not fully disclose the assets managed by their investment vehicles. In addition to SWFs, some countries have launched other public entities that manage investments in specific sectors. For example, in Qatar, Barwa and Qatar Diar operate in real estate worldwide. Dubai Port focuses on transport facilities and logistics.

Table 13.1: The world's largest sovereign wealth funds

Country	*Fund name*	*Assets (in US$ billion)*	*Inception year*	*Origin*	*Linaburg-Maduell Transparency Index*
UAE – Abu Dhabi	Abu Dhabi Investment Authority	875	1976	Oil	3
Norway	Government Pension Fund – Global	396.5	1990	Oil	10
Saudi Arabia	SAMA Foreign Holdings	365.2	n/a	Oil	2
Singapore	Government of Singapore Investment Corporation	330	1981	Non-commodity	6
China	SAFE Investment Company	311.6**		Non-commodity	2
Kuwait	Kuwait Investment Authority	264.4	1953	Oil	6
China	China Investment Corporation	200	2007	Non-commodity	1
China – HK	Hong Kong Monetary Authority Invest. Portfolio	173	1998	Non-commodity	7
Russia	National Welfare Fund	162.5*	2008	Oil	5
Singapore	Temasek Holdings	159	1974	Non-commodity	8
China	National Social Security Fund	74	2000	Non-commodity	5
Qatar	Qatar Investment Authority	60	2003	Oil	5
Australia	Australian Future Fund	58.5	2004	Non-commodity	9
Libya	Libyan Investment Authority	50	2006	Oil	2
Algeria	Revenue Regulation Fund	47	2000	Oil	1
UAE – Dubai	Investment Corporation of Dubai	X	2006	Oil	4
UAE – Federal	Emirates Investment Authority	X	2007	Oil	1

Country	*Fund name*	*Assets (in US$ billion)*	*Inception year*	*Origin*	*Linaburg-Maduell Transparency Index*
US – Alaska	Alaska Permanent Fund	39.8	1976	Oil	10
Ireland	National Pensions Reserve Fund	30.8	2001	Non-commodity	8
Brunei	Brunei Investment Agency	30	1983	Oil	1
South Korea	Korea Investment Corporation	30	2005	Non-commodity	9
Malaysia	Khazanah Nasional	25.7	1993	Non-commodity	4
Kazakhstan	Kazakhstan National Fund	21.5	2000	oil	2
Canada	Alberta's Heritage Fund	16.6	1976	Oil	9
US – New Mexico	New Mexico State Investment Office Trust	16	1958	Non-commodity	9
Chile	Social and Economic Stabilization Fund	15.5	1985	Copper	1
Taiwan	National Stabilization Fund	15	2000	Non-commodity	1
New Zealand	New Zealand Superannuation Fund	13.8	2003	Non-commodity	10
Iran	Oil Stabilization Fund	12.9	1999	Oil	1
Nigeria	Excess Crude Account	11	2004	Oil	1
Bahrain	Mumtalakat Holding Company	10	2006	Oil	6
UAE - Abu Dhabi	Mubadala Development Company	10	2002	Oil	6
Oman	State General Reserve Fund	8.0	1980	Oil & gas	1
Botswana	Pula Fund	6.9	1966	Diamonds & minerals	1
Saudi Arabia	Public Investment Fund	5.3	2008	Oil	3

Country	Fund name	Assets (in US$ billion)	Inception year	Origin	Linaburg-Maduell Transparency Index
China	China-Africa Development Fund	5	2007	Non-commodity	4
US Wyoming	Permanent Wyoming Mineral Trust Fund	3.9	1974	Minerals	8
Azerbaijan	State Oil Fund	5.0	1999	Oil	9
US – Alabama	Alabama Trust Fund	3.1	1986	Gas	6
East Timor	Timor-Leste Petroleum Fund	3.0	2005	Oil & gas	6
Vietnam	State Capital Investment Corporation	2.1	2006	Non-commodity	4
UAE – RAK	Ras Al Khaimah Investment Authority	1.2	2005	Oil	3
Venezuela	FIEM	0.8	1998	Oil	1
Trinidad & Tobago	Heritage and Stabilization Fund	0.5	2000	Oil	5
Kiribati	Revenue Equalization Reserve Fund	0.4	1956	Phosphates	1
Mauritania	National Fund for Hydrocarbon Reserves	0.3	2006	Oil & gas	1
Angola	Reserve Fund for Oil	0.2	2007	Oil	1
	Total oil- & gas-related	2,381			
	Total other	1,473			
	TOTAL	3,854			

* This includes the oil stabilization fund of Russia. **This number is a best-guess estimation. ***All figures quoted are from official sources, or, where the institutions concerned do not issue statistics of their assets, from other publicly available sources. Some of these figures are best estimates as market values change day to day.

Source: SWF Institute.

only $3.4 billion. This compares with foreign assets held by Saudi sovereign entities estimated at between $300 billion and $500 billion. Furthermore, the Saudi government has expressed the intention to open this fund to international institutional investors, a novel approach that could actually represent a sensible way to allay concern raised in the West about transparency and undue influence. In essence, this Saudi fund would be more of an investment company than an SWF.

The combined wealth managed by the SWFs is expected to grow at 15% per annum until 2015, reaching $10 trillion. For many countries, especially in the Arabian Peninsula, this means that they will increasingly become asset-based rather than commodity-based economies, because the revenues from foreign assets will exceed their commodity revenues. As an example, for Abu Dhabi variations in world interest rates matter more than the price of oil.

Macroeconomic imbalances: their financial market repercussions

The controversy sparked by the recent spate of acquisitions by SWFs, many of them based in the Gulf, can be seen through a different lens. The starting point is to disentangle the specious arguments, tinged with populist overtones, from the genuine worries about financial markets' soundness.

In developed economies, financial markets are viewed by the general public, by policy-makers, by banks and by most economists as a place where private investors trade securities in the pursuit of profits. Accordingly, governments' participation in these markets is limited to the issuance of public debt (through intermediaries) and occasionally the sale of state-owned companies. In essence, governments are positioned on the sell side. Central banks routinely carry out open market operations and, more rarely, foreign exchange interventions, but these are monetary policy tools, not intended to turn a profit. It is therefore awkward to realize that public entities are engaged in financial transactions as if they were private entities. Is this an aberration or should it be considered a legitimate course of action, and under what conditions?

To answer these questions and to put into proper perspective the activities of SWFs we follow two intertwined lines of analysis: 1) the macroeconomics of current account surplus management (which provides a rationale for the setting up of SWFs); and 2) the political sensitivities aroused by state-owned entities acquiring a controlling stake in privately owned large foreign companies.

The macroeconomics of current account surpluses

Current account surpluses must be invested abroad to enable a country with a structural surplus to build up a stock of foreign assets. These investments, according to the prevailing view (and to historical experience), are carried out primarily by the private sector and, to a much lesser extent, by the public sector through the central bank. Crucially, central bank reserves are maintained in low-risk assets in order to ensure that domestic economic agents have access to foreign currency, needed for their business, travel or portfolio choices. Central banks are not supposed to engage in active asset management.

This situation exists because in developed economies, exporters (and asset-managers) are predominantly private companies and the government sector provides public (non-tradable) goods. But in the case of the GCC countries, a large share of their economy is dominated by the public sector, which owns and manages the stock of natural resources and therefore accumulates most of its revenues. Furthermore, economic theory tends to neglect the influence on asset prices of foreign investment activities because traditional models assert that current account imbalances are temporary, as real exchange rate corrections and/or productivity adjustments reduce the competitive advantage of net exporters. Also, the magnitude of these surpluses is deemed to be small relative to the stock of outstanding financial assets, especially in developed countries. Finally, it is presumed (somewhat unrealistically) that the bulk of these net foreign assets are held in almost riskless government securities and do not significantly affect other asset prices.

From the mid-1990s, these assumptions looked increasingly simplistic, as the US continued to run a widening current account deficit and countries such as China and Japan (together with other Asian countries and, to a lesser extent, Germany) maintained large permanent current account surpluses. Moreover, when energy and commodity prices increased after the invasion of Iraq, the GCC countries (and other commodity exporters) saw their surpluses skyrocket. These surpluses clearly are not temporary, and we should wake up to this new reality.[3] It was estimated by the Institute of International Finance that between 2002 and 2006, the GCC countries accumulated $1.5 trillion, twice as much as in the previous five years. As a matter of comparison, this figure is equivalent to about 10% of the domestic market capitalization of the New York Stock Exchange

3 Another way to look at this phenomenon is to consider the increase in energy prices as a tax levied on consumers by a government (albeit a foreign one). Part of the 'tax' receipts will be spent on providing public goods or infrastructure and the rest will increase government savings, which in turn will be invested in the private sector (domestic or foreign).

at the end of 2007, more than one-third of the Tokyo Stock Exchange, the Euronext exchanges and the NASDAQ, and it would have almost been sufficient to buy all the companies listed in the Deutsche Börse at the end of 2006. Obviously, not all the windfall has been invested abroad, but its magnitude has reached such a level that global financial markets are being seriously affected.

However, economists, policy-makers, financial institutions and the media have continued to view the world through the lenses of an outdated economic theory, valid perhaps for the 1960s but not for today's reality. Therefore the activities of the SWFs have often been misunderstood, little analysed and widely portrayed through specious arguments. In the next section we try to explain why SWFs, especially from small economies, are an unavoidable consequence of economic reality and what should be the most appropriate policies in this new environment.

The rationale for establishing SWFs

The basic question to address is why export revenues are not reinvested mostly in domestic projects. The answer differs greatly depending upon whether one has, say, Russia or Qatar in mind. In the former it is a symptom of broad institutional failure; in the latter it is a matter of objective constraints on development owing to the size of the domestic economy compared to the magnitude of export revenues. To be more specific, Russia is not a functioning market economy. The rule of law and even the basic protection of investors are, at best, patchy. Despite the desperate need of capital for infrastructure, manufacturing, raw materials extraction, etc., few viable investment opportunities exist. The private corporate sector, i.e. companies outside the stranglehold of national or local governments, plays a negligible economic role. As a consequence, the Russian government invests abroad those resources that would be more desirably used to lift the living standards of the population. Qatar, to the contrary, is a country of only 234,000 nationals[4] and limited territory, mostly barren. Its government has launched a massive programme of infrastructure building and structural transformation of the economy in areas such as financial services, tourism, transport services and petrochemicals. As a result, the size of the economy more than tripled in the seven years to 2007 when measured in nominal dollars. Investments represent more than 40% of its GDP, and new investments planned over the next few years are estimated at about three times its current GDP. Expatriates already make up about

4 The rest of the resident population, which is estimated at about one million, is made up of foreign workers and their families.

Table 13.2: Energy exports – values and shares of total exports

	Energy exports ($bn)			*Energy exports (% of total)*		
	1996	*2001*	*2005**	*1996*	*2001*	*2005**
Bahrain	3.2	3.9	8.0	67.3	70.3	79.4
Kuwait	14.9	15.0	40.5	95.5	92.4	94.6
Oman	5.9	10.5	15.9	80.3	83.3	84.9
Qatar	3.2	9.8	22.9	84.8	92.4	88.9
Saudi Arabia	54.3	59.9	163.3	89.4	88.0	89.6
UAE	18.4	24.1	47.4	49.4	49.8	48.2

* Estimates
Source: Gulf Organization for Industrial Consulting.

three-quarters of the resident population. Any further acceleration in this breakneck expansion activity would run into insurmountable bottlenecks – which are already evident in terms of housing scarcity, labour and raw materials shortages and infrastructure deficiencies – and exacerbate inflation, which already exceeds 13%.

Similar observations can be made of the UAE and, to a lesser extent, the other GCC countries. In essence, they are compelled to invest abroad a large portion of their export revenues because the size of their domestic economies, notwithstanding the enormous progress made so far, is limited. Stated differently, for small countries such as Qatar, the UAE and Kuwait, but also the likes of Norway and Singapore – which have already attained a high per capita income and face objective constraints in further expanding their domestic economies – it makes sense to transfer the wealth accumulated through exports (especially of non-renewable commodities) to future generations. A parallel motivation is diversification: if a shock hits its domestic economy, the country can be at least partly shielded. Large countries such as Russia or China would be better off if they channelled more of their export proceeds into their domestic economies after liberalizing their business environment and, to a lesser extent, all other GCC countries whose dependence on energy exports is extreme (Table 13.2).

To summarize the argument, small economies face the problem of the absorptive capacity of export revenues as determined by the size of their economy, their population and their territory. Large countries face the problem of absorptive capacity as determined by their institutional and legal set-up, which in turns results in lower productivity.

The Gulf countries' strategy for foreign investments

GCC member states have invested petrodollars in the West since the 1970s (see Table 13.3), generally without attracting much attention or criticism. These investments have been sizeable: in 2005, the net purchases of US mutual funds shares was $260.3 billion. In the same year, the total energy-related export revenues of the GCC countries reached $297.9 billion. If two-thirds of this money were reinvested abroad, it would be more than enough to sustain share prices across the globe. So the capital flowing from energy and, more generally, from commodity exporters (not only from the GCC) has contributed to reducing the volatility of the stock markets and has exerted downward pressure on long-term interest rates in recent years.

The international activity of Gulf investors in 2007 (see Table 13.4) and 2008 was due to the new opportunities that opened up in the aftermath of the subprime crisis. This was a major force underlying the resilience of not only mergers and acquisitions (M&A) markets but also stock exchanges in general. But overall it did not represent a change in the asset-management strategies of the SWFs.

Broadly speaking, actors, destinations and motivations can be classified in four clusters. First, obviously, there are higher returns through a diversified portfolio. For example, Kingdom Holding, a Saudi state-owned company that has been an active private equity firm since the 1980s, targets blue-chip shares and luxury hotels in developed countries, as well as emerging firms in developing countries, including in Africa. In Bahrain, Investcorp and Arcapita Bank use their private equity arms to purchase majority shares in companies in Europe and the United States. The Dubai government, through its private equity firms, has made some significant cross-border equity acquisitions, including the purchase of P&O through

Table 13.3: FDI from the GCC countries, 1981–2006 (US$m)

	1981–85	*1986–90*	*1991–95*	*1996–2000*	*2001–05*	*2006*
Bahrain	–1	25	1	141	661	980
Kuwait	72	451	0	–275	143	7,892
Oman	–0	2	345	0	115	247
Qatar	1	–2	9	14	126	379
Saudi Arabia	40	349	0	197	376	753
UAE	7	–4	0	246	1,515	2,316

Source: UNCTAD (2007), *World Investment Report*, http://www.unctad.org/Templates/Download.asp?docid=9156&lang=1&intItemID=3277.

Table 13.4: Top foreign equity acquisitions by GCC investors, 2007

Date	*Target*	*Acquirer*	*Value ($bn)*
21 May	GE Plastic (USA)	SABIC (Saudi Arabia)	11.6
13 Dec	5 Dow Chemical plastic divisions	Kuwait Petroleum	9.5
15 Nov	4.9% of Citigroup	Abu Dhabi Investment Authority (UAE)	7.5
16 Apr	3.1% of HSBC (UK)	SAAD (Saudi Arabia)	6.6
9 Aug	OMX (Sweden)	Borse Dubai (UAE)	4.9
24 Sep	Prime West Energy Trust (Canada)	Abu Dhabi National Energy (UAE)	4.6
26 June	Binariang GSM, PT Natrindo (Malaysia)	Saudi Telecom Saudi Arabia)	3.1
22 Aug	50% of City Center (USA)	Dubai World (UAE)	2.8
28 May	Northrock Resources (Canada)	Abu Dhabi National Energy (UAE)	2.0

Source: Reuters.

the state-run DP World, the world's third-largest ports operator. Mubadala Development, a wing of the Abu Dhabi government, bought a 7.5% stake in Carlyle Group, the big US buyout firm. Mubadala, according to Carlyle, got a 10% 'liquidity discount', presumably by paying cash. The investment strategy of the GCC countries' SWFs has also produced some notable effects on financial markets. On the one hand, sizeable cash injections to recapitalize major financial institutions have contributed to preventing systemic repercussions from the credit crisis. On the other, in terms of influence, the strategy has shifted the centre of gravity from the major financial centres where liquidity has dried up to the periphery where liquidity is still abundant and growth prospects appear more resilient to the global turmoil.

Second, economies of scale and synergies provide additional motivations in sectors where GCC companies already have a competitive advantage and play a significant role. Petrochemical industries have invested in the Far East, especially to secure long-term contracts for their oil resources. For example, Kuwait and the Guangdong provincial government in China are planning to build a refinery and petrochemicals complex for $5 billion. A new $3.6 billion refinery and petrochemicals plant was inaugurated in Fujian (China) by Saudi Aramco (which has a 25% share) along with China's state-owned Sinopec (50%) and ExxonMobil (25%). Crude oil for the plant is to be supplied by Saudi Arabia, China's largest oil supplier.

Third, other companies from the region have invested in mature sectors, such as real estate, banks and utilities to generate a steady flow of returns. Real estate companies have invested in India, North Africa and the Middle East, home to most GCC immigrants. Cross-border M&As in West Asia saw an increase from $0.6 billion in 2004 to $14 billion in 2005.[5] Intra-regional M&As, accounting for 65% of the total value, played an important role in this growth. A pioneer has been the Majid Al-Futtaim Group, which has exported its shopping mall concept across the Middle East after its great success in Dubai. In recent months, Tecom of Dubai has purchased 35% of Tunisie Telecom, and Emirates Telecommunications Corporation (Etisalat) has acquired a 26% stake in Pakistan's state-owned Pakistan Telecommunication Company Limited. Mubadala owns a 5% stake in Ferrari, the luxury automobile company, and other GCC investors have also played an important part in large-scale acquisitions in services, mainly telecommunications and banking, in Turkey. Emirates Airlines has owned 43.6% of Sri Lankan Airlines since 1998, and wholly managed the airline (although the contract was not renewed after March 2008). Many of the high-profile rescue operations in the banking sector (hit by the subprime crisis), such as the acquisition of 4.9% of Citicorp by ADIA (Abu Dhabi Investment Authority), must be seen in this context.

Finally, the emergence of a pan-GCC market (thanks to the unified external tariff) and the necessary allowance of foreign ownership and investment in order to meet WTO rules have created a level playing field that has benefited regional firms more than their foreign competitors. For example, Etisalat from the UAE set up a mobile telephone network in Saudi Arabia following the Saudi Telecommunications Company's loss of its monopoly over mobile services. A smaller example is the establishment of a branch of the Emirates Bank Group in Riyadh, with a nationwide network due to be rolled out shortly. At the same time, Kuwaiti and Saudi investors have rushed to buy real estate in Dubai, taking advantage of a new local approach to freehold ownership.

Most of the time, the actors implementing these different strategies are entities collectively indicated as SWFs, but this simplification hides a more variegated reality. The largest funds have a mandate to transfer wealth to the next generations, and therefore adopt a strategy akin to pension funds. Actually, in most cases investment decisions are delegated to an external asset manager. Other types of fund defined as 'strategic investors' adopt more aggressive strategies, target opportunistic acquisitions and take more speculative positions. In essence, their strategy is similar to those of private

5 UNCTAD (2006), *World Investment Report*, tables II.9 and II.10.

equity funds. A third type is publicly funded companies, which pursue a broader range of ventures in specific sectors, especially real estate and utilities. Strictly speaking, these are not SWFs, but often it is their acquisitions that spark controversy.

Three paradigmatic cases

It is ironic that the first high-profile operation to cause political reactions to SWFs involved not an SWF but DP World, the state-owned company that runs the port of Dubai. In winter 2005–06, it tried to acquire P&O, a British company with important operations in the United States. Opposition to this focused primarily on the security consequences of having management by a foreign entity in the sensitive area of access to US territory. When the (US Treasury) Committee on Foreign Investment in the United States (CFIUS) approved the deal in February 2006 after a standard 30-day review, DP World agreed to an additional 45-day security review. In March, following a 62:2 vote in Congress forbidding the acquisition, it agreed to spin off the US assets.

As the *New York Times* put it at the time in a leader on the P&O deal, 'it is not irrational for the United States to resist putting port operators, perhaps the most vulnerable part of the security infrastructure, under [the] control [of an ally whose] record in the war on terror is mixed.'[6] After stoking a fear of terrorism in the public mind, it was of course an irony that the Bush administration could be accused of being soft on security matters. In practice, this anxiety was overblown, as security arrangements in the United States are determined not by the port facilities operators but by security and law-enforcement agencies. And the ports are definitely not the most vulnerable part of the security infrastructure, as proved by the hundreds of thousands of illegal aliens reaching the United States by land – not to mention the hundreds of miles along the western coastline guarded by only a handful of patrol troops.

Rational arguments, however, cannot hide the fact that concern about security and other essential national interests is on the rise. Many countries have taken steps to safeguard essential interests that, although not necessarily 'protectionist' in nature, have nevertheless generated much public debate. Some European countries have shown unease about international mergers in strategic sectors, and some have taken regulatory action. In the United States, the Foreign Investment and National Security Act of 2007 has strengthened the security clearance of investment projects. China has

6 'The President and the Ports', *The New York Times*, 22 February 2006.

recently tightened procedures for cross-border M&As. The Russian and Indian authorities are reassessing their position on foreign control of sensitive enterprises.

To highlight that emotional arguments often play a larger role than thoughtful analysis, one can point to the battle for the acquisition of Sweden's stock exchange. In August 2007, Borse Dubai, the Dubai International Financial Exchange's (DIFX) holding company, announced plans to buy at least 25% of OMX Group, the Stockholm stock exchange. A protracted fight started with the NASDAQ stock market. This ended in September when the two suitors agreed to join forces not only in an OMX bid but also in a far-reaching deal that could have broad implications for the fast-growing and rapidly consolidating universe of financial exchanges. Borse Dubai will continue to advance its $4 billion cash bid for OMX Group. But NASDAQ will acquire its OMX shares in a cash-and-shares arrangement that will leave Borse Dubai with nearly 20% of NASDAQ, although its voting rights will be restricted to 5%. NASDAQ will also become the principal commercial partner and a strategic shareholder in the DIFX, which will be rebranded NASDAQ and use trading technology from NASDAQ and OMX. Finally, Borse Dubai will acquire NASDAQ's 28% stake in the London Stock Exchange, for around $1.6 billion.

The outcry in the United States about whether an entity owned by the government of Dubai is acceptable as a major shareholder in a key US financial exchange was limited. There were calls for CFIUS to intervene but Dubai's voting rights will be restricted to 5%. On the other hand, the Swedish government is to pass a new law to protect the country's stock market from being 'Americanized'. The government was concerned that the sale of OMX Group might undermine its competitiveness by exposing it to US corporate governance rules. But in the end the deal went through.

Finally, the attempted takeover of the British food retailer Sainsbury's by the Qatar Investment Authority (QIA) serves as a reminder that not all SWFs have the skills to carry out complex financial operations. The Delta Two investment fund, which is backed by the QIA, started negotiating the purchase in early summer 2007 and proposed a cash element of around $7 billion. Unite, Britain's largest union, expressed fears about Qatar's long-term intentions for Sainsbury's, and the company's founding Sainsbury family, still a sizeable minority shareholder, was allegedly opposed to the sale. Once it appeared that the fallout from the US subprime mortgage crisis might make obtaining finance harder, Sainsbury's shareholders naturally sought to reduce the proportion of debt in the deal, and Qatar gradually upped its cash injection to close to $10 billion of the $21.6 billion total cost. The UK's Takeover Panel imposed 8 November as the final deadline to 'put up or shut up'. And in early November the Qataris indicated turmoil in the credit markets as the main reason for their decision to abandon the acquisition. Although some analysts have said that the QIA has been prudent in pulling out of the deal because of the rising cost of borrowing, in reality, due to its stubborn determination not to pay the extra sum it actually lost a larger amount, over $1 billion, in the final few days as the share price retreated. The *Financial Times* quoted one person involved in the bid as saying that 'Qatar's reputation as a credible financial investor of international assets has been seriously damaged and it will be a while before another British public company enters into exclusive negotiations with them again. We used to think private equity's behaviour could be low but what Qatar has done is lower than a snake's belly.'[7]

Final remarks

SWFs and similar entities launched by small countries accomplish an indispensable function by investing current account surpluses into a well-diversified asset portfolio as a means to share the accumulated proceeds with future generations. The prominence of SWFs' activities must be seen in the broader context of regulatory changes in FDI and efforts to make financial markets more transparent. Since 2004, a spate of regulatory changes around the world, less favourable to foreign investors, has prompted many pundits to declare an end to the era of liberalism and to raise concern about the advent of a new era of protectionism or perhaps strategic interventionism.

In reality, even nowadays the vast majority of regulatory changes lessen the impediments to foreign investors. Nonetheless, episodes such as the attempt by DP World to acquire P&O draw attention to the activities of SWFs and other state entities and to their potential consequences. One argument, popular in Europe, stresses that shortly after governments have completed the privatization process of key sectors, it would be ironic if, for example, airlines, utilities and banks were to fall prey to a foreign government whose purposes might not be entirely linked to economic considerations. Russia and China appear to be stirring specific fears.

This anxiety is more nuanced in the case of GCC countries. They have been in accord with the United States (and the West in general) and their interests are broadly aligned with those of developed countries. But a degree of ambiguity resurfaced, especially in the US, after 9/11. A former US Treasury Secretary, Larry Summers, whose views are becoming increasingly

7 'Standing of Qatar Laid Low Following Surprise Exit', *Financial Times*, 6 November 2007.

protectionist, has voiced concern about various possibilities, ranging from supposedly hidden motivations behind investment strategies to the danger that SWFs might move the operation of blue chips to their countries and use their political connections to force a bailout should their investment be disastrous. These worries did not prevent his successor, Henry Paulson, from flying to the UAE in an effort to persuade the Abu Dhabi Investment Authority to rescue Citibank when it ran into trouble generated by the subprime crisis. The ensuing deal, worth $7.5 billion, took the shape of a convertible bond with an 11% interest rate over two years – a favourable term for the SWF but hardly excessive given the liquidity crunch on the international financial markets. Analogous terms were negotiated by the Swiss authorities when they asked Singaporean and Saudi public entities to inject funds into UBS. In later visits to the Gulf Mr Paulson has essentially given a political assurance that undue limitations to investment by GCC entities in the US would be removed. These examples show that at times of crippling liquidity worries, SWFs have acted to restore a degree of confidence in the markets.

In essence, it would be pointless and counterproductive to stem capital and FDI flows because as the integration of international trade progresses, a natural consequence will be increasing capital flows from countries that run a current account surplus into those that run a deficit. OECD governments are conscious of the need to keep restrictions to a minimum, ensuring that markets will remain open to investment by SWFs and other entities. However, it will also be desirable that any institution active in the financial markets should conform with governance standards that allow markets to function efficiently. About some SWFs very little is known other than their name and the country from which they operate. Sometimes even the names of key officials are confidential, and their balance sheets and asset holdings are not disclosed. It must be pointed out that often these questionable practices are tolerated by market regulators. For example, the habit of concealing the terms of certain deals or the amount paid for stakes in listed companies is simply unacceptable.

Furthermore, a fundamental principle of reciprocity must be implemented. Countries whose markets and companies are not fully open to foreign investors cannot expect their SWFs or other publicly owned entities to be given complete freedom to acquire ownership or a controlling stake in companies from countries adhering to market freedom. In a nutshell, greater disclosure of SWFs' activities, sound governance, timely reporting of deals and openness to foreign investors will assuage the fears raised by arguments of a nationalistic or, worse, paranoid tenor and minimize restrictions on the operations of SWFs.

Appendix 1: Capital injection in banks by SWFs

Date of announcement	*Financial institution*	*Write-down (of financial institution)*	*SWFs and other investor(s)*		*Amount (% of total stakes from SWFs and other investor(s))*		*Immediate market response (change after announcement compared to previous transaction day)*	
			SWFs	*Other investor(s)*	*SWFs*	*Other Investor(s)*	*Stock price (%)*	*CDS (%)*
26 Nov 2007	Citigroup	$6bn in 2007: Q3	Abu Dhabi Investment Authority		$7.5bn (4.9%)		–1.2	–6
10 Dec 2007	UBS	$18bn in 2007	Government of Singapore Investment Corporation	Unknown Middle Eastern investor	$9.7bn (10%)	$1.8bn (2%)	1.4	–9
19 Dec 2007	Morgan Stanley	$9.4bn in 2007: Q4	China Investment Corporation		$5bn (9.9%)		4.2	0
21 Dec 2007	Merrill Lynch	$8.4bn in 2007: Q3	Temasek Holdings	Davis Selected Advisors, L.P.	$4.4bn (9.4%)	$1.2bn (2.6%)	1.9	0
15 Jan 2008	Citigroup	$18.1bn in 2007: Q4	Government of Singapore Investment Corporation, Kuwait Investment Authority	Sanford Weill, Saudi Prince Alwaleed bin Talal, Capital Research Global Investors, Capital World Investors, New Jersey Investment Division	$6.8bn from Government of Singapore Investment Corporation (3.7%) and $3bn from Kuwait Investment Authority (1.6%)	$2.7bn (1.5%)	–7.3	–5

15 Jan 2008	Merrill Lynch	$14.1bn in 2007: Q4	Korea Investment Corporation, Kuwait Investment Authority	Mizuho Financial Group Inc.	$2bn (3.2%) from Korea Investment Corporation and Kuwait Investment Authority respectively	$2.6bn (4.1%)	−5.3	−12
18 Feb 2008	Credit Suisse	$2.85bn	Qatar Investment Authority		Approximately $500 million (1%–2%); the purchase was on the open market		3.2	2
18 Jul 2008	Barclays		Qatar Investment Authority, Temasek Holdings	China Development Bank (CDB) and Japanese bank Sumitomo Mitsui (SMFG)	Qatar SWF (6.2%), Qatar ruling family member (1.9%), Temasek (2.5–3%)	CDB – ~3%, SMFG – ~2%		

Sources: Bloomberg LP, Citigroup and IMF staff estimates.
Note: The stock price of Citigroup rose 6.5% on 28 November 2007, three days after the announcement of the first capital injection. The stock price declines of Citigroup and Merrill Lynch on 15 January 2008 could not be entirely attributed to the SWF operations, owing to the simultaneous announcement of huge write-downs and dilution of the shareholders' value.

14 How to spend it: distinguishing the origins of sovereign wealth funds

Helmut Reisen

Introduction

Sovereign wealth funds, government-controlled investment vehicles, are stimulating protectionist sentiments in some OECD countries. Their asset size (more than $3 trillion) and their owners (governments) create fertile ground for conspiracy theories, such as fear of industrial espionage or geopolitical threats. These fears were sensationally summarized on CNBC on 18 January 2008 by the maverick TV anchorman Jim Cramer: 'Do we want the communists to own the banks, or the terrorists? I'll take any of it, I guess, because we're so desperate.'

Sovereign wealth funds: development motives and financing sources

This section explains that the basic principles of public finance and development economics leave little room for conspiracy theories and that funding sources and economic motives differ between commodity and non-commodity SWFs.

The funds with assets greater than $100 billion ('heavy' SWFs) are, as Table 14.1 shows, either from oil-exporting countries or from East Asia. Table 14.1 also displays the respective countries' saving rates, both gross national and 'genuine'. Unless exhaustible resources are reinvested in financial, physical or human capital, oil-rich countries will deplete their total capital and their 'genuine' savings will be negative. The World Bank has calculated that many resource-abundant economies have negative 'genuine' saving rates and become poorer each year. Table 14.1 shows as well that the 'genuine' savings performance in countries with 'heavy' SWFs are strikingly different: Asian countries save too much; the Gulf states may save too little.

As the economics underlying oil-exporting countries' SWFs are different from the economics of East Asian funds,[1] so too are the appropriate policy

1 The largest SWFs, as depicted in Table 14.1, are either financed from export receipts earned from

Table 14.1: SWFs: their assets and savings rates

Country	*Fund*	*Assets ($bn) (as of 9/2007)*	*Source*	*Gross national savings (% of GNI), 2000*	*'Genuine' savings (% of GNI), 2000*
United Arab Emirates	Abu Dhabi Investment Authority	875	Oil	n.a.	n.a.
China	China Investment Corp. Ltd, Central Hujin Investment Corp., State Foreign Exchange Investment Corp.	500	Non-commodity	38.8	25.5
Singapore	Govt. of Singapore Investment Corp., Temasek	438	Non-commodity	47.7	35.2
Norway	Govt. Pension Fund – Global	322	Oil	36.9	18.5
Saudi Arabia	Various funds	300	Oil	29.4	−26.5
Kuwait	Kuwait Investment Authority	250	Oil	40.0	−12.9
Hong Kong, China	Hong Kong Monetary Authority Investment portfolio	140	Non-commodity	31.8	21.4
Russia	Stabilization Fund of the Russian Federation	127	Oil	37.1	−13.4

Sources: Kern (2007) and World Bank (2006).

answers. Development economics can explain both the sources of savings and the motives that have led to the recent SWF boom, thus helping to avoid investment restrictions in OECD countries.

Public finance, monetary and development economics point to several major motives/considerations for countries to build up sovereign wealth funds instead of merely accumulating official foreign exchange reserves:

- Foreign exchange reserves, mostly held in US treasury bonds, are judged excessively large. From a certain level, interest rate and currency risk embodied in official reserves start to militate in favour of portfolio diversification (especially when FX reserves are huge – see China), in order to contain losses on the dollar or on the face value of US treasury bonds.

a non-renewable resource, or they result from very high corporate or household saving rates and saving surpluses.

Central banks find it increasingly difficult to control monetary aggregates when official reserves grow too large, as local financial markets are not deep enough to allow a reduction in the domestic component of the money supply needed to counterbalance the rise in foreign exchange. At some point, either inflation or an upward float of the currency has to be accepted by monetary authorities under an effectively open capital account. Either way, this means real currency appreciation.

- Next to the shifting out of excessive reserves, economic diversification and efficiency gains are major economic motives for establishing SWFs. For raw material-rich countries, reducing resource dependence through vertical and horizontal sector diversification is a major development goal. Sovereign wealth funds can serve this goal in several ways: for example, by helping to limit unwarranted currency appreciation, they contain the competitiveness burden for non-traditional industries ('Dutch disease'). The United Arab Emirates are using their fund for rapid diversification of their economies away from oil towards tourism, aerospace and finance. Diversification is as legitimate a motive as the desire to raise the efficiency of their economy through acquiring stakes in leading global companies.
- By investing in world-class businesses, technology transfer and network benefits can be fostered and production efficiency can be raised as a future driver of growth; by investing in infrastructure, in particular that with regional links, private-sector business can be stimulated. This motive is particularly relevant in those (Asian) countries where future growth cannot be based on mere factor accumulation but requires more reliance on greater efficiency in the use of accumulated production factors. The desire to raise efficiency in the allocation of funds may well explain the recent rush by SWFs to take stakes in US financial intermediaries battered by the subprime lending crisis.
- Intergenerational equity concerns and expected demographic pressures entail the need to smooth consumption levels over time for future generations, also for a period when resources will be exhausted. This motive becomes more important to the extent that policy-makers want to limit immigration. It also presupposes that the problems of political economy that typically have led to the 'resource curse', the appropriation of raw material rents by sitting governments, have been overcome. This assumes that the stream of natural resource revenues and what is done with it is completely transparent.

The largest funds, specified in Table 14.1, either are financed from export receipts earned from a non-renewable resource or result from very high corporate or household saving rates and savings surpluses. Griffith-Jones and Ocampo (2008) rightly emphasize that from a development perspective, it makes sense only to finance a sovereign wealth fund from a surplus in a country's current account of the balance of payments. In the absence

Table 14.2: 'Heavy' SWF countries: motives and financing, 2007

Main motive / *Financing*	*Diversification of foreign exchange reserves*	*Economic diversification*	*Economic efficiency*	*Intergenerational equity*
Commodity earnings	Russia	United Arab Emirates		Kuwait, Norway, Saudi Arabia
Structural savings surplus	China	Singapore	China, Singapore	

Source: Author's assessment.

of a current account surplus, it is difficult to rationalize the creation of SWFs, as these would be created merely on the basis of external financing and thus would constitute a form of financial intermediation of 'borrowed money'. Countries with important SWFs must have a savings surplus.

As for the source of the savings surplus, SWFs can be divided into two types: commodity-based funds, which are established through the receipts from commodity exports owned or taxed by the government, and non-commodity funds, which are usually financed by a transfer from the official foreign exchange reserves, thus via a country's central bank. Table 14.2 puts the major motives and financing sources into a matrix, calibrated for those countries with SWFs that currently exceed $100 billion. The next sections discuss the rationale for commodity and non-commodity SWFs in greater detail.

The rationale and case for commodity SWFs

In their choice of how best to spend the income from their natural resources, authorities in resource-rich countries depend on information – resource reserves, future commodity prices and rates of return on exploration – that is highly uncertain and interrelated. Essentially, the choice is between extraction and preservation of exhaustible resources; between consumption and investment once the decision for extraction is made; between foreign investment and domestic investment; and between foreign investment and repaying the national debt. I rely on two excellent surveys (Collier 2007; Van der Ploeg 2008) to build Table 14.3, which provides the decision tree faced by authorities in resource-rich countries.

A country exporting oil or any other exhaustible commodity should be indifferent to whether it keeps the oil under the ground (in which case the return is the expected rise in future oil prices) and also to getting a

Table 14.3: A decision tree for managing public-sector commodity booms

Decision	*Rule*
How much to deplete? Arbitrage: the country should be indifferent between keeping the natural resource under the ground, in which case the return is the capital gain on the reserves compared to selling the resource, and getting a market rate of return on it.	*The Hotelling/Solow rule* This rule requires that the price of natural resources should grow at the world rate of interest and that under some conditions the rate of depletion should equal the demand elasticity times the world rate of interest. The steady-state depletion rate stipulates that societies with fast-growing populations should deplete their natural resources less rapidly than countries with little population growth.
How much to save? To maximize intergenerational utility, the question is which saving rate will sustain a stable consumption per capita over time. Consuming rents from exhaustible resources is literally consuming capital.	*The Hartwick rule* To sustain a constant per capita income if there is no population growth, all resource rents must be invested in capital, including education. If consumption per head were rising (falling) over time, social welfare could be increased if earlier (later) generations saved and invested less or consumed capital at the expense of later (earlier) generations.
The mid-term saving decision is ruled by concern about stabilization and diversification. Fiscal policy is superior to monetary policy in dealing with the first; active diversification involves the use of funds for new activities (as in the UAE, Norway and Chile).	*The commodity price-smoothing rule* Unlike the savings generated according to the Hartwick rule, savings by the commodity price-smoothing rule are intended to finance subsequent consumption during periods when the oil price is below its long-term path. There is thus a strong case for holding these assets in liquid form, which implies the acquisition of financial assets abroad.
How much to invest at home?	Excess return of home investment
	The construction price-smoothing rule Requires domestic investments to be stretched to avoid domestic price bubbles in the non-tradable sector.
How much to invest abroad vs repaying the public debt?	Excess cost of public debt over global return.

Source: Based on discussion in Collier (2007) and Van der Ploeg (2008).

market rate of return on its sale (the Hotelling/Solow rule for efficient depletion (see Table 14.3)). Extracting and selling oil amounts to running down capital unless the receipts are fully reinvested in financial, physical or human capital (the Hartwick rule for intergenerational equity (see also Table 14.3)). Sovereign wealth funds can be helpful too in stabilizing notoriously volatile raw material prices. The law of diminishing returns forces oil exporters to invest a large share of the savings abroad.

In *Where Is the Wealth of Nations?*, the World Bank (2006) has calculated that many resource-abundant economies do not follow the Hartwick rule: they have negative 'genuine' savings rates and become poorer each year. This highlights the important policy question of what resource-rich economies can do to avoid the resource curse. A fund can help, in that oil receipts are eventually transformed into other forms of wealth.

Oil exporters would be forced to disregard both the Hotelling/Solow and the Hartwick rules if SWFs could not invest in OECD countries. The former rule warns that lowering the returns on investment from oil receipts, by preventing investments by SWFs from oil-rich countries, would lead to a smaller oil supply and higher oil prices. Thus a protectionist stance against commodity SWFs can clearly damage the interest of the SWF host country, by stimulating a higher transfer of purchasing power to the oil exporters as oil prices rise. In oil-rich countries, such capital protectionism would lead to more intense waste and corruption today and lower consumption tomorrow, possibly with harsh geostrategic implications.

Table 14.3 shows that there are good theoretical reasons for investing a substantial part of the windfall abroad initially: the return on investment would fall below the world interest rate if the windfall were used entirely for domestic investment. Investing abroad offers an escape from diminishing returns: foreign assets can be repatriated gradually and used for domestic investment. The construction price-smoothing rule can be employed to dampen rising capital costs, such as typically occur in a construction boom, by deferring domestic investment until the construction boom abates. However, in practice an efficient balance between domestic and foreign assets is politically difficult to sustain. Domestic debt repayment may solve this dilemma, and is lucrative as long as domestic debt cost exceeds expected foreign returns. It has the added advantage of making foreign asset accumulation difficult to reverse by future predator governments.

Non-commodity SWFs: 'dynamic inefficiency' and currency misalignment?

In contrast to SWFs of oil-rich countries, those from East Asia are financed through transfers from foreign exchange reserves. For a decade, China has been providing 'cheap savings' to the United States as it extended supplier credits to pay for the 'cheap goods' the country used to export, holding the accumulating reserves mostly in low-coupon US treasury bonds. Eventually, with reserves at $1.5 trillion, currency and interest risk was deemed excessive, and monetary control was lost owing to exhausted sterilization capacity as the central bank becomes unable to keep the domestic component of money supply sufficiently low to avoid inflation.

To be sure, official foreign exchange reserves allow countries to smooth domestic absorption in response to sudden stops in capital inflows. Popular rules of thumb for policy-makers have been linked to the current account, such as maintaining reserves equivalent to three months of imports, or to the capital account, notably the Greenspan-Guidotti rule of full coverage of total short-term external debt. Covering all foreign short-term debt *plus* three months of imports would require China to hold $500 billion in reserves, roughly one-third of what it actually holds. These excess reserves plus future saving surpluses represent the funding potential for China's sovereign wealth funds. (Note, however, that the level of 'optimal' reserves may be higher than suggested by the popular rules of thumb, depending on the output cost and the probability of capital-flow reversals.)

Although in most OECD countries growth is driven by productivity gains, it is factor accumulation that has explained growth in East Asia (Young 1995). The relevance of this finding to the sustainability of Asia's rapid growth is that factor accumulation tends to be self-limiting. Eventually, you run out of labour, and supplying a given labour force with more and more capital equipment leads to diminishing returns. This may suggest that Asian SWFs are the result of 'dynamic inefficiency'. This is defined as capital over-accumulation.

Abel, Mankiw, Summers and Zeckhauser (1989) show that an economy is 'dynamically efficient' if gross capital income consistently exceeds gross investment (where capital income is defined as the sum of profit, rental and interest income). If this is the case, then the financial sector is making more resources available for future consumption than it is using. Conversely, if investment consistently exceeds capital income, then the financial sector is draining resources from the economy. This is inefficient, because the whole point of investing is to augment future consumption possibilities.

In countries with 'dynamic inefficiency', so much capital has been accumulated that investment spending tends to exceed capital income; investment is draining resources from the economy rather than augmenting future consumption possibilities. Note that the pension motive should not apply to SWFs from 'dynamically inefficient' countries when their growth rates exceed the global capital return. Ironically, 'pay-as-you-go' (PAYG) pensions would generate higher returns for beneficiaries than would fully funded pensions.

In East Asia, rapidly ageing populations and limited immigration suggest the need for high savings in order to sustain consumption levels in the future. When savings become excessive and capital returns drop below the growth rate, however, tax-financed pensions achieve that goal better than fully funded pensions. Mandatory savings and excessive capital accumulation have resulted in 'dynamic inefficiency' in both China and Singapore, as shown by recent empirical research (Kasa 1997; He, Zhang and Shek 2007). The root sources of excess savings differ between the two countries.

In Singapore, much of saving is 'forced'. Since 1955, the government has operated a compulsory savings programme, the Central Provident Fund, which is a fully funded defined-contribution public pension scheme. It requires a 'contribution' from both employees and their employers. The compulsory contribution rates are on average 20% for employees and 13% for employers, for a total of 33% in 2008. Forced savings help to explain that gross national savings averaged 47% of GDP in 2007, and the current account surplus was 24.3% of GDP. Predictably, such excessive savings have generated very low returns for Singapore's pension beneficiaries. Asher and Nandy (2006) estimate that the Central Provident Fund has generated a meagre 1.2% real rate of return during the period 1987–2004.

China's high savings are linked ultimately to a surge in corporate profits thanks to an undervalued currency. In contrast to Singapore, China has seen a strong rise in corporate and government savings over recent years, but household savings have remained flat (Kuijs 2005). Between 2000 and 2005, gross corporate savings increased from 16% to 23% of China's GDP, and government savings rose from 5% to 10%. Household savings remained roughly constant at 16%. Mattoo and Subramanian (2008) cite estimates of China's exchange rate to suggest a sizeable undervaluation for the 2000–07 period, ranging from 20% to 60%. Eliminating this undervaluation, it is estimated, would reduce China's current account surplus by between 6 and 12 percentage points of GDP.

Ferguson and Schularick (2007) make a convincing case that China's current account surplus and corporate savings are linked with the undervaluation of the yuan. They show that Chinese companies, many of them state-owned, have taken over large parts of the domestic market from foreign competition, depressing imports, and have expanded their market share abroad, thereby increasing exports. The surge in corporate profits in China has come mainly from two industrial sectors: manufacturing and mining. Purely domestic-orientated industries have seen much less dramatic profit growth. The reason for the profit boom has not been a widening of margins, which have been more or less stable. It has been a dramatic increase in sales volumes and gains in market share both abroad and at home. Profits have surged and the dollars have piled up as official reserves at the People's Bank of China before being partly divested into China's SWFs.

Outlook

From the perspective of development economics, then, there is little need for conspiracy theories to explain what drives the funding and motivation of sovereign wealth funds. Although a clear case can be made for commodity SWFs from a development perspective, the issue is much more complicated as far as Asian non-commodity SWFs are concerned as they may be funded from excessive savings and reflect dynamic inefficiency, as explained above. For China, a large but still relatively poor and underdeveloped country with eroding public safety nets, the case for investing the country's savings in overseas markets is ambiguous. Unlike many commodity exporters, China, and also Singapore, tend to save too much.

A partial solution to global imbalances, and a strong barrier to rapid asset growth of SWFs, will occur with the inevitable real appreciation of currencies, not only in China and Singapore but also in the Gulf countries. As for China and Singapore, current consumption should be stimulated – in China, first and foremost through a transfer of corporate profits to the (rural) household sector; in Singapore, by establishing a focus on capital return rather than accumulation and by further reducing contribution rates to the Central Provident Fund. Sovereign wealth funds in general should not be restricted by industrialized countries as long as they pursue return objectives. Doing so when they stem from oil-rich countries would harm oil-importing countries most, as oil prices would rise further in response to capital protectionism, as suggested by the Hotelling and Hartwick rules.

References

Abel, Andrew B., N. Gregory Mankiw, Lawrence H. Summers and Richard J. Zeckhauser (1989), 'Assessing Dynamic Efficiency: Theory and Evidence', *Review of Economic Studies*, 56: 1–20.

Asher, Mukul G. and Amarendu Nandy (2006), *Social Security Policy in an Era of Globalization and Competition: Challenges for Southeast Asia*, Working Paper 06-06, National University of Singapore, January.

Collier, Paul (2007), *Managing Commodity Booms: Lessons of International Experience*,

Paper prepared for the African Economic Research Consortium, Oxford University, January.

Ferguson, Niall and Moritz Schularick (2007), '"Chimerica" and the Global Asset Market Boom', *International Finance*, 10(3): 215–39.

Griffith-Jones, Stephanie and José Antonio Ocampo (2008), *Sovereign Wealth Funds: A Developing Country Perspective*, Columbia University (www.policydialogue.org), February.

He, Dong, Wenlang Zhang and Jimmy Shek (2007), 'How Efficient Has Been China's Investment? Empirical Evidence from National and Provincial Data', *Pacific Economic Review*, 12 (5): 597–617.

Kasa, Kenneth (1997), 'Does Singapore Invest Too Much?', *FRBSF Economic Letter* 97-15, Federal Reserve Bank of San Francisco, May.

Kern, Steffen (2007), *Sovereign Wealth Funds – State Investments on the Rise*, Deutsche Bank Research, Frankfurt/Main, September.

Kuijs, Louis (2005), *Investment and Saving in China*, World Bank Policy Research Working Paper No. 3633, June.

Mattoo, Aaditya and Arvin Subramanian (2008), *Currency Undervaluation and Sovereign Wealth Funds: A Case for the World Trade Organization*, Peterson Institute for International Economics, Working Paper 08-2, January.

Van der Ploeg, Frederick (2008), *Challenges and Opportunities for Resource Rich Economies*, OxCarre Research Paper 2008-05, Oxford University, January.

World Bank (2006), *Where Is the Wealth of Nations? Measuring Capital for the XXI Century*, Washington, DC.

Young, Alwyn (1995), 'The Tyranny of Numbers: Confronting the Statistical Realities of the East Asian Growth Experience', *Quarterly Journal of Economics*, 110: 641–80.

15 The transparency of sovereign wealth funds

Andrew Rozanov*

Introduction

Sovereign wealth funds are increasingly becoming a major part of the global financial system. Owing to persistently high commodity prices and burgeoning foreign exchange reserves, many developing countries are launching new funds, and existing SWFs are developing their assets by leaps and bounds. This trend has prompted many policy-makers and market commentators in the developed world to express concern about the potential impact of these institutions, especially given the perceived lack of transparency of many of them. Some observers also worry about the tendency of certain SWFs to engage in private equity-style transactions, taking large minority stakes or even controlling positions in individual companies.

The Middle East boasts some of the largest and oldest sovereign wealth funds. Indeed, Kuwait established its government investment operation as far back as 1953 and is currently estimated to have in excess of $264 billion under management. The Abu Dhabi Investment Authority (ADIA), which was established in 1976 and is allegedly the largest SWF in existence today, has an estimated asset size well in excess of $500 billion. The Saudi Arabian Monetary Agency, although technically not an SWF, has for decades managed a very sizeable non-reserve portfolio on behalf of the Saudi government. Together with the Government Investment Corporation (GIC) and Temasek Holdings of Singapore, these entities have a long track record of investing in Western financial markets. Over the years, they have developed a reputation as sophisticated investors who operate in a responsible and market-friendly way. It is therefore with some surprise

* Andrew Rozanov is Managing Director and Head of Sovereign Advisory at State Street Global Markets. The views expressed in this chapter are those of the author and do not necessarily reflect the views of State Street Global Markets or any affiliated entity. All material has been obtained from sources deemed to be reliable, but its accuracy is not guaranteed. Views expressed are through July 2008.

and disappointment that they suddenly find themselves on the receiving end of some very negative publicity surrounding the SWF phenomenon.

The biggest problem that most Western commentators seem to have with sovereign wealth funds in the Gulf region is their considerable lack of transparency. Coupled with the recent string of high-profile private equity-style transactions, this has led to increased pressure on SWFs to become more open and transparent and to consider subscribing to a code of best practice and a common set of rules. In view of the increased size and market presence of SWFs and their expected growth trajectory, it is not surprising that many countries on the receiving end of sovereign wealth flows feel the need to understand these funds and to get more comfortable with them. A meaningful increase in transparency and the amount and quality of information disclosed by SWFs generally, and the Gulf Cooperation Council states' funds in particular, will certainly go a long way towards accommodating this need. However, the issue of transparency and public disclosure is much more nuanced and complex than it may appear at first glance. This chapter attempts to explore these issues from a market practitioner's point of view.

The different aspects of transparency

Although there is considerable room for SWFs in the Gulf to increase their overall level of transparency, the utmost care must be exercised when determining exactly what information can and should be disclosed. When the political establishment in the West demands more transparency from the SWF community, the latter should respond by requesting that these demands be couched in much more detailed and concrete terms. Exactly what information would be required, why and at what level of detail? What would be the frequency and timing of such disclosure? Who would be the intended recipients of this information and how would they propose to use it?

Once the discussion gets down to this level of detail, some interesting, and much more fundamental, questions emerge. What exactly do we mean by transparency? Can there be one set of rules that would apply equally to funds that are very different in nature? And what happens if the level of transparency of a particular fund is perfectly adequate for domestic purposes but is found to be lacking by international standards? Can such a fund square the circle by opening up to international organizations and to national regulators in recipient countries on a confidential basis, thus avoiding full public disclosure?

The SWF debate is happening at a time when regulators and market commentators are pondering very similar issues as they relate to other parts of the financial system, namely private equity and hedge funds. There are indeed some interesting parallels. Consider, for example, the following quote from George Soros's testimony to the US Congress back in 1994 in which he deliberates on the question of transparency and disclosure by hedge funds:

> I should like to draw a distinction between supervision and regulation. I am for maximum supervision and minimum regulation. I should also like to draw a distinction between information gathering and disclosure. I think the authorities need a lot more information than the general public. In fact, information we are legally obliged to disclose has, on occasion, caused unwarranted price movements.[1]

Arguably, these two distinctions – between supervision and regulation and between information-gathering and disclosure – go to the heart of the matter, not only in the hedge fund debate, but also with regard to SWF transparency. There are two reasons for this.

First, each sovereign wealth fund operates in its own country under a set of rules that are considered optimal by domestic standards. Whatever level of transparency and disclosure these funds maintain *vis-à-vis* local constituents is a matter of sovereign choice in each individual country. However, once these funds expand their investment activity overseas, they may face legitimate concern on the part of international organizations and national regulators in recipient countries. Any sensible sovereign wealth fund should be sympathetic and sensitive to such concern and should be prepared to engage and work with its counterparts in a meaningful and productive way. It is when increased transparency is equated to increased disclosure of information to the general public – above and beyond what may be considered optimal for domestic purposes – that SWFs may find it politically difficult to accommodate these demands.

Secondly, increased transparency and public disclosure may carry a real economic cost. This is what George Soros alluded to when he referred to 'unwarranted price movements'. Whatever one may think of hedge funds and their role in the financial system, the one sin of which nobody can accuse them is harbouring a political agenda or being motivated by non-economic considerations in their investments. In terms of their goals and objectives, hedge funds are the ultimate money-making machines: they

1 George Soros, 'Hedge Funds and Dynamic Hedging', in Ronald Lake (ed.), *Evaluating and Implementing Hedge Fund Strategies: The Experience of Managers and Investors*, 3rd edn (London: Euromoney Institutional Investor, 2004), p. 426.

seek maximum return with minimum risk, preferably within the shortest possible time horizon. If these institutions find it advantageous to operate with minimum levels of transparency and public disclosure, then surely they do it for no other reason than to maximize profits and to protect their economic interests.

Of course, SWFs are different from hedge funds in many respects, and one should be careful not to draw too many direct parallels when it comes to formulating a policy response. But the point still stands: if some SWFs appear reluctant to embrace full transparency and public disclosure, it may have less to do with their political agenda or any strategic considerations and more to do with legitimate economic and financial concerns. Consider the following quote from *The Economist*:

> Murkiness brings unpredictability, which financial markets do not like. If the Abu Dhabi Investment Authority, with an estimated $875 billion under management, decided to unwind a big position and nobody knew why, it could start a panic. For their own good, sovereign funds should follow Norway's example and open up a little.[2]

It is debatable whether one can state quite so categorically that financial markets dislike unpredictability. The whole purpose of financial markets is to price assets under conditions of uncertainty. Although some traders and investors may be hurt by increased volatility, others thrive on it. To demand increased transparency from a large institutional investor solely on the grounds that it would help to reduce market uncertainty and increase the confidence of other traders and investors in their own risky bets does not seem to be a particularly convincing or logical argument.

Much more importantly, if an institutional investor of ADIA's size were to decide to unwind a big position, the last thing it would want is for everyone in the market to know about it. As any market practitioner will attest, investing or divesting a sizeable portion of a portfolio is challenging enough owing to the risk of pushing market prices against the fund. It gets even trickier if the market segment or instrument in question is not particularly liquid. And it can be next to impossible if the institution in question is so large and systemically important that other traders and investors follow its every move in an effort to profit from any expected portfolio shifts. In these circumstances, for any institutional investor to show its hand to the market would mean helping other market participants to profit at the expense of the fund's beneficiaries. Such transparency would be illogical, and it would go against the letter and spirit of the basic principle of fiduciary responsibility.

2 'Governments Go Shopping', *The Economist*, 26 July 2007.

The cost of transparency

At times it is not inconceivable for increased transparency to be dangerous to one's financial health. Two very different episodes from recent financial history may help illustrate this point. The first case study comes from a book called *A Demon of Our Own Design* by Richard Bookstaber, an experienced market practitioner who has worked for many years in bulge-bracket investment banks and large hedge funds. In it he describes in detail how in 1998 Salomon Smith Barney's new management decided to close down their proprietary fixed-income arbitrage unit, which was effectively an in-house hedge fund. A key point in this discussion, and indeed an important insight for any large institutional investor, is the question of transparency. As the arbitrage unit prepared to unwind its huge positions in various fixed-income markets, it knew that transparency was its enemy:

> The next question was how to engineer the closing. The key factor in this decision was – or at least should have been – to minimize transparency. The arbitrage unit was sitting on billions of dollars' worth of positions ... These positions took months to build and, even in a cooperative market, would take just as long to sell off ... And other firms held similar positions ...
>
> Most investors do not appreciate the issue of transparency because it is only when positions are so large that their liquidation can affect the market. But when you have to put billions of dollars to work and there are only so many good ideas to execute, the individual positions can take days or even weeks to work into the market and later liquidate. If other funds know that you have a large position and are in the process of closing it out – and especially if the reason for closing it out is that the price has been going against you – they will start to sit on the sidelines or even trade the other way.[3]

If there is a risk that the nature and approximate size of the positions that need to be built up or divested can be guessed by other market participants, then it becomes doubly important to maintain a low profile and to keep the trade execution programme as secret as possible, preferably for as long as possible. In these circumstances, opacity and a long time horizon are the fund manager's best friends, and transparency and a short execution window are the worst enemies. According to Bookstaber,

> Because the positions were no longer opaque, it was imperative that the winding down be kept as quiet as possible. If the market sniffed Salomon's selling, especially if it knew the selling was based on marching

3 Richard Bookstaber, *A Demon of Our Own Design* (London: John Wiley & Sons, 2007), p. 88.

> orders from senior management, then the liquidation would turn into a fire sale. The best course of action was to gradually and silently take the positions down ...
>
> Outside the firm, the announcement [of the imminent position closure over a relatively short time] changed perceptions of the markets. Every trader around the globe could expect Salomon to unload its huge positions. No one could say when, but no one wanted to be on the same side of the market when the floodgates opened ... Everyone knew there would be an overhang, and no one wanted to be on the other side of the first trade. Who wants to buy the first $100 million of $10 billion of inventory knowing another $9.9 billion will follow?[4]

Some might argue that what is natural and appropriate for a private-sector entity may not be so for a public institution: if a fund is managed by the government in the interests of the general public, then surely full transparency is always and unequivocally a good thing? But consider the following counter-argument.

Sovereign wealth funds are typically set up in order to provide better investment returns, broader diversification of national wealth and more efficient management of public finances. In fact, this is one of the key tenets espoused by Western critics of SWFs. They advocate, in no uncertain terms, that any sovereign fund should be run on purely commercial terms and market-based principles. If that is indeed the case, then it would be perfectly natural and appropriate to apply to SWFs the same principles that govern the investment behaviour of private-sector entities.

Also, even in the non-profit-orientated part of the official sector, transparency can sometimes be harmful or even potentially lethal. Consider the second case study, the recent Northern Rock débâcle, which produced the first run on a British bank in 140 years. The lessons of this incident are still being digested by both the authorities and the general public, but one particular point made by Mervyn King, Governor of the Bank of England, in his statement to the House of Commons Treasury Select Committee is especially relevant to this discussion. He said that he would have preferred to offer covert aid to the troubled bank. However, according to him, the EU Market Abuse Directive prevented the Bank from doing so, as it would have required public disclosure of any covert support.[5] Instead, the authorities were forced to act overtly, which sparked worries about Northern Rock's solvency and led customers to queue to withdraw their deposits.

Many market participants believe that the débâcle could indeed have been avoided, or that at least its costs could have been contained, had the

4 Ibid., pp. 91–3.

5 'Mervyn King Attacked over Northern Rock Rescue', *Times Online*, 20 September 2007.

Bank acted covertly to supply funds to Northern Rock in the early days of the crisis. Instead, the costs to the taxpayer have ballooned and the crisis is yet to be resolved at the time of writing. These higher costs can be attributed, at least in part, to the unintended consequences of a well-meaning set of regulations mandating transparency and public disclosure.

The two cases above represent two very different sets of circumstances and motivations. In the first, a private-sector institution was trying to act in a non-transparent way in order to maximize profits or to minimize losses. In the second, a public-sector institution expressed a strong preference for a non-transparent way of dealing with a major public policy problem. But in both cases, the underlying reason to shun transparency was the same: the dynamics of public markets and the market psychology that drives them.

The lesson for all proponents of more transparency and tighter regulations in financial markets is that sometimes it may be more efficient and beneficial to all parties involved to have less transparency. Therefore, in designing regulations and putting together codes of best practice for SWFs, it is important to recognize that increased transparency may come at a cost, both to the funds themselves and to the financial system overall. At the very least, this calls for building some flexibility into the policy response, whatever shape it may take.

Norway or Singapore as a model?

As evidenced in the *Economist* quotation above, one often hears calls for all SWFs to follow the Norwegian model. Norway's approach is appealing to Western observers for two reasons. First, its level of openness and disclosure is exceptional: its fund is fully transparent, to the point of listing individual portfolio holdings in its financial reports. Secondly, as a matter of policy, Norway's fund caps any shareholding at 5% of outstanding shares, and in most cases it holds much smaller positions. So why cannot all SWFs be like that?

One can argue that Norway may be a special case. During its first 10 years of existence, its fund invested 60% in highly liquid bonds and 40% in highly liquid equity markets. It constructed and managed broadly diversified portfolios in both asset classes, controlling its active risk within a fairly tight 1.5% tracking-error range, in effect ensuring that it maintained investment exposures that were very close to broad market indices. It had no liabilities explicitly attached to the fund. With such characteristics, Norway's fund could afford the luxury of being fully open and transparent.

Not all SWF countries have the same luxury. Some, like China, have interest-bearing, local currency-denominated liabilities that support their SWF assets. This introduces an additional complication for the managers of the fund, in the form of a potentially very high 'hurdle rate' that they need to beat in order to make the fund economically viable over the long term. Others, such as some GCC funds, may face the difficult task of investing large and growing amounts of petrodollars in decidedly less liquid and more challenging asset classes and instruments. In both cases, these SWFs will be seeking higher investment returns and broader portfolio diversification than has been practised by Norway so far. And as a result, they will need to venture out into riskier, less liquid and more complex asset classes and instruments. Given the size of these SWFs and the increasing attention paid to them by other market participants, it may be difficult for them to achieve as high a level of transparency as Norway.[6]

On the basis of this, one can make the following general observation. All else being equal, if a fund is relatively small, does not have explicit liabilities attached to its assets, prefers to invest in liquid asset classes and instruments, takes modest amounts of active risk, maintains index-like exposures and caps positions in individual issuers, then it is reasonable to expect from it maximum openness and transparency. If, on the other hand, the fund is very large, has liabilities attached to its assets, invests in relatively less liquid asset classes and instruments, takes relatively more active risk, maintains less index-like exposures and has the risk appetite to take on large and concentrated positions, then it would not be reasonable to expect it to offer maximum levels of transparency.

A better, more instructive model for at least some SWFs in the Gulf may be that of Singapore's Temasek. Its more concentrated, private equity-like strategic investment style has delivered compounded annual returns in excess of 18% over the 33 years of its history. During most of that period, Temasek maintained a very low profile, with very little by way of meaningful transparency. However, in the past few years it has undergone a major transformation. Today, one can find a fair amount of information on its investment policy, asset allocation and portfolio holdings, as well as its approach to governance, structure and operations. The fund is becoming much more open and transparent, even as it maintains its relatively concentrated strategic investment style. But the most encouraging aspect of Temasek's experience, at least with regard to the above discussion, is that it has managed to increase transparency without hurting returns. If

6 For a more detailed discussion of this point, see A. Rozanov, 'Will China Follow the Norwegian Model?', *Professional Investor*, summer 2008, pp. 34–5.

anything, returns since its transformation have been considerably higher than the long-term average.

But is Temasek's model the answer? Can its approach to transparency, if adopted by its peers, assuage concern in the West over SWFs? On the one hand, there is some positive supporting evidence. Consider the relative ranking of Temasek in the 'Scoreboard for Sovereign Wealth Funds' published in October 2007 by Edwin Truman, a senior fellow at the Peterson Institute for International Economics and an acknowledged authority on central bank reserves and, more recently, SWFs. In his paper, the author evaluates 32 SWFs in 28 countries according to four basic categories: structure, governance, transparency/accountability and behaviour. In terms of the overall score, Temasek came in at a very respectable eleventh position, scoring 13.50 out of a possible total of 25.00 points. This is noticeably higher than the mean of 10.27 and considerably above the median of 9.00 points. In terms of the 'Transparency and Accountability' sub-category, Temasek has done even better, coming in behind only six other funds.[7] So if this 'scorecard' approach is indicative of the way that Washington's policy community would evaluate SWFs, then the Temasek model looks promising.

On the other hand, Temasek's relatively high level of openness and transparency did not shield it from the headline risk and political backlash that it incurred following some of its recent foreign investments, namely the purchase of a controlling stake in Shin Corporation in Thailand or the more recent controversy over its telecoms holdings in Indonesia. This suggests that increased transparency and accountability, although clearly important, do not offer SWFs sufficient protection against political risks and threats of protectionism. A much more comprehensive solution is required if the policy response on both sides of the SWF divide is to be robust and equitable.

The GCC countries' policy response

What can policy-makers in the Gulf do to address these issues? If SWFs want to avoid further controversy and make sure that recipient countries keep their markets open for business, they should pre-empt further scrutiny and criticism by taking the lead in this debate. Specifically, they may want to consider taking the following three steps.

7 Edwin Truman, 'Sovereign Wealth Fund Acquisitions and Other Foreign Government Investments in the United States: Assessing the Economic and National Security Implications', Testimony before the Committee on Banking, Housing and Urban Affairs, US Senate, 14 November 2007.

First, SWFs should signal clearly to the West that they fully understand and acknowledge the source of concern and the legitimate nature of calls for more transparency. They should seek to engage with the developed world in a dialogue about how best to achieve increased transparency. However, in the course of this dialogue, they should insist that the West clarifies exactly what information is required, on what grounds, and exactly how the recipients of such information will use it.

Secondly, SWFs should take the whole transparency debate to a much more sophisticated level. As discussed above, increased transparency may come at a cost and its effects may be limited. SWFs need to understand and weigh the various implications of increased transparency and how it may affect their performance, liquidity and other key parameters of their operations.

Finally, GCC countries may want to consider using this opportunity to take the lead in organizing a dedicated policy forum for SWF states where they could discuss various issues of mutual concern and interest. The recipient countries of the developed world already have their own fora at the G-7 and the OECD, where they discuss and coordinate policy towards SWFs. It would only be fair for SWF states to have a similar policy forum of their own. Some analysts have already suggested a catchy term – the 'Super Seven' – which would include two SWFs from Singapore and one each from Abu Dhabi, Norway, Kuwait, China and Russia.[8]

Calls for the increased transparency of sovereign wealth funds are timely and legitimate, but they must be addressed in a calm and balanced way, taking full account of all potential implications, both positive and negative, for all the parties involved. Large and systemically important sovereign wealth fund states, especially those in the Gulf, can and should rise to the challenge.

8 Gerard Lyons, 'State Capitalism: The Rise of Sovereign Wealth Funds', Standard Chartered Bank, 15 October 2007.

Index